ANXIOUS WEALTH

ANXIOUS WEALTH

MONEY AND MORALITY AMONG CHINA'S NEW RICH

JOHN OSBURG

STANFORD UNIVERSITY PRESS ∎ STANFORD, CALIFORNIA

Stanford University Press
Stanford, California

Printed in the United States of America on acid-free, archival-quality paper

Library of Congress Cataloging-in-Publication Data

Osburg, John, author.

Anxious wealth : money and morality among China's new rich / John Osburg.

pages cm

Includes bibliographical references and index.

ISBN 978-0-8047-8353-8 (alk. paper) — ISBN 978-0-8047-8354-5 (pbk. : alk. paper)

1. Rich people—China—Chengdu. 2. Businessmen—China—Chengdu. 3. Elite (Social sciences)—China—Chengdu. 4. Social networks—China—Chengdu. 5. Sex role—China—Chengdu. 6. Entrepreneurship—Sex differences—China—Chengdu. 7. Chengdu (China)—Social life and customs. 8. Chengdu (China)—Moral conditions. I. Title.

HC428.C453O57 2013

174.0951'38—dc23

2012035314

ISBN 978-0-8047-8535-8 (electronic)

Typeset by Bruce Lundquist in 10/14 Minion

CONTENTS

FIGURES

ACKNOWLEDGMENTS

I would like to thank the many mentors, colleagues, and friends who made the completion of this book possible. First thanks are due to Susan Gal and Judith Farquhar for their intellectual guidance and moral support. Prasenjit Duara, John Kelly, and Danilyn Rutherford provided invaluable comments and suggestions and played key roles in my development as a scholar.

Several institutions also made this book possible. My field research was supported by a fellowship from the Social Science Research Council, with funds provided by the Andrew W. Mellon Foundation, the Wenner-Gren Foundation, and a Fulbright-Hays Fellowship from the U.S. Department of Education. The writing of the earliest version of this book was made possible by generous support from the Chiang Ching-kuo Foundation and by a Mark Hanna Watkins Post-Field Fellowship at the University of Chicago. I am grateful to these institutions for all of their financial support. Thanks go as well to my colleagues at the Center for Gender Studies at the University of Chicago for their insightful comments on my work and for providing me with an all-important office in which to write the initial draft. Julie Chu, Jason Ingersoll, Teresa Kuan, and Lili Lai all provided valuable feedback on the earliest versions of the manuscript. Anne Ch'ien, the superhuman administrator of Chicago's Anthropology Department, deserves my eternal gratitude for the assistance and guidance she provided throughout my graduate school career.

I was fortunate to spend a year as a post-doctoral fellow at Stanford University's Center for East Asian Studies. Versions of chapters from this book were presented at workshops and colloquia there. Thanks go to the helpful feedback I received from attendees of these presentations and, in particular, to Paul Festa, Matthew Korhman, Jean Oi, and Andrew Walder for their valuable comments on my work. I am also grateful for the feedback I received from my colleagues at the College of William and Mary, especially Brad Weiss and Jonathan Glasser, who read and commented on drafts of sections of the book.

Thanks to Stacy Wagner, my editor at Stanford University Press, for her enthusiasm, encouragement, and very thoughtful guidance in bringing this book to completion. I am very fortunate to have such wonderful colleagues in the Anthropology Department at the University of Rochester—Ayala Emmett, Bob Foster, Tom Gibson, Eleana Kim, and Dan Reichman. I greatly appreciate their support, advice, and stimulating intellectual company. Ro Ferreri helped make my transition to Rochester easy and has provided a wealth of practical advice.

I owe a special debt of gratitude to the two anonymous readers who reviewed the initial draft. Both went above and beyond their duties as readers and provided me with some truly insightful suggestions and new directions in which to take my material. Many of their suggestions and comments will continue to inform my future work. And a final thanks to Ben Eastman for reading the final draft.

To all my friends and colleagues in China who helped with my research, shared aspects of their personal lives, and imparted to me their insights into contemporary China, I wish to express my heartfelt gratitude. Many of those people appear in this book under pseudonyms. Marc and Kara Abramson, Shawn Mahoney, Rich Meyer, and Richard Morgan all provided me with important insights and introductions for my fieldwork and made my time in Chengdu even more enjoyable. Finally, thanks to the people of Chengdu for their hospitality and for being so willing to discuss my sometimes sensitive research questions.

My deepest gratitude goes to my families in America and in China—Mom, Dad, Barb, Steve, Ben, Liz, Molly, Ba, Ma—for their unwavering support of my intellectual pursuits despite my slow pace by "real-world" standards. Finally, I benefited greatly from the love and support of Jiao Qian and our son, Evan. They kept me going during the ups and downs of researching and writing.

Note on Translations

All translations of textual and spoken materials from Chinese to English that appear in this book were done by the author. The Pinyin system for Romanizing Chinese characters is used throughout the text. Statements made in the Chengdu or other Sichuan-area dialects are transcribed with standard Mandarin pinyin spelling for ease of understanding.

ANXIOUS WEALTH

1

INTRODUCTION

In 1997, I arrived in Guangzhou, the booming capital city of Guangdong province, to begin teaching English at a provincial education college. Like many casual observers of China, I was captivated by the irony of a wealthy, entrepreneurial class in an ostensibly socialist country and the social tensions and contradictions brought by China's market reforms. My students were primarily high school English teachers in their twenties from small towns in rural Guangdong. They were attending two years of professional training in Guangzhou before being sent back to their schools. Over late-night snacks and beers in outdoor sidewalk restaurants, they talked about their hopes for the future and anxieties about the present. I quickly learned that the broader social and economic transformations of the previous two decades, while improving their standard of living, had overturned many of their certainties about Chinese society and their place within it. They felt both threatened by and drawn to the expanding world of business, angry about its injustices but seduced by its promises of excitement, status, and riches.

While the new rich were a common topic of discussion, many of the conversations we had about this group quickly evolved into discussions of marriage, romance, and sexual morality. In many ways, among my students it seemed that anxiety about growing social inequality in China manifested in moral discussions about men and women.

My male students frequently complained that in their hometowns uneducated entrepreneurs and nouveau-riche peasants were taking "their women."

They claimed that just a few years earlier the level of education and the lifestyle afforded by their occupations had given them moderate status in their rural home communities, enough status at least to attract another hometown teacher as a wife. Now they felt that the relatively paltry material benefits of their jobs— low incomes and dependence on their schools for cramped, dilapidated housing—ranked them lower in the marriage market than uneducated but wealthy entrepreneurs who often had private cars and personal residences bought in the commercial housing market. Their female classmates, they complained, had it easy. Because they were educated (but not overeducated), poorly paid (relative to a potential husband), and employed in jobs considered morally appropriate for their gender, these women had no trouble finding a suitable (and wealthy) spouse.

For these male students, an increasingly normative masculinity based on taking entrepreneurial risks and achieving success in the market economy had very real consequences for their life decisions. As a result of their difficulty getting married, many were looking for ways to leave their schools. However, because their work units (*danwei*) had funded their two-year stints at the education college, the only way out of their teaching commitments back home was for them to reimburse their schools for all the money spent on their behalf.[1] Ironically, this led quite a few of them to skip classes in search of business and money-making opportunities in Guangzhou. In fact, some had viewed attending the college in Guangzhou from the start as little more than a means of getting to the city to find better employment, a better quality of life, and, they hoped, a wife along the way.

They experienced their dependence on the state sector as a form of emasculation. Their outdated sense of entitlement, derived from their status as non-laboring "intellectuals" (*zhishifenzi*), informed their indignation over "their women" marrying nouveau-riche fish farmers and auto parts dealers who would have been both morally and politically suspect just a decade earlier. This example points to the gendered logic and consequences of stratification in contemporary China. The emergence of a new, class-inflected masculinity, revealed in this case in the domain of marriage, reoriented the ambitions of these teachers and altered their sense of themselves as producers, consumers, and men. And for the female teachers it helped reinforce a reemerging "traditional" femininity—that women should cultivate their feminine virtues and physical attractiveness along with the goal of marrying well. As many popular allegories now proclaim, overachievement in education and business would only make finding a husband more difficult.

There was a saying often repeated to me in these conversations: "As soon as a man gets rich, he goes bad; as soon as a woman goes bad, she becomes rich" (*nanren yi youqian jiu huaile; nüren yihuaile jiu youqian*). This statement suggests that to many of my students both the lure of wealth and the experience of prosperity affect men and women differently. They understood wealth not only to reveal basic differences between men and women, but to have a transformative effect on their motives, characters, and relationships as well. In short, the social stratification brought by China's economic reforms has produced new ideologies and relations of gender, and these are in turn affecting the course of social and economic change in China (Gal and Kligman 2000).

This book examines the rise of elite networks composed of nouveau-riche entrepreneurs, state enterprise managers, and government officials. These powerful new groups have exerted increasing dominance over many aspects of Chinese commerce and politics during the reform era, which began in the late 1970s. The book considers these networks, which are composed mostly of men, as gendered social formations governed by an ethics of brotherhood, loyalty, and patronage. Using ethnographic data gathered from interviews, experiences as the host of a Chinese television show, and countless evenings accompanying businessmen entertaining their clients, partners, and state officials, I analyze the ways in which relationships are formed between elite men through shared experiences of leisure—banqueting, drinking, gambling, and cavorting with female hostesses—and the importance of these relationships in organizing business ventures, orienting personal morality, and performing social status.

This "masculinization" of the sphere of private business and deal-making in China has generated challenges for women entrepreneurs, who are often accused of using their sexuality to get ahead, and has given rise to a new class of young women who live off the patronage of China's new-rich businessmen and corrupt state officials. These young women are central to mediating relationships and mirroring status among elite men and are integral to the emergence of a growing, semi-legitimate "beauty economy" (*meinü jingji*) in urban China, which seeks to exploit the youth and attractiveness of young women for commercial gain.

I also examine the rise of new forms of leisure and consumption, new patterns of marriage and sexuality, and the proliferation of official corruption in China, all as aspects of shifting templates of interpersonal morality. I contend that these phenomena are key to understanding new forms of economic inequality and gender discrimination in contemporary China, as well as many aspects of China's current political configuration.

China's Market Reforms
and the Rise of Entrepreneurs

After the death of Mao in 1976 and after a brief Maoist interim period led by Hua Guofeng, the Communist Party, under the leadership of Deng Xiaoping, began to reassess many of the tenets of Maoist economics such as collectivization and the centralized allocation of resources. In the domain of ideology, Deng proclaimed that the fundamental contradiction in Chinese society was no longer between classes, but between "the backward and the advanced forces of production," and therefore called for the unleashing of the latter, even if it meant the appearance of "transitional" forms of social inequality. Deng grounded his new theory of "socialism with Chinese characteristics" in a selective reading of Maoist thought that stressed pragmatism over theoretical dogmatism, an approach summarized by Mao's oft-quoted phrase, "seek truth from facts." Deng and the Party legitimated their reform program largely as a reorganization of the economy in accordance with certain "natural laws" of the market. Market reforms, were, and continue to be, legitimated as scientific and rational means of achieving the socialist ends of national economic prosperity, social stability, and prestige in the international political arena.

In 1978, the Third Plenum of the Eleventh Party Congress introduced the first reforms that marked the beginning of the Reform and Opening Policy (*gaige kaifang*) and what has become known as the reform era. This period has been marked by a decline in central economic planning and an increasing reliance on market mechanisms for the distribution of capital, resources, and goods. The "opening" component of the Reform and Opening Policy also signaled an opening to cultural and economic exchanges with the capitalist world—the United States, Japan, Hong Kong, and Taiwan in particular. It also signaled a turning away from the "nonaligned" countries of the third world (Rofel 2007: 11).

Reforms began in rural areas in 1980 with the introduction of the household responsibility system. However, following a general theme of the reform era, practices on the ground tended to precede their official sanction in state policy. Under this system, individual households contracted for a portion of collectively owned land and farm equipment, which they "paid" for in taxes and grain quota obligations to the state. Households were allowed to organize production in any way they saw fit and to sell their surplus for profit. Although the household responsibility system improved agricultural output and raised the standard of living throughout rural China, reforms in rural industry benefited a smaller portion of the country and produced a class of rural industrialists which included many cadres and their kin.

Post-Mao reforms also included a reorganization of state power. The Communist Party apparatus was formally dislodged from the government bureaucracy (though not disconnected in practice), and the daily operation of the government became less subject to the intense politicization that characterized the Cultural Revolution years (1966–1976). The Party's role was envisioned as formulating goals, agendas, and priorities, while the government's role would be to develop and implement policies that realized these goals (Fairbank and Goldman 1998: 420). Deng called for the rationalization of bureaucratic rule, emphasizing professional qualifications over ideological purity among the official ranks (Meisner 1999). Both economic and political decision-making were partially decentralized, granting greater autonomy to local-level governments and cadres. While this change helped facilitate rapid economic growth in many areas, it also gave local officials the power and administrative space to personally profit from economic reforms. They were able to do so largely because many of the new market-oriented businesses were built on the bureaucratic architecture of the previous collective, state-run economy.

"Township-village enterprises" (TVEs) were one such example.[2] They evolved from collective and brigade-run industries started during the Great Leap Forward (1958–1960). The dramatic success of TVEs in the mid-1980s spawned the first class of "new rich"; and "rural entrepreneurs" (*nongcun qiyejia*) and nouveau-riche "upstarts" (*baofahu*) emerged as social categories around this time. Though officially classified as part of the collective sector of the economy, TVEs were run independently of planned economic decisions by the state, a common theme of much market-oriented business during the first decade of reforms.[3] They were officially registered as collectives (known as "wearing a red hat" [*dai hongmaozi*]), but most were run like profit-oriented private businesses. In fact, many "privately run" businesses to this day are still started with state-controlled capital, affiliate themselves with a state-owned enterprise or ministry, or invite one or more government officials to serve on their governing board, practices that allow them to reap the tax benefits, regulatory flexibility, and political protection afforded by close ties to the state (Wank 1999; Tsai 2007; Huang 2008).

Small-time entrepreneurs first appeared in urban areas in the early 1980s as "independent households" (*getihu*). For the most part, this term referred to a petty capitalist class of shop owners, peddlers, taxi drivers, and restaurateurs who were independent of the state-controlled work-unit (*danwei*) structure, made their own production decisions, and received few or no state-sponsored benefits such as medical care and housing. Businesses classified as getihu were envisioned by policymakers as units of household production and were legally limited to eight employees. Up until the early 1990s, most urban Chinese viewed this class with suspicion and disdain.[4] Many early getihu who prospered in the nascent market economy were in fact men and women with low political status and sometimes criminal backgrounds on the margins of the state-run economy who had little to lose by engaging in semi-legal business. They included unemployed youth and intellectuals who had recently returned to urban areas after being sent down to the countryside during the Cultural Revolution, as well as former political prisoners.

Reflecting on this era, many of my informants described the first group to get rich from market-oriented small businesses as "daring" (*danzi da*) because of the semi-legal nature and uncertain political status of many of their activities. According to narratives of the time, because they already lived a marginal, insecure existence, successful getihu were not afraid to suffer or "eat bitterness" (*chiku*). In the 1980s, many parents would have been reluctant to allow their daughters to marry an entrepreneur, which at the time was still perceived as a politically insecure status (Yang 1994: 160).

The power and scope of the market economy in urban areas increased significantly in 1984 when the Communist Party leadership called for the increased efficiency and autonomy of state enterprises. Cut off from public funds and facing bankruptcy if unable to show a profit, most urban enterprises began to be run like profit-minded businesses, and some aspects of production (as well as entire enterprises) were contracted out (*chengbao*) to entrepreneurs, many of whom were the current managers of the businesses being privatized. Until the mid-1990s, however, the majority of these enterprises used their increased revenues to provide for employees by constructing housing and creating jobs for their employees' children, thereby continuing to fulfill their socialist-era welfare obligations (Andreas 2008: 127). While many managers themselves became shareholders in or proprietors of formerly state-owned enterprises through managerial buyouts and "insider privatization", others profited both directly and indirectly from their sale. According to several of my interviewees, as failing and unprofitable state enterprises started to be dismantled, countless numbers of them were sold at well below market prices to relatives and associates of the cadres overseeing their sale who manipulated the value of the company's assets.

In 1988, private firms (*siying qiye*) received official legal sanction, and private businesses were allowed to legally hire more than eight employees. In practice, it was still difficult for them to obtain bank loans, they were subject to higher rates of taxation than their "red hat"-wearing or state-run counterparts, and they were (and still are) barred from certain sectors of the economy. As Kellee Tsai (2007: 54) puts it, it wasn't until after Deng Xiaoping's 1992 Southern Tour (*nanxun*) that "the red hats started to come off" and the number of legally registered private enterprises began to mushroom.[5] Many state-run and collective enterprises were dismantled or privatized, resulting in over 50 million public sector workers losing their jobs. Those state enterprises that remained were increasingly run like profit-oriented businesses, shedding many of the welfare obligations to their employees (Andreas 2008: 131). Around this time the flow of rural migrants to cities and prosperous rural regions such as the Pearl River Delta, which had started in the early 1980s, became a flood. These migrants filled the service and manufacturing jobs created by the newly legitimated private sector.

After 1992, foreign investment, the bulk of which initially came from Taiwan and Hong Kong, also took off, creating more opportunities for entrepreneurs as factory managers and export merchants. China's Special Economic Zones, as well as other coastal cities open to foreign capital, attracted much of this investment, which was primarily used to support export-oriented manufacturing. During the 1990s and 2000s, foreign investment continued to grow exponentially as other cities and provinces were opened up to international capital. Most of the early foreign corporate ventures in China came in the form of joint ventures, which paired foreign companies with Chinese state-owned and privately owned enterprises. But since China's entry into the World Trade Organization (WTO) in 2001, foreign investment has increasingly taken the form of wholly foreign-owned enterprises (WFOEs). By 2008, 80 percent of foreign investment assumed a "wholly-owned" structure (Walter and Howie 2010: 7).

Seeing the success and official sanction of profit-making, by the mid-1990s members of nearly all occupational groups and economic strata of China's cities began to moonlight in private enterprises to supplement their work-unit incomes. Many left their work units or dropped out of school to form private businesses in the hope of making a fortune in the market economy (Gold 1991). Despite the preponderance of tales of hard work and self-sacrifice serving as the basis of rags-to-riches success, entrepreneurs with official connections succeeded at a much higher rate than ordinary citizens (Pieke 1995; Buckley 1999; Meisner 1999: 477).

The means of profit-making for the officially connected often bordered on the illegal. One legacy of the restructuring of 1984 was a dual pricing system in which state industries paid a low fixed price for resources that could then be sold for much more on the free market. Many early fortunes of the new rich (largely composed of former cadres, state enterprise managers, and their friends and relatives) were made through practices that exploited discrepancies between the planned and market economies. Smuggling of imported luxury goods, films, music, electronics, and cars from Hong Kong, Japan, and the West was rampant in southern coastal areas as well.

The early 1990s saw a mass departure of "intellectuals" (*zhishifenzi*)—teachers, scientists, and engineers—from their work units into the market economy as well, a phenomenon known as *xiahai*, "jumping into the sea." Also in the mid-1990s, an influx of foreign capital led to the creation of another category of nouveau riche—"white-collar" workers (*bai ling*)—highly skilled employees and managers of foreign or joint-venture companies. This group, which is concentrated in large eastern cities, tends to be better educated and more cosmopolitan than the stereotypical entrepreneur and is often disdainful of the crudeness and lack of sophistication of many of China's nouveau riche from the interior provinces. The growing success of large Chinese private and state-owned companies has also contributed to the rise of this white-collar class.

In a speech on July 1, 2001, China's then president, Jiang Zemin, gave official approval to the status of entrepreneurs. He declared that entrepreneurs from the nonpublic sector of society were "working to build socialism with Chinese characteristics." Jiang proposed that entrepreneurs should join workers, farmers, intellectuals, cadres, and soldiers as the foundational elements of the socialist Chinese nation. This speech also officially condoned what was by that time already a common trend—wealthy entrepreneurs becoming Communist Party members and occupying posts at local levels of government. It seemingly marked the end to a debate on whether "Red Capitalists" should be allowed to join the Communist Party (Li 2001).

Even with some lingering resistance from leftists within the Party, the official embrace of entrepreneurs continues to move ahead. In the spring of 2002, exemplary entrepreneurs became eligible to be considered for model worker honors (Ruwitch 2002). Then, in 2004, the constitution was amended to explicitly protect private property rights, although this has not yet led to dramatic changes in how the state manages property rights in practice (Tsai 2007: 71).

Despite their increasing acceptance by official ideology and vanishing fears of a leftist retreat from reforms, China's entrepreneurs are still intertwined with and dependent upon the state. The majority of entrepreneurs, far from being a class spawned by an unruly, latently democratic market that potentially poses a threat to Communist Party rule (as many Western observers would like to see them) are still largely dependent on the Chinese state for capital, certain commodities (such as land), beneficial policies, and access to business opportunities in many industries. The political, cultural, and economic conditions in which entrepreneurs have arisen complicate attempts to place them within universalizing social science categories such as the "bourgeoisie" or "middle class," who inevitably come to demand political rights and representation to protect their accumulated capital (see Goodman 2008). In fact, instead of autonomy from the state, many entrepreneurs actively seek ways to forge closer relationships with state officials (although many do so grudgingly), as these still afford them a competitive advantage in virtually all areas of business.

New-Rich Men and the Effects of Wealth

Following the late-1990s commercialization of housing, the rise of private auto ownership, and the explosion of exclusive bars, restaurants, and nightclubs in urban areas, a distinctive elite emerged in nearly all Chinese cities. Drawing from the practices of Hong Kong and Taiwanese businessmen, images of Western life in Hollywood films, and prerevolutionary Chinese gentry culture, this new elite has created a distinctive lifestyle that has served as the subject of countless political, economic, and moral discourses on the future of China, alternately receiving praise and condemnation.

The smashing of the "iron rice bowl" (*tiefanwan*)—the end of state systems guaranteeing social services, lifelong employment, and housing—has generated greater uncertainty for most Chinese, but it has also created opportunities for individuals to dramatically alter their material wealth and social status. As the influence of the market economy on many aspects of people's lives grows, the authority of the socialist work unit (*danwei*) in such realms as marriage decisions, housing allocations, and career choices has virtually disappeared, allowing for greater personal freedom and autonomy. Many Chinese view post-Mao society as having more space for the expression of individuality, providing more opportunities for economic advancement, and offering more choice and greater freedom in marriage, career, and lifestyle. Urban Chinese often characterize the present as a return to more "natural" gender relations after the prohibitions of the Maoist years. The lifestyle of China's new rich is understood by many to exemplify these trends.

In addition to being hailed by the government for their enlightened business practices through "model worker" awards and Communist Party membership, new-rich entrepreneurs, the vast majority of whom are male, are often the most sought-after marriage partners, trendsetters in consumption and fashion, and the most prominent patrons of urban China's exclusive restaurants, nightclubs, and department stores. Advertisements, fashion magazines, and romance and dating-themed television and radio shows draw from the experiences and images of the new rich to produce and market a new elite masculinity for emulation by consumers from all strata of Chinese society. Furthermore, elite masculine forms of entertainment and leisure—banqueting, drinking, singing karaoke, playing mahjong, receiving massages and foot baths (*xijiao*)—have come to form the core practices for the cultivation of personal relationships (*guanxi*) with both government officials and fellow businessmen essential for making deals in China (Liu 2002; Zhang 2002; Zheng 2006; Uretsky 2007). Much of this entertaining involves young women, who play a mediating role in projecting an idealized masculinity onto the men involved (Allison 1994). Elite masculinity thus is gradually becoming institutionalized and codified by state and market alike, and in the process it is becoming the normative masculinity around which all urban men's practices are oriented and measured.

At the same time, many Chinese see prosperity as having had a negative impact on people's character, personal relationships, and morality, as exhibited by the excesses of male entrepreneurs. The Chinese media abound with stories of happy marriages turned bad once the husband got rich, tales of businessmen who keep unofficial second wives (*bao ernai*), and accounts of women lured into extramarital affairs by the luxurious lifestyles of entrepreneurs (Xu 1996). Intellectuals and reformers decry the betrayal of socialist goals of gender equality by young women who cultivate their feminine charms in the hope they can marry well or "live off moneybags" (*bang dakuan*). Young people of both genders complain that marriage has been rendered little more than a material transaction (*jiaoyi hunyin*).[6] Campaigns launched at both national and local levels have sought to tone down the consumption activities of the new rich and regulate the businesses that cater to them.

Another legacy of the new rich is divorce. Divorce rates among the new rich are much higher than among the Chinese population as a whole (Tang 2009).

So-called buyout divorces (*gaojia xieji lihun*) have emerged in which a wealthy entrepreneur offers his first wife a significant share of his wealth in exchange for a quick and easy divorce, and, because he has not technically abandoned his family, the moral upper hand.

The Chinese marriage law was reformed in 2001 largely to deal with the problems associated with the newly wealthy such as de facto polygyny, abandonment of spouses, and divorce and prenuptial settlements involving significant amounts of wealth. While many single women express their desire to find a man with "good economic conditions" (*you tiaojian*—usually referring to the possession of a car, house, and high salary), they also complain that men at this income level cannot be trusted to be faithful. Furthermore, for Chinese men lacking the resources to enter the ranks of the new rich (or even a vaguely defined car- and house-owning middle class), exclusion from this lifestyle is often experienced as a form of "emasculation"—difficulty finding a spouse, loss of status and prestige, and a dwindling social network.[7] Given their status as both exemplary and excessive, male entrepreneurs of the new-rich class thus embody many of the contradictions of the reform era.

Who Are the New Rich?

When people in Chengdu asked me about my research topic, my most economical answer was simply, "the new rich," which I most often described with the phrase "the rich stratum (*furen jieceng*), "high society" (*shangliu shehui*), or simply the "new rich" (*xinfu*).[8] By far the most common question that followed was, "How much money does someone need to have to be considered rich?" Sometimes I suggested a monthly salary that I considered put one in the ranks of the new rich, but my interlocutors often responded that that wasn't enough or that there were lots of people who made that kind of money. Another response questioned the value of my topic: "Why do you want to study them? They're all corrupt." Or, "We're trying to learn from famous American entrepreneurs like Bill Gates. Why would you want to study Chinese entrepreneurs?"

These exchanges did lead me to ponder the problem of just who constituted the new rich. Because I didn't have access to my informants' bank statements, and many were less than forthcoming about their personal net worth and its sources, I could only use the external trappings of money such as their cars, wardrobes, houses, club memberships, and circle of friends and associates as indicators of their wealth, a tactic that proved mostly effective.[9] This approach followed from my understanding of the new rich as not a coherent class defined by income level or occupation, but an unstable and contested category that is constituted by the practices and performances of a diverse group of entrepreneurs, professionals, artists, and government officials.

To most of the Chinese with whom I spoke, the new rich were the public new rich—the entrepreneurs and heads of enterprises that appear on *Forbes* magazine's or *Hu Run Report*'s list of China's richest people and who are profiled in the Chinese and international media. Or they are high-ranking officials and their the sons and daughters (the so-called princeling party [*taizidang*]) who now occupy key positions in many major state-owned companies and are frequently employed by large multinational corporations doing business in China hoping to benefit from their high-level guanxi.[10] The Western media, on the other hand, are often quick to lump the new rich in with an emerging "middle class" in China that, they presume, will help usher in political reform. As measured by their income, however, this new "middle class" constitutes a small slice of even urban China, let alone China as a whole, and thus they resemble a minority elite more than a middle class.[11]

Using World Bank standards of average world income adjusted for purchasing power in China, a Chinese National Bureau of Statistics Survey from 2005 reported that only 5 percent of China's population could be considered middle class by these global standards (Renmin Wang 2007).[12] In an editorial entitled "The New Rich in China: Why There Is No New Middle Class," David Goodman (2007) argues that new-rich entrepreneurs in China, judged by political, ideological, or economic standards, fail to resemble a middle class as it is idealized in the West and cautions us not to see them simply as "the PRC manifestation of a universal middle class" (Goodman 2008: 1). In their numbers, relative incomes, and political behavior, he contends that they resemble something closer to an "haute bourgeoisie," a minority elite with close ties to the state. He argues that labeling the new rich the "middle class" is comforting both to Westerners, who believe this class will usher in liberal democracy, and to many Chinese, who can see them as a growing middle stratum rather than a divergent elite (2007). In short, the notion of the middle class carries a great deal of ideological baggage and partakes in the mythology of China's inevitable evolution toward democracy.[13]

Thus, for these political, analytic, and demographic reasons, I label most of my wealthy informants members of the "elite" or the "new rich." Although most of my research subjects lacked the wealth, power, and connections of the national elite (that is, they were not heads of national enterprises or members of the "princeling party," for example), many of their practices, privileges, and anxieties are similar. They have close ties and access to local (and sometimes provincial-level) state officials, sometimes serving on local People's Congresses (*Renda*) and joining the Communist Party themselves. Many enjoy extralegal protections, and some are awarded government privileges, from special license plates to official titles. Many have their own private chauffeurs, and nearly all employ domestic servants in their homes. Like the children of their national-level counterparts, their children attend the best domestic schools and often enroll in elite boarding schools and universities in other countries. Although some are resentful of the fact, many rely on the current Chinese regime for their success and protection, and the majority fears a major political shakeup in China.

Entrepreneurs in China, and the new rich in general, have diverse backgrounds with varying economic interests and political attitudes and thus should not be considered a "coherent class" (Tsai 2007: 71). As the above history suggests, the category "entrepreneur" includes individuals in a wide variety of private and state-owned industries. In fact, the very diversity of backgrounds and paths to success among China's new rich generates a great deal of anxiety and boundary work among their ranks. Every entrepreneur is haunted by a category closely associated with his or her occupation—that of the *baofahu*, a derogatory term for the nouveau riche. Baofahu, who are stereotypically from a rural background, are considered culturally unsophisticated, poorly educated, and lacking the "taste" (*pinwei*) and personal quality (*suzhi*) to spend their wealth properly. The paths to success for baofahu are often suspect as well, and they are depicted both as lucky beneficiaries of opportunities and as unscrupulous profiteers. Thus, entrepreneurs I knew often concealed their rural backgrounds from me at first and were at times reluctant to provide a detailed account of how they made their money.

Virtually all of the entrepreneurs in my study are private entrepreneurs, operating businesses that are legally separate from the state-run economy (though by no means disconnected from it). Except where noted, most of them came from ordinary families with little wealth and few political connections. Despite their high levels of wealth and status relative to the vast majority of Chinese, most of the entrepreneurs I worked with still characterized Chinese society as a domain in which only those with "background" (*bejing*—political connections, wealthy families, influential friends) were guaranteed long-lasting success. For the most part they differentiated between themselves and what they termed the "nobility" (*guizu*—the same term used for the European aristocracy), which usually referred to high-level government officials and their families and the publicly known super-rich. In contrast to the privileged *guizu*, most of my informants referred to themselves and their social group as members of the "upper-middle stratum" (*zhongshang jieceng*) or "high-salaried stratum" (*gao shouru jieceng*).

State enterprise managers and government officials are another component of the new rich. They were a constant presence during evenings of entertaining hosted by my businessmen informants, and I met many during the course of my research. Because of the sensitive nature of my research interests, which often touched on semilegal and illegal practices in China's economy, they were usually reluctant to serve as research informants. When discussing this group, entrepreneurs tended to lump together state enterprise managers, leaders of party- or state-controlled institutions (such as the military, scientific research institutes, and universities), members of the Communist Party's various bureaucracies, and members of the government into a single category usually referred to as "officials" (*guanyuan, dangguande*), "cadres" (*ganbu*), or "leaders" (*lingdao*). Thus, when I refer to government officials below, I am following the practice of my entrepreneur informants and mean anyone whose status was derived primarily from his or her position in a bureaucracy. Although I tried to ascertain the positions and affiliations of officials who were introduced to me, many were reluctant to identify the institutions to which they belonged.

Despite their growing political and social acceptance, the new rich I encountered were beset with an array of anxieties about their position within Chinese society and how they were perceived by both their domestic peers and the outside world. Many were unhappy with aspects of their professional and personal lives and critical of the lifestyles and values of their peers. Several had become legal residents of Western countries and planned on leaving China once they made their fortunes. Most had sent or planned to send their children abroad for their education. Others had sent their entire families to live abroad and planned to join them in retirement. Most expressed a conflicted attitude toward the current regime. On the one hand, they resented the power and influence the state wielded over their affairs. But at the same time they acknowledged how they had profited from ties to the state and feared the chaos dramatic political transformation might bring. Few harbored an optimistic outlook on China's long-term political and economic prospects.

Research Chronology and Methods

I conducted this study during several extended periods of research in Chengdu, the capital of Sichuan province, from 2002 to 2006, a total of thirty-five months of primary fieldwork supplemented by short follow-up visits in 2008, 2010, and 2011. In early 2003, I became involved with a local Chengdu television show, serving as a co-host, translator, and writer. The show received all of its revenue from advertising, and thus a large portion of my work consisted of accompanying the show's producer and sales representatives to area businesses to court sponsors for our show. I also was charged with helping to maintain the show's relationship with cadres in the state-run television station, whose sponsorship was crucial to its existence and plans for expansion to other networks. I met many of my initial research subjects through this experience, including restaurant owners, real estate developers, government officials, and entrepreneurs with diverse business ventures who were the program's sponsors and whose businesses were profiled on the show. Through these individuals I gradually was able to meet other members of their social networks, many of whom helped me with my research. During my time at the TV show, I also learned the importance of cultivating and maintaining relationships with clients and official patrons and became familiar with the techniques involved in what the Sichuanese refer to as *goudui*, the courtship of important people for an instrumental purpose.[14]

I ended my association with the television show in the spring of 2004, and in the fall of 2004 I began full-time fieldwork. Building on the contacts I made through the TV show, I spent much of the first few months doing favors for entrepreneurs, including emceeing business ceremonies (because of my television experience) and translating their companies' promotional literature into English. Once I had established a core group of about twenty-five entrepreneurs, I found myself with a fairly full social agenda, meeting people for tea or coffee in the afternoons and attending banquets and going out to karaoke clubs in the evenings. Though I met most of my subsequent research informants through this group, I also met a few key individuals by chance at bars and nightclubs frequented by the new rich.

My core informants ranged in age from their mid-twenties to late forties. Older entrepreneurs, those in their fifties and sixties, were often less accessible to me partly because their lifestyles differed from their younger counterparts. They were less likely to frequent clubs, and because their business ventures tended to be more well established, entertaining was a less crucial component of their business. They were also more likely to engage in less-visible forms of leisure such as gambling in teahouses and trips to saunas. My research thus focused on this younger age group largely because they were accessible, and this accessibility was a product of the stage of their careers as well as the industries in which they did business. Furthermore, this younger group constitutes the core demographic of entrepreneurs in China, and it is their business culture that has attracted the most scholarly and popular attention, both in China and elsewhere.

The bulk of the participant-observation component of my research consisted of accompanying entrepreneurs as they entertained their business associates and clients in the evenings and on weekends. During the day I often accompanied my informants to a tea- or coffeehouse, where they played cards, met with business associates, and managed their enterprises over their mobile phones. With a few exceptions, I had little access to their workplaces, and thus their relationships with staff and forms of management fall outside the scope of this ethnography. Most bosses in Chengdu preferred to conduct their business away from their offices, in teahouses, restaurants, and karaoke clubs and by mobile phone. Most of my data were gathered during these informal conversations in the afternoon and evening. During the last several months of my fieldwork, I also conducted extended semi-structured recorded interviews with several of my key informants.

Many of my informants came to see me—a male, Chinese-speaking American familiar with banquet protocol—as a useful resource in conducting their business entertaining who could help build their social networks. Sometimes I was invited along to help court an important client or official. At other times my presence as a foreigner served to vaguely suggest the international reach of an entrepreneur's social circle. The status afforded to me as a white, American male, and the novelty of being a Chinese-speaking foreigner in Chengdu, which has a much smaller foreign population than many of China's eastern cities, no doubt helped me gain access to my informants' social networks. As a foreigner with whom they had no business ties, I was safely positioned outside their business and social circles. Thus many of my informants felt that they could discuss personal dilemmas with me that would have been too sensitive to discuss frankly with other members of their social networks, for fear that such revelations would adversely affect their reputations. Many also actively sought an outsider's perspective on the changes occurring in Chinese society and were eager to discuss their observations with me. My outsider status, however, also imposed limitations on the types of people willing to talk to me and the kinds of information they were willing to divulge.

Chengdu as a Fieldsite

In the English-language social science literature on China one rarely finds mention of the importance of local discourses of regional cultural difference. To most Chinese, however, each region and city is associated with a character type, some aspects of which locals self-identify with, others of which they reject. These tropes figured heavily into how my research subjects talked about gender relations, business practices, and the overall direction of change in China during the reform era.

Regional "character" was used to explain particular behaviors, and they frequently cited regional cultural differences to account for the representativeness or uniqueness of Chengdu in economic and cultural matters. Sichuan as a whole and Chengdu in particular has a reputation for being more "laid back" (*xiuxian*) and slower-paced than other regions of China. To account for this, Chengduers often noted that their city had been less affected by many of the wars and natural disasters of the past several hundred years than the eastern regions of China. Sichuan's climate is also well suited for agriculture, giving it the nickname "land of abundance" (*tianfu zhi guo*). Urbanites would often assert that even the farmers in Sichuan enjoyed their leisure and could be seen playing mahjong year-round. Many locals also explained that the irrigation works at the nearby city of Dujiangyan, which helped prevent floods and facilitated agriculture in the Sichuan basin, was a major contributing factor to the laid-back mentality of most Sichuanese.

Chengdu, with a population of around 9 million (14 million if you include the surrounding rural districts), is the financial, commercial, and transportation center of western China. Located at the western edge of the Sichuan Basin, Chengdu is surrounded by mountains on all sides, shielding it from harsh northerly winds but also condemning it to fewer sunny days than London. The region's geography and its resulting reputation as a place that promotes hedonism and whittles away the ambitions of young people have led to a popular saying that Sichuan is not a good place for young people to go to seek their fortunes (*shao buru chuan*). Some people even used Chengdu's topography to emphasize this point: "Sichuan is a basin; once you fall in, it's very hard to get out."

Throughout China, next to its spicy cuisine, Chengdu and Sichuan are most famous for the purported beauty of the local women. The most common explanation for this is the nearly sunless climate, which, it is claimed, allows the local women to maintain white, unblemished skin. Chengdu also has a reputation for being sexually more "open" than most Chinese cities and certainly more than any other city in the interior.[15]

Virtually all the Chengduers I encountered agreed that their reputation for being laid back and enjoying life was accurate, the evidence of which was often

FIGURE 1.1. Chengduers playing cards and mahjong outside a teahouse. All photographs by the author.

visible and frequently commented on by Chinese from elsewhere. While having tea in a Chengdu teahouse on a weekday afternoon with a visitor from Guangzhou, my friend expressed shock that there were "so many capable, working-aged men in a teahouse playing cards in the middle of the afternoon." Many of the entrepreneurs who owned or managed their own businesses spent their days in teahouses, often playing cards and discussing entrepreneurial ventures with their business associates. However, in emulation of their bosses' habits, many junior managers also spent their days in (less expensive) teahouses doing the same. Thus, most concrete tasks were eventually delegated to assistant managers and low-ranking employees who were stuck at their offices and places of business.

Despite the weight Chengduers gave to regional culture in accounting for their behaviors and attitudes, many of the practices I examine in this book have a national reach. All of the entrepreneurs I worked with had business networks that extended to other major Chinese cities, and most had both Chinese and non-Chinese business associates in other countries. They viewed some of the practices of relationship cultivation (*gao guanxi* or *goudui*) as more exaggerated in Chengdu but as not fundamentally different from what they encountered in other Chinese cities and rural areas. In fact they saw the relative importance of guanxi and the practices used for guanxi cultivation as varying more by industry than by region. In areas such as construction, real estate, and mining they are essential, while in fields such as advertising and information technology (IT) arguably less so.

At times they characterized Chengdu as being a little more economically "backward" (*luohou*) than cities such as Guangzhou and Shanghai, which was evidenced by the relative lack of foreign investment (at the time of my research) and the more "traditional" management style of Chengdu's bosses. Entrepreneurs who had lived and worked in eastern Chinese cities often complained about the poor efficiency and lack of drive of many Chengduers. Businessmen from elsewhere (nearby Chongqing in particular) accused Chengduers of being superficial (*xurong*) and deceitful (*jia*). I constantly heard the phrase "They make many promises but deliver on few of them" to characterize both Chengdu government officials and businessmen.

Most media attention and scholarly work on China's new rich or "middle class" has focused on wealthy eastern cities such as Beijing, Shanghai, Shenzhen, and Guangzhou that are well integrated into the global economy. The vast majority of foreign firms who do business or manufacture products in China are located in these cities or in surrounding regions, in particular the Pearl River Delta region of Guangdong and the Yangtze River Delta region around Shanghai. Because of its distance from ports, at the time of my research, Chengdu played a fairly small role in export-oriented manufacturing compared with many eastern cities. However, because of its cheaper labor costs, China's interior is very quickly attracting more and more manufacturing. Transportation has also improved with the construction of thousands of miles of highways that link western China to the coast.

Given its role as the commercial center of western China, the entrepreneurs with whom I worked were more likely to be involved in various forms of trade, from the distribution of liquor to the sale of foreign automobiles, than in manufacturing. What manufacturing does exist in Chengdu is concentrated primarily in the pharmaceutical, aeronautics, electronics, food, and liquor industries. Even though they were the owners and operators of private companies, these entrepreneurs had many contacts and ties to the "state sector." State-owned companies, owing to their deep pockets and reputation for accepting kickbacks, were some of their most important clients.

In 1999, the central government announced the "Develop the West" (*Xibu Da Kaifa*) program, a plan to speed up the development of China's western regions, whose growth has lagged behind that of coastal cities. This plan consists of incentives for foreign and domestic firms to invest in China's western regions, the creation of special technology zones in selected western cities, and several infrastructure improvement projects. Since the introduction of this policy initiative, Chengdu has been actively promoted as a high-tech center, and in 2006, Intel, lured by tax incentives and cheap labor, opened a plant in the Chengdu suburbs. Many local and foreign businessmen saw Intel's arrival as signaling the "discovery" of Chengdu by foreign capital, and several other Fortune 500 companies, especially those in the IT industry, including Foxconn in 2010, have since established research centers and manufacturing facilities in Chengdu. The recent reports on working conditions at the Chengdu Foxconn plants that manufacture iPhones and iPads has thrust Chengdu into the international spotlight.[16]

Like virtually all major cities in China from 2002 to 2011, Chengdu was undergoing a real estate boom. Soviet-style architecture from the Maoist era was being torn down all over the city and replaced with office towers and gated apartment complexes. Centuries-old one-story wooden houses (*pingfang*), which once dotted the city center and gave Chengdu a distinctive character, had all but vanished by the time I left Chengdu in 2006. Farmland surrounding the city was rapidly being appropriated for housing developments, industrial parks, and designated green spaces. Farmers who once occupied the land were being resettled in high-rises in newly urbanized areas. The vast majority of my informants, if not involved in real estate development as their primary business, were buying up land and apartment units as part of their portfolio of investments. Many entrepreneurs I interviewed who were struggling to find new ventures pinned their hopes on real estate.

The networks of entrepreneurs with whom I conducted my research were deeply financially and socially intertwined. They were shareholders in each other's companies and bought each other's products and services. They exchanged information, offered advice, provided both material and nonmaterial assistance, and served as intermediaries in bringing together business partners, introducing clients, and soliciting patrons in the government. Because it is still difficult for small and medium-sized private companies to obtain bank loans in China, many relied on their social networks for the bulk of their capital (see

FIGURE 1.2. View to the south from a luxury high-rise in Chengdu. Before the late 1990s this entire area was farmland.

Tsai 2002). After making their initial fortune in one business, most had diversi-fied by investing in their friends' ventures to such an extent that it was often difficult to pin down their primary business. In addition to shares based on the amount of capital invested, entrepreneurs were sometimes awarded shares in their associates' companies based on their relationship to other sharehold-ers or in recognition of nonmaterial contributions such as innovative ideas or important connections. These shares were referred to as "dry shares" (*gangu*). For example, a businessman with a relative in the transportation bureau might be allotted a number of shares to reflect the deals his connection to the govern-ment would likely generate. Similarly, important officials were offered shares and/or seats on a company's governing board.

At the time of my research, because there were fewer foreign firms and large private enterprises in Chengdu than in eastern cities, Chengdu lacked the large white-collar class that characterizes cities such as Beijing, Shanghai, and Shenzhen. Owing to the lack of prestigious, high-salary positions, most of my informants looked down on all forms of salaried work, dismissing it as a form of "working for others" (*gei bieren dagong*).[17]

Most viewed being the boss of one's own company as the only means to elite wealth and status. This attitude resulted in a context in which everyone, from a low-level salaried worker to a foreign researcher, was presumed to be a potential entrepreneur on the lookout for business opportunities. Investment opportunities and business dilemmas were constant topics of conversation, not just among the entrepreneurs I worked with but among ordinary Chengduers hoping to escape salaried jobs as well. As an illustration, once, a local doctor, while diagnosing my illness, pitched a business plan to me involving a website that would sell collectible Chinese stamps and coins to foreign customers.

Avoiding involvement in my informants' business schemes took consider-able energy on my part and required constant explanation. The entrepreneurs I worked with were baffled by my seemingly irrational commitment to an un-profitable career as an academic and skeptical of my ability to look after my own self-interest.

The Evolution of *Guanxi* in China's Business World

A key component of my informants' social worlds and a constant topic of dis-cussion among themselves and with me were their social networks or guanxi-wang. Despite what countless business guides to China might lead one to believe, guanxi is not an unchanging essence of Chinese culture, nor a preprogrammed way that Chinese people do business. In everyday usage, the term guanxi refers to webs of social relations through which an individual can achieve various ends.[18]

Guanxi connections can help an ordinary citizen grease the wheels of a slow-moving bureaucracy, or it can provide a businessman with a government contract to build a road. Although guanxi networks (*guanxiwang*) are used to accomplish tasks from the mundane to the fortune-making, this does not mean that guanxi is therefore by definition purely "instrumental" or "utility-maximizing." Guanxi relationships are composed of mixtures of interest, affect, and morality, a mixture that distinguishes them from other types of relationships. As Andrew Kipnis argues, in guanxi relationships "feeling and instrumentality are a totality" (1997: 27).

Not all relationships are considered guanxi, but one can cultivate guanxi in virtually any social interaction. Closely associated with guanxi is the notion of *renqing*, a multifaceted term that defies a single definition. Literally translated, *renqing* refers to "human sentiments," and in practice it can refer both to affective relationships between kin, friends, and colleagues and "the norms and values that regulate interpersonal relationships" (Y. Yan 2009: xxxiv).[19] The cultural discourse of renqing, rooted in Confucian notions of relational ethics, forms the ethical and moral framework through which guanxi is cultivated, maintained, and put into operation (Yang 1994: 71). In everyday usage renqing has a positive moral connotation, while guanxi has a slightly derogatory one. The distinction between guanxi and renqing, however, is often one of perspective and moral framing rather than analytic category. For example, a businessman acquaintance of mine referred to his relations with the local government as renqing, relations that any outside observer would no doubt characterize as a form of guanxi, if not outright corruption.[20]

Two other features of guanxi important to this study are the reciprocity inherent in guanxi and the relationship between guanxi and social prestige. Once a guanxi relationship is established between two people, each can ask a favor of the other with the expectation that the favor will be repaid sometime in the future (Yang 1994). There is, however, no "time limit" on the repayment, and hasty repayment of a favor might be perceived as an attempt to dissolve the mutual indebtedness at the heart of the relationship. Second, guanxi is related to power and prestige, or "face" (*mianzi*), in complex ways, and relative prestige can shift over the course of the relationship (Hwang 1987; Pye 1992; Y. Yan 1996). During my research, I observed that prestige accrued to those who possessed expansive *guanxiwang* and could mobilize them to get things done for others. As Yunxiang Yan (1996) points out, gifts tend to flow to those who have the most power and prestige and are thus most likely to be able to assist others with weaker guanxi networks. Many of my informants often went out of their way to do favors, offer gifts, or deepen a relationship with a powerful boss or official even when no immediate favor was being sought since these actions allowed them to broaden their guanxiwang.

The fact that guanxi relationships cannot be reduced to being either purely affective, instrumental, or moral has generated much disagreement among social scientists searching for the underlying "truth" behind guanxi (see Gold, Guthrie, and Wank 2002: 8).[21] The logic of guanxi, often understood as a traditional "gift economy," is also thought by some scholars to be fundamentally incompatible with market rationality and the rule of law (Hwang 1987; King 1991: 79; Guthrie 1998).[22] Even those who subscribe to the notion that in guanxi "feeling and instrumentality are a totality" often posit an implicit traditional/ modern divide in guanxi practices, assuming that, in rural areas, guanxi has more to do with sentiment and is grounded in renqing; while in urban centers it is more instrumental and subject to calculations related to the market economy (see, e.g., Y. Yan 1996; 2003).

While some have framed guanxi as the legacy of a planned economy and doomed to be swept away as markets expand (Guthrie 1998; King 1991), other scholars have emphasized the adaptability and continuing evolution of guanxi in the reform era (see Wank 1996, 1999, 2002; Bian 1994, 2002; Pieke 1995; Ong 1999; Potter 2002; Yang 2002).[23] Building on the work of these scholars, my research supports the notion of guanxi as an evolving cultural practice whose existence cannot be derived from the presence or absence of particular institutional structures.[24] The cultural institution of guanxi predates both the PRC and the reform era, and its practices and forms have evolved along with the shifting political and economic regimes of modern China (Yang 1994: 146–72; Y. Yan 1996: 230). For example, during the late Maoist era guanxi networks, often referred to as "going through the back door" (*zou houmen*), played a key role in helping individuals obtain scarce goods, a role they rarely play in today's economy of consumer abundance (Davis 2000). In the context of business, David Wank (2002) argues that markets have not replaced guanxi and clientelist ties between the entrepreneurs and the state, but rather market reforms are structured by and operate within a clientelist framework.

Thus I am skeptical of accounts that view guanxi as the product of a "transitional economy" still trying to shake its socialist legacy or as a relic of traditional culture resistant to modern state and market logics. In the reform era, guanxi networks have proliferated in particular political domains and industries, while they have declined in others. Moreover, they are not simply constituted out of the fabric of "traditional" social relations—such as kinship and native-place ties—but are increasingly forged between business associates in the new spaces of leisure in China's urban centers. Following Yunxiang Yan's characterization of Xiajia villagers, I would agree that most of my informants perceived guanxi to be "the foundation of society—the local moral world in which they live their lives" (Y. Yan 2003: 39).

Increasingly, however, the practices and ideologies associated with guanxi exist "in tension with" the rise of the individualism (Mason, forthcoming) and discourses of self-reliance and self-cultivation in China (Rofel 2007; Ong and Zhang 2008; Y. Yan 2009). Anxieties and frustrations are generated when increasing expectations of self-fulfillment and independence meet the need to rely on social networks for both business success and broader social recognition. Thus, while the moral, financial, and social lives of my informants were still structured by the practices and moralities of guanxi, many felt highly ambivalent about its pull on their lives. They articulated a desire to be free from social networks and allowed to follow their own paths.

This tension between individualism and guanxi mapped onto gender in interesting and unexpected ways. In her seminal study of guanxi, Mayfair Yang (1994: 316) sees the alliances generated by guanxi as inherently feminine, which she contrasts with a "masculine" rationalist objective legal system. She states that the "flexible lines extending social relationships and networks across social groups and divisions" are "more compatible with a female gender construction." In an essay on the growing appeal of Christianity to women in rural Shandong, Andrew Kipnis (2001: 87), however, argues that women are largely excluded from the domain of male banqueting and karaoke singing (two of the key sites of guanxi formation in post-Mao China) that serves to generate a form of association he dubs "particularized male relationality." Drawing on Margery Wolf's (1972) work on women in the patrilineal Chinese family, Kipnis suggests that women are more drawn to the individualism implicit in Christianity, which serves as a "gendered critique" of the outside world of male networks.

Similarly, I found women entrepreneurs to be highly critical of the masculine networks they saw structuring business. They were often dismissive of men whose business success (in their view) derived from the power of their guanxi rather than their own abilities. Invoking notions of individualism and self-reliance, women entrepreneurs often claimed that they, unlike men, were the "real" entrepreneurs in that they relied solely on their individual talent and hard work rather than their guanxi to succeed. Furthermore they often scoffed at the conspicuous, extravagant spending of nouveau-riche businessmen, which they viewed as a hollow performance for the benefit of others rather than a meaningful reflection of their personal character or taste (see Chapter Four).

Interest, Affect, and Gender under Capitalism

Entrepreneurs use an evolving repertoire of practices to cultivate guanxi, and the networks they build and come to rely on have a profound effect on their business ventures, interpersonal ethics, and consumption habits. My account of interpersonal relationships in the world of business in China differs from previous studies in its emphasis on two domains largely neglected by the scholarly literature on China's entrepreneurs: the role of gender in guanxi practices and networks and the evolution of practices of relationship cultivation (entertaining, banqueting, etc.) during the reform era (cf., e.g., Bruun 1993; Wank 1999).[25]

Given that these elite social and business networks are largely composed of men and often formed in clubs and venues that cater to men, I place gender at the center of the ethnography.[26] Although some of these networks are based on ties of kinship and native place, the bulk of the relationships that make up these networks are forged and maintained through ritualized leisure—experiences of shared pleasure in venues catering to the desires of elite men. These experiences are crucial to creating homosocial intimacy, which then can serve as the basis for affective ties between men. These networks, built on ideologies of male solidarity, not only constitute a key component of business but also comprise the "elementary structures" of corruption and organized crime in China.[27]

As Maoist political cosmology has lost its salience in people's interpersonal relationships, gendered notions of interpersonal morality and authority, rooted in kinship and renqing, have increasingly served to legitimate everyday forms of power and ethics. In his study of Xiajia Village in North China, Yunxiang Yan describes how, as the state and the class-based morality it promoted have retreated from everyday life, villagers have fallen back on the ethics of kinship and guanxi as the foundation of their local moral worlds.[28] He argues that kinship ties have become "absorbed into the more general and open-ended structure of guanxi networks" and are becoming increasingly "instrumentalized" and less rooted in morality and sentiment (Y. Yan 2003: 38–40). While I agree with Yan that guanxi rhetorics and practices are often employed when dealing with strangers for instrumental purposes, this dichotomy between sentimental and moral forms on the one hand, and instrumental forms on the other, fails to capture the more dynamic and fluid nature of guanxi in practice (see also Wilson 2002).

As I describe in Chapter Two, businessmen often deliberately try to transform relationships of short-term instrumentality into ones rooted in morality, sentiment, and mutual aid (Wank 1999). This is why entrepreneurs often spend an inordinate amount of time carousing with their clients, partners, official patrons, and associates. Many of the wealthy men I worked with aspired to transcend mere calculation, instrumentality, and interest in their relationships with others. Even when clearly acting in their own individual interests, businessmen often framed it as "helping a friend" or pointed to the nature of a relationship to explain their behavior—"We're brothers" (*xiongdi*), or "We're [part of] one family" (*yijiaren*). Despite the fact that kinship terms were sometimes deployed in a cynical and calculated manner, the overlapping social and business relationships I studied were suffused with the language of kinship. In short, given that businessmen tried very deliberately to mix the instrumental with the affective, the calculated with the moral, and contracts with kinship, it became very difficult to sort out types of guanxi on the ground. Instead, degrees of distance and closeness were constantly evolving as new relationships became more salient and older ones faded away.

In her study of Italian family firms, Sylvia Yanagisako (2002) challenges the dichotomies that have structured much Western social theory, in particular the assumption, inherited from Max Weber (1978) via Talcott Parsons, that economic action is "rational" and rooted in "interest" whereas family ties and friendship are governed by irrational forms of affect.[29] This dichotomy can also be traced to the work of Karl Polanyi (1944) who understood modern European economic history in terms of the attempt to disembed economic activity from other domains of social life.

Anthropologists, influenced by Polanyi as well as Marcel Mauss (1990), typically have tended to see economic life as embedded in other social relationships and their corresponding moralities in noncapitalist societies, but as disembedded in capitalist ones. More recently, however, anthropologists examining actors in capitalist societies have begun to question this distinction

(Parry and Bloch 1989; Dilley 1992; Yanagisako 2002; Ho 2009). Yanagisako (2002: 6), for example, argues that the interests of Italian firm owners are not the product of "the singular logic of capital" but are the "product of historically situated cultural processes," which include both sentiments and desires. This dichotomy between interest and affect is also deeply rooted in Western understandings of the family as a domain of nurturance and affect standing in opposition to the competitive, interested relations of the market (Collier, Rosaldo, and Yanagisako 1997).

Here, following Yanagisako and others (Granovetter 1985; Granovetter and Swedberg 2001), I employ a theory of economic action that "treats all social action—including capital accumulation, firm expansion, and diversification—as constituted both by deliberate, rational calculation and by sentiments and desires: in other words, as cultural practices" (Yanigisako 2002: 21). As Karen Ho (2009: 31) asks in her study of Wall Street investment bankers, "Given that 'the market' has for so long assumed a place of taken-for-granted power in the social scientific literature, what would it mean to conceptualize and approach markets only as a set of everyday, embodied practices"?

This book thus questions the assumption that capitalism and "the market" are transforming business practice, and for that matter, social life in China according to a singular monolithic logic. Instead of taking it for granted that the market disembeds economic activity from other social relationships, I demonstrate how "marketization" in China is best understood as a process of embedding new economic structures and opportunities into existing and emergent social networks that straddle state and society. Rather than rendering guanxi less important, I describe how, in many ways, it has become even more important. In making this assertion, however, I am not arguing for a distinctive Chinese "guanxi" capitalism rooted in relationships that combine interest and affect in opposition to a fully rational modern Western capitalism rooted in law and contracts.[30]

Actually, existing capitalism in the United States, as opposed to ideologically derived models of it, is too embedded in complex social relations, culturally motivated desires, and political structures just as in China. But the character of those relations, the practices through which they are formed, and the cultural idioms through which they are understood are no doubt different. In short, in any cultural or historical context, the ways in which capitalism becomes integrated into social and cultural forms needs to investigated rather than assumed (Sahlins 2000).

Masculinity and Networks in Post-Mao China

Notions of old boys' networks, men's clubs, and smoke-filled rooms are familiar American folk theories of power and often assumed to be integral components of global capitalism (Ling 1999; Connell 2001). The notion that networks of men control and structure key aspects of business and politics in China will likely strike no one as surprising.[31] Yet, partly owing to the power of the dichotomy in which women are equated with the domestic domain of affect and men with the market domain of instrumentality, scholars have tended to interpret business ties between men in terms of interest (or perhaps some notion of primordial male bonding). While a great deal of scholarly literature references (and condemns) these institutions, there is surprisingly little work that shows how networks of male solidarity are formed through men's interactions and how they generate forms of value and obligation that structure business and politics.

Much work on masculinity is very good at showing how "hegemonic masculinity" is reinforced and reproduced in men's interactions,[32] but I would contend that it has been less successful in showing how networks of male solidarity are formed and reproduced through institutionalized practices—in other words, how "old boys' clubs" come into being in the first place.[33] This folk theory of power is, however, a good starting point; these archetypal sites of gendered interactions and assessment—the bar, the locker room, the country club, and the karaoke club—are sites in which anthropologists can analyze these interactions. They accomplish much more than what American businesspeople refer to as "networking." In addition to establishing new relationships, during evenings of banqueting, drinking, gambling, and singing new desires are created and new selves are constituted.

Male, sex-segregated social networks have been at the heart of many late imperial and modern Chinese institutions, from scholarly academies and the civil service exam to secret societies and bandit groups (Mann 2000: 1602). Among the entrepreneurs I worked with in China, business relationships were often couched in a rhetoric of male solidarity, brotherhood, paternalism, mutual aid, and *yiqi* (honor or a sense of obligation in personal relationships). One template for these relationships is the hierarchical and gendered idiom of kinship. Patrons and well-connected bosses are often referred to as "elder brothers" (*dage*), and their status depends on fulfilling paternalist obligations and providing for the well-being of the other members of their networks. Associates and underlings are usually referred to as "iron brothers" (*tiegemen'er*) or simply "brothers" (*xiongdi*). They are expected to put their fictive brotherly relationships above all other commitments, sharing their success and using positions of power to the advantage of other members of their network.

Given the strong rhetoric of brotherhood and loyalty among these groups of men, another template for these relationships is that of *jianghu* culture and the tradition of male brotherhoods in China.[34] *Jianghu* refers to the knight-errant culture depicted in the classic fourteenth-century Chinese novels *Romance of the Three Kingdoms* (*San Guo Yan Yi*) and *The Water Margin* (*Shuihu Zhuan*), sometimes given the English title *All Men Are Brothers*). The peach orchard scene at the beginning of *Three Kingdoms*, in which the three main characters pledge their loyalty to one another, was widely imitated by underground brotherhoods (*banghui*) in Qing China. To this day many criminal sworn brotherhoods in Hong Kong, Taiwan, and the PRC base their initiations on the "peach garden pledge" (*taoyuan jieyi*) from this novel. Guan Yu, the deified main character from *Three Kingdoms*, is also worshipped by many of these groups as the embodiment of the code of brotherhood and "honor in personal relationships" (*yiqi*) (see Ownby 1996; Boretz 2011).

While some of the networks I encountered in my research were organized, underground (criminal) brotherhoods with a well-defined hierarchy and a clearly delineated membership, commonly known as *heishehui* (literally, "black society") in China, many others more loosely mimicked the forms, terms of address, and ideology of China's tradition of sworn brotherhoods.[35] In Republican China (1912–1949) sworn brotherhoods were frequently intertwined with the state to help with the policing and governance of particular unruly populations (Zhou and Shao 1993: 563–72), a relationship that, as I discuss in Chapter Three, is not all too different from their role today. Drawing as much from this tradition as from Hong Kong gangster movies in developing their ethos, formal underground brotherhoods (*heishehui*) exert an increasing influence over local state organs in China, play a key role in real estate development, and control much of China's vast "underground" economy.

In entertaining and leisure interactions, elite men establish forms of solidarity, cooperation, and obligations. Rather than view their practices as part of a "supposedly universal psychology of male bonding" (Kipnis 2002: 92n16), I situate them within the complex social field of contemporary China. In other words, a starting point of my analysis is that masculinity is not a universal essence or biological impulse, but a culturally and historically variable construction that requires constant maintenance through performances.[36]

Carousing in nightclubs with girlfriends and paid hostesses thus should not be interpreted as a release of suppressed masculinity after the prohibitions of socialism or simply as just what men, by nature, are programmed to do. Rather, by drinking, singing, and being flattered by female companions in nightclubs, men are both creating and enacting a particular version of masculinity associated with being a man of status and wealth in post-Mao China.

Lyn Jeffrey (quoted in Rofel 1999: 97) asserts that in the 1980s and 1990s, as the state sector of the economy became less profitable and lost status, it came to be viewed as "feminine," while the private sector was seen as more and more "masculine." This book examines how this gendering of the world of business came to be and the ways in which it is constantly reproduced through forms of network building and deal making in contemporary China. What kinds of subjectivities are produced in these spaces? How do forms of elite play create a space of homosocial intimacy that serves as the basis for building affective ties between men? How are (heterosexual) sexuality and desire marshaled in the service of building alliances between men? When the participants return home and sober up, and after their maids (*baomu*) have washed the cigarette smoke and spilled whiskey from their clothes, what kinds of bonds and desires linger from the previous night?

Elite Networks, Corruption, and the State

In this book I describe the strategies entrepreneurs use to create embeddedness (Polanyi 1944; Granovetter 1985) with their clients, partners, and patrons in the government. Although many scholars have interpreted China's post-Mao economic reforms in the context of a global tide of neoliberalism (e.g., Harvey 2005; Wang 2003), this book suggests that while some of China's policies over the past three decades might be loosely translated as "neoliberal" (e.g., the retreat of the state from the provision of housing and health care, the auctioning and privatization of state-owned businesses and assets), the projection of a neoliberal order onto China distorts key features of China's current political and economic configuration (Kipnis 2007, 2008; Nonini 2008)—namely the rise of elite networks of entrepreneurs and state officials governed by complex moral economies.

Although the concept of a moral economy is most often associated with the poor and marginalized in resisting market forces which benefit the powerful (e.g. Thompson 1971, Scott 1976), I use it as an overarching term to describe the overlapping and intertwined kinship ideologies, reputational economies, and gift economies that organize elite social relations. I argue that the moral economies of elite guanxi networks are at the very heart of "capitalist" development in urban China. This is not to say that they are "moral" in the sense of being somehow more fair and equitable, but rather that these networks are institutions with their own roles, rules, obligations, and entitlements that structure business transactions rather than being structured by them (Granovetter 1985; Kelly 2007).

Among the (overlapping) business and political elite, these moral economies serve to exclude outsiders and consolidate power. They create a limited network of exchange that disadvantages competitors and grants special privileges to insiders. They do not, however, function as isolated fields of exchange closed off from other social and economic spheres. Rather, elite networks (along with the Chinese state) exploit different modes of exchange and forms of authority in their various "power projects," which often combine individual enrichment with state-directed development goals (Schneider and Schneider 2003a). A well-connected entrepreneur might persuade his official patron to use the state's legal regime to punish a business competitor just as the local government construction bureau, at a banquet with a local underworld (*heishehui*) boss/demolition entrepreneur, might enlist his organization to help force residents off land marked for development.

These elite networks provide protection and opportunities for the accumulation of wealth and status for both state and nonstate elites, and they are also the networks through which the state-driven goals of economic growth are achieved. While entrepreneurs and underworld leaders cultivate relationships with members of the state to obtain protection, insider access, and government privileges, state officials rely on entrepreneurs to achieve development goals that advance their careers, and they depend on unofficial incomes and deeds to support the extra-bureaucratic "face" appropriate for a powerful official in the reform period. Elite networks are thus the social formations that organize corruption and govern its transactions through their "unwritten rules" (*qianguize*).

Masculinity is a key component to understanding corruption as well. As members of these networks, businessmen, state enterprise managers, government officials, and members of the underworld all aspire to and emulate a similar "boss-patron" ideal—as a generous dispenser of assistance and opportunities for whom all are eager to do favors, and someone who commands a large and powerful *guanxiwang*. The power and status of an elite man is measured, above all other factors, by his ability to accomplish goals, both for himself and others, through his social network. Furthermore, male government officials, as high-status men, are not exempt from being measured according to the symbolic code of elite masculinity—mistresses, imported cars, luxury brand clothing and accessories. Thus many forms of extralegal moneymaking should be understood as attempts to support a lifestyle that maintains their status and recognition within their broad social networks.

My emphasis on elite networks thus challenges "individualist" approaches, which explain corruption in terms of the incentive structures that either foster or inhibit corrupt activities. I argue that corruption is not the result of institutions failing to keep individual desires in check; instead it needs to be understood as a fundamentally social activity involving culturally produced desires, obligations, and duties. In other words, corruption is less about the proliferation of rotten apples undermining a healthy organizational logic for their own "private" ends than about the spread of elite networks that distribute state resources according to their own logics. In short, the pervasive corruption found in contemporary China is primarily the end result of government officials becoming enmeshed in the moral economies of elite networks and their corresponding codes of elite masculinity.

Organization of the Book

This chapter provides historical and theoretical background on the new rich in China and an introduction to my fieldsite and my research subjects. Chapter Two examines the formation of elite networks in China's new spaces of leisure and entertainment—private banquet rooms, karaoke clubs, foot massage parlors, and saunas. I trace the inflationary dynamic of elite forms of entertaining and relationship cultivation during the reform period. Building on anthropological work on Chinese banqueting, I argue that the goal of business entertaining is to transform (though not always successfully) interested, calculated, commodified relationships into ones rooted in "irrational" sentiment and affect. In particular, this type of courtship of government officials is seen as essential in a context in which businessmen are "lining up at their doors to offer bribes." Much of this entertaining involves young women who, as mistresses or paid hostesses, play a crucial role by projecting an idealized masculinity onto the men they accompany. Given the prominent role of young women in these forms of entertaining, I also examine how elite men conceive of their different sexual relationships.

Chapter Three broadens the book's ethnographic scope by analyzing the operation of some of the networks formed through elite alliance-building practices and the contending spheres of morality, interest, and social obligation that corrupt officials and their dependent businessmen must negotiate.

This chapter's argument is drawn from three case studies. I begin by examining the published confessional narrative of a corrupt official, Li Zhen, in an attempt to elicit a preliminary understanding of the "moral economy of corruption" in China and the ways in which informal networks and their modes of power intersect with official bureaucracies. I examine how Li Zhen frames the reputational economy of "face" (*mianzi*) as the most important component of a government official's power. Face is derived less from official titles, deeds, and accomplishments than from perceived influence in informal networks.

Next I look at the organization and ideology of a sworn criminal brotherhood in Chengdu and examine its ties to other businessmen and officials. Rather than viewing them as a hostile threat to the state, I argue that organized criminal brotherhoods (*heishehui*) provide forms of governance and revenue for government officials.

Finally, through an account of a real estate entrepreneur's career, I analyze the intersection of multiple modes of power—official, underground, and economic—in capitalist development in urban China. In real estate development projects, local governments often collude with entrepreneurs in the appropriation of publicly owned land for commercial development, and they rely on the underground force provided by organized criminal brotherhoods to force reluctant residents off their land or to persuade them to accept often illegally low compensation for their property.

Chapter Four considers some of the consequences and effects of elite networks on the dynamics of consumption and status in urban China. Through an examination of elite license plates, banqueting practices, and extensive interview material, I argue that many characteristics of elite social circles in China challenge understandings of leisure and conspicuous consumption derived from the experience of capitalism in the West, including the dynamic of taste and distinction outlined by Pierre Bourdieu (1984).

China's new rich emphasize the legibility of economic value above all other qualities in their consumption practices, rendering notions of taste and connoisseurship of secondary concern. Many new rich characterize their social networks as exerting a controlling influence over their consumption habits and lifestyles. They view consumption as a domain of social obligation and calculated performances rather than one of individual cultivation and taste. Given the obligatory, ritualized nature of many their consumption practices, many elites view autonomy and invisibility, often captured by the phrase "living for oneself," as a key mode of distinction. However, attempts to distance themselves from their social circles and focus on individual hobbies and forms of self-cultivation tend to undermine the foundation of their elite status and recognition—as patrons and providers in their social networks. (It also potentially threatens their financial ventures, which are deeply intertwined with other members of their network.) This contradiction between how being elite is imagined and the demands made on elites in their social lives has led many of my informants to actively seek out other models for a "quality" elite lifestyle, which often draw on the (imagined) lifestyles of Western elites.

Chapter Five compares the experiences and narratives of two different groups of women who navigate the masculine sphere of Chinese business— women entrepreneurs and the mistresses of wealthy men. I examine the terms that have arisen during the reform period to categorize different "character types" of women in China—including "beauties" (*meinü*), rich ladies (*fupo*), white-collar women, and female entrepreneurs. Each of these stereotypes is differently positioned within a matrix of wealth, sexuality, and morality.

Because of the masculine associations of the business world, the sexual virtue of female entrepreneurs is constantly under scrutiny by many of their peers, and they regularly face accusations that their success is based on the manipulation of men rather than their own work and talent. In their personal narratives, however, female entrepreneurs often stress the earned nature of their wealth in contrast to elite men (who rely on their ties to other men) and young women who exploit their femininity and sexuality to (in the words of female entrepreneurs) "take the shortcut" to success.

Many wealthy men's mistresses are also participants in what has come to be termed a "beauty economy" (*meinü jingji*, literally "beautiful woman economy") in reform China. This term refers to the increasing use of attractive young women in corporate ceremonies, in live commercial performances, and as sales agents for everything from insurance to real estate. I examine instances in which young women who participate in the "beauty economy" frame themselves as entrepreneurs utilizing their "feminine capital" to achieve material success.

The book's conclusion uses my ethnographic material to challenge many dominant narratives of China's political and economic evolution. While many scholars have depicted guanxi as either counter-state or counter-market, I argue that this approach underestimates the "institutionality" of elite networks, which serve to structure and organize state power and economic opportunities to the advantage of the privileged and powerful.

I also examine the loss of collectivist ethics that many Chinese feel characterizes the reform period and assess some potential sources for a new public oriented morality. The practices of accumulation engaged in by elite networks generate tragic consequences for the public good—shoddy construction (referred to as "tofu dregs construction"), contaminated food, and stark material inequalities, revealing the limits of the relational ethics of guanxi.

While some scholars have interpreted the term *suzhi* (personal quality) as evidence of a totalizing discourse of neoliberalism used to measure the economic value of human subjects, I contend that suzhi has been appropriated by many Chinese to point out the moral failings of the new rich and their lack of public concern. In fact, the most common phrase uttered about the new rich during my research was, "They might have money, but they lack quality" (*suzhi*). The new rich themselves are searching for domains of distinction and cultivation that resist reduction to pure money values, which may foster a greater concern with philanthropy and generate new forms of moral distinction.

2

"ENTERTAINING IS MY JOB"

Masculinity, Sexuality, and Alliances

Among Chengdu's Entrepreneurs

Doing a hundred good things for the leader is not as
good as doing one bad thing with the leader.[1] If the leader
takes you to do a bad thing together, that means there
will be a hundred good things waiting for you!

—Saying popular on Chinese Internet forums in 2011

Compared with his lifestyle just a few years earlier, Mr. Gao had fallen on hard times.[2] Lounging in the private room of a foot massage parlor (*xijiaofang*), our feet soaking in a hot medicinal bath, Mr. Gao recounted tales from his halcyon days: "I used to spend 10,000 RMB on an evening of entertainment with some government officials, and that 10,000 would become a [future profit of] 100,000 overnight. I made money just by lying in bed dreaming."[3]

At the peak of Mr. Gao's success, as a contractor undertaking construction projects for local state agencies, he owned a car and several apartments, each occupied by a mistress he supported financially. He had moved from a county seat in rural Sichuan to the provincial capital of Chengdu and started taking English classes at the local university, envisioning a future when his business ventures would frequently take him overseas. When I met him in 2003, however, only two apartments (and one mistress) remained, and he was contemplating selling his car. The foreign capitalists he had dreamed about never came knocking on his door, and he was desperately searching for a new business venture and hoping that I could help. He had treated me to this particular foot massage in order to pitch a business proposal involving exporting dried rose petals to the United States and Europe. He was hoping that I could help with finding U.S. customers and navigating the relevant customs regulations. When I told him that he didn't need to pay for my foot massage in order to ask for my assistance, he replied, "It's easier to talk this way" (*zheyang shiqing haoshuo yixie*).

Mr. Gao knew that I was a graduate student in anthropology with no business experience to speak of, but we had become friends over the previous several months. I had helped Mr. Gao with his spoken English, and we frequently dined and drank together. The fact that Mr. Gao was looking to me for assistance with a product and industry I knew next to nothing about was a sign of just how far he had fallen. But given the amount of time we had spent together, he felt he could trust me and that our relationship was deep enough that I wasn't likely to refuse his request for a favor. The weeks spent treating me to dinners and foot massages were an attempt to cultivate a relationship with me, a practice referred to as *goudui* in the Sichuan dialect.

Mr. Gao attributed his decline to a failure to maintain his past relationships and to use them to generate new opportunities. A few weeks before our conversation over foot massages, I had encountered a dejected Mr. Gao carrying a shopping bag full of 100 RMB bills. He had just failed in an attempt to bribe an official. When I asked him what went wrong, he explained, "He [the official] must have someone else in mind." In other words, the official already had an established relationship with an entrepreneur who was going to receive the contract, and Mr. Gao's bribe by itself was insufficient to persuade the official to offer it to him instead.

This chapter focuses on the evolving repertoire of practices that entrepreneurs use to cultivate relationships with both state officials and other entrepreneurs and the effect of these social networks on their business ventures and interpersonal ethics. I argue that viewing these networks as gendered social formations is crucial to understanding their structure and ethos.

Although there are many highly successful women entrepreneurs in China, the vast majority of entrepreneurs in post-Mao China are men.[4] This is largely due to the fact that business networking requires entering spaces (such as nightclubs and saunas) and participating in activities (drinking, gambling, and sex consumption) that are not viewed as appropriate for "proper" women.[5] These networks, built on ideologies of male solidarity, not only constitute a key component of business but also provide the foundation for corruption and organized crime in China (discussed in Chapter Three). Although some of these networks are based on ties of kinship and native place, the bulk of the relationships of which these networks are composed are forged and maintained through ritualized leisure—experiences of shared pleasure in venues catering to the desires and enjoyments of elite men, including karaoke clubs, saunas, nightclubs, high-end restaurants, and teahouses.

The forms and venues of elite entertaining have changed with the shifting regulations and policies of the reform period (Wang 2000). Like the price of housing and the monthly salary of the ideal husband, elite entertainment has been subject to inflation. While once drinks and a banquet might have been enough to secure a business deal in the early 1990s, officials and businessmen now demand increasingly expensive, illicit, and rare pleasures and enjoyments in their dealings with one another—flirting with hostesses, "business" vacations, and sex consumption.

The late 1980s and early 1990s were characterized by an explosion in banqueting in the private rooms of restaurants in China, especially among government officials and entrepreneurs.[6] By the time of my fieldwork in 2004, however, most of my informants operated in a context that I term "banquet saturation," in which the formerly festive forms of the Maoist era and early reform period were now part of the routine work lives of most elite businessmen. Most of my informants had nightly dinner invitations or hosting obligations that were an integral part of their business ventures. Banquet saturation has led to a corresponding inflation in the etiquette, expense, and forms of business-oriented entertainment. While a dinner in an upscale restaurant accompanied by expensive liquor, extravagant dishes, and exotic animal meat might have been enough to seal a deal in the mid-1980s, by the mid-1990s business dinners were increasingly followed by trips to karaoke clubs, saunas, and massage parlors that provided sexual services.

By the late 1990s sexual entertainment had become an integral part of many business deals. Travel, expensive gifts, and introductions to potential mistresses had become features of this entertaining as well.[7] However, by 2004, lavish dinners, drinking in a nightclub, and sex with a hostess were no longer viewed as sufficient in themselves to ensure the loyalty of officials and fellow businessmen. As I will argue below, the inflation in forms of commodified pleasure has begun to reach its limit, and businessmen are seeking ways to generate more "authentic" sentiment and solidarity through their entertaining practices.

The volume and intensity of business-related entertaining have also increased to such an extent that the lines between "work" and "play" are blurred for many Chinese businessmen. Entrepreneurs complained to me that they lack any "true" leisure time because the majority of their evenings are spent hosting and attending banquets and carousing with business associates, appointments that are obligatory and essential to their business success. (If my own field-work experience is any guide, the remaining free evenings are spent recovering.) Many entrepreneurs I knew in Chengdu even considered entertaining and being entertained with groups of businessmen and government officials as the most essential part of their work. As one government contractor, Mr. Wu, put it, "Entertaining *is* my job" (*Yingchou jiushi wode gongzuo*).[8]

These new sites of elite entertainment—karaoke clubs (also called KTVs, an abbreviation for karaoke television), saunas, and massage parlors—in urban China are gendered spaces in that they cater to heterosexual male pleasure. I argue that these venues are key sites for the performance and reproduction of the ideologies and practices of a post-Mao elite masculinity. Access to these spaces is integral to elite status, and these forms of entertaining are increasingly emulated (with important differences) at lower levels in the socioeconomic hierarchy. In massage parlors and saunas, migrant women from the country-side massage and service urban male bodies, while in karaoke clubs hostesses provide an "ego massage," projecting an idealized masculinity onto their patrons (Allison 1994). In these sites, relationships between men are forged quite literally over the bodies of women.

Masculinity and Sexuality in Post-Mao China

In the domains of gender relations and sexuality, many urban Chinese characterize the present as a time of "opening" (*kaifang*) after the prohibitions of the Maoist years, invoking the familiar narrative of sexual repression. They praise the present as a time when romance and marriage can finally be rooted in private emotions rather than be the product of political, familial, or financial pressures (see Farquhar 2002: Chapter 4). However, instead of the final realization of companionate marriage based on mutual affection between equals and sexual equality for women, which have been goals of Chinese reformers since the May 4th Movement of 1919, the reform period has been marked by the rise of hierarchical, patron-client forms of sexuality, especially among the elite. Mistresses, multiple wives, and extramarital affairs are the norm among wealthy entrepreneurs and government officials, and the sex industry has developed in pace with the rest of China's economy and become an integral part of nightlife for China's newly rich men.

Some observers see the explosion in divorce and extramarital affairs, and the rise of the sex industry in China, as the result of a hyper-masculinity now surging forth after decades of suppression. Meanwhile, the state is eager to blame these phenomena on the "spiritual pollution" that is a byproduct of China's opening to the outside world (Uretsky 2007). Examination of the sexual practices of elite men, however, suggests that this is not just another instance of "men gone wild," fueled by a potent mix of new wealth and hormones, of a "castrated" generation of men reclaiming their lost virility, or of a conservative sexual culture succumbing to Western-inspired sexual freedom.[9] While the retreat of the state from the domain of private life has no doubt opened up the possibility for new forms of sexual expression, the emergent forms of masculinity and femininity and their corresponding sexualities are not unmediated reflections of pent-up private desires (Farquhar 2002). Rather, masculinity and femininity have been actively constructed and reconstructed during the reform period in dialogue with economic changes, global influences, and reimagined and reinvented traditional gender forms (Rofel 1999, 2007; Schein 2000; Brownell 2001; Evans 2002).

Many scholars have pointed to the mass media and consumption (often encapsulated by the term "the market") as sites where new Chinese subjectivities, desires, and genders are being formed (Davis 2000; Brownell 2001; Schein 2001). Others have emphasized the domain of "public culture" where Chinese cultivate new desires and forms of subjectivity through the negotiation of public allegories found in movies, novels, advertisements, and television shows (see, e.g., Rofel 2007). However, as I discuss in Chapter Four, many of the entrepreneurs I worked with confront the forms of cosmopolitanism promoted by global mass media and the modes of citizenship promoted by the state with considerable ambivalence. While most new-rich Chinese hope to be recognized as members of a global elite, the forms of masculine entertainment that predominate in urban China are not straightforward imitations of elite lifestyles from Chinese television, Hong Kong, or Hollywood films. Rather, the more proximate others and more pressing concerns of their social networks and business ventures exert a powerful influence in orienting their desires and practices. Furthermore, as many scholars of postsocialism have pointed out, the legacies of socialism and the memories of bodies matter in figuring postsocialist desires (Farquhar 2002).

The markers of male status and the forms of elite enjoyment in contemporary China resonate with both Maoist era and prerevolutionary practices. Elite entertainment, despite its superficial resemblance to global leisure culture, draws on notions of male power and privilege with a longer historical trajectory in China (Uretsky 2007). I argue that a closer examination of the new spaces of leisure and entertainment frequented by the entrepreneurial elite suggests a more complex mechanism for the production of new elite, masculine subjects than interpellation by a global discourse of neoliberalism.

Much work on male alliance building in the North American context emphasizes that the lurking fear of homosexuality delimits the forms and contexts for expressing and enacting homosocial desire (Kimmel 1994; Kiesling 2005). However, in the context of elite entertaining in China, the fear of having their actions and utterances construed as homosexual or feminine was not an overriding concern for most of the men I studied. Partly because homosexuality was "unthinkable" for most of these men, there was little policing of behaviors and utterances that expressed affection for other men. In fact, successful evenings of entertaining included declarations about relationships and physical displays of affection; for example, it was common for a man to put his arms around a fellow reveler or a hand on another man's leg.[10]

The challenge of an evening of *yingchou* (business entertaining) was not how to generate desire in the context of lurking homosexuality (as in North America), but rather how to create intimacy out of conventional, ritualized, and increasingly routine forms of entertaining—drinking, banqueting, singing karaoke—or, as the quote at the beginning of this chapter expressed, how to get the leader to accompany you in doing "bad things."

The Inflationary Dynamic of Business Entertaining

The patron-client relationship between state officials and entrepreneurs in China and the importance of social capital that includes ties to the government has been well documented by social scientists (Smart 1993; Pieke 1995; Buckley 1999; Wank 1996, 1999; Liu 2002). China's economic reforms notwithstanding, state agents still control access to capital, business licenses, and land. Furthermore, in many industries strong ties to the state offer one a competitive advantage.[11] Well-connected entrepreneurs are more likely to win government contracts or obtain insider information about the auctioning of public assets (land in particular), and they are the first to learn about shifts in policy.[12] As David Wank (1999) has argued, they also rely on the state both for protection from other predatory state agents (such as tax collectors) and for leverage should any business disputes arise. Wank characterizes the relationship between state officials and businessmen as "symbiotic clientelism": entrepreneurs obtain protection and many benefits that enhance their business success, while state agents both generate revenue for local government agencies and obtain illicit income (through bribes and kickbacks) that often dwarfs their official salaries (Wank 1999: 11).

By distributing favors, privileges, contracts, and protection, officials are able to build their own networks of entrepreneurs to accomplish various projects, both public and private. Entrepreneurs and government officials alike increasingly aspire to a similar masculine "boss" ideal: they aim to become dispensers of favors and opportunities, people who can command the assistance of powerful individuals with just a phone call. Participation in these networks as both patron and client is fundamental to post-Mao ideologies of masculinity. These entrepreneur-bureaucrat relationships are often forged over banquets and in KTVs.

Many scholars both within and outside of China have described these informal networks as a form of "privatization of the state" or as conducting "transactions in money for power" (*qianquan jiaoyi*) (e.g., Sun 2004). But many other forms of value circulating in these networks besides money. My research suggests that elite entertaining and the forms of consumption it demands should be understood as an *effect* of overwhelming commodification—in which everyone and everything (government patronage, sex, loyalty) is understood to be for sale and available to the highest bidder. Entertaining is understood by its participants as a (not always successful) attempt to inject forms of value that are resistant to commodification into business relationships, to transform relationships of cold calculation into particularistic relationships embedded in moral economies of sentiment.[13] This transformation is realized through the incommensurable, shared experiences of intimacy, vulnerability, and transgression that elite entertaining enables (but does not always achieve).

The entrepreneurs I worked with hoped that by paying for an evening on the town their client or official patron would walk away not simply feeling "indebted" to the host for his lavish expenditure but also with an embodied memory of shared pleasure and a latent sense of fondness, or *ganqing*, for their host. In his description of how banquets transform relationships in China, Andrew Kipnis (2001: 88) states, "Psychologically, *ganqing* may be described as a sentimental memory of indebtedness and shared experience. . . . The more exceptional the memory created the better." In other words, anyone can offer a bribe or a kickback; so only those who can generate more durable ties rooted in ganqing rather than just financial interest have an advantage. *Yingchou* (business entertaining) thus should be understood as an attempt to embed market relationships into gendered social relationships.

As Farrer and Sun (2003: 14) note in their analysis of discourses surrounding sexuality in reform era Shanghai, feelings and sentiment (ganqing) have increasingly served as a counter-discourse to money in post-Mao China and have taken on a very positive moral connotation. By framing their behavior as motivated by feelings rather than money, I believe my informants also were claiming a particular kind of elite moral subjectivity, implying that they were secure enough financially to be free from being governed by crude material interest alone. In this context, my informant friends frequently framed their business transactions and patron-client relationships as "helping friends" (*bang pengyoude mang*) or as rooted in "feelings" (*ganqing*) for others. To appear to be overly calculating and greedy and focused on a short-term transaction rather than the relationship itself was to risk being accused of having a "poor peasant mentality" (*xiao pinnongde liezhixing*). Such behavior was viewed as a sign of both desperation and untrustworthiness and likely to raise the suspicions of business partners and official patrons. Generosity was at the core of the boss-patron ideal that many of my informants emulated, and several of my interviewees told stories of friends and acquaintances who had borrowed money and gone into considerable debt to maintain the generous displays demanded of elite masculinity.

This is not to say that these networks were islands of brotherly love and feelings in a commodified world. Although the businessmen mostly enjoyed banqueting, drinking, and cavorting with hostesses on their own, they resented being obligated to entertain clients, partners, and officials they did not like on a personal level and the considerable amount of time, money, and energy consumed by this entertaining. They also complained about obligations to help out a business associate or to promote his product or service. One memorable example involved an entrepreneur, Mr. Cai, who owned the distribution rights to a brand of moon cakes considered by many to be inferior in taste. Around the Mid-Autumn festival, when moon cakes are traditionally given as gifts, they nonetheless dutifully purchased the dry, crumbly moon cakes from Mr. Cai to distribute to other members in their social networks.

Some also saw the constant drinking in KTVs and the hiring of sex workers as the mark of an unsophisticated (and presumably rural) nouveau riche (*baofahu*), and they sometimes looked down on clients and officials who demanded this form of courtship. Some contrasted China's business world with an idealized West in which their talents and abilities alone would be sufficient to win

FIGURE 2.1. A high-end teahouse and seafood restaurant. The car parked in front is a Bentley.

contracts and attract partners. Many of my interviewees complained that their endless social obligations to business associates, government officials, and other members of their social networks prevented them from pursuing their own business and leisure interests. Several of my interviewees explained that successful, wealthy individuals in particular are forced to "live for others" (*weibeiren shenghuo*) rather than for themselves. Many wished they could just give a bribe or a kickback and be done with it; but the inflationary pressures of entertaining had rendered the production of relationships rooted in irrational, incommensurable sentiment all the more crucial to business success. Increasing market competition has made the cultivation of guanxi more important rather than less.

The Typical Scene: Business Entertaining in a KTV

In journalistic accounts of the "new China," with the possible exception of luxury shops, no venue is cited more often as evidence of China's opening up than the disco. To Western journalists and scholars, the disco represents the epitome of globalized modernity. It is the exemplary site for liberatory leisure, status consumption, and hedonistic sexuality. Disco dance floors are where neophyte consumers' tastes in fashion and beverages are assessed, where the youth partake in transnational youth culture, and where ostensibly Western sexual mores are practiced and propagated (Farrer 1999).

Discos of this kind can be found in most of China's big cities, but they constitute only a portion of the nightlife establishments that have sprung up during the reform period. The majority of my informants, from their early thirties to late forties, preferred the controlled, private spaces of rented rooms in teahouses, massage parlors, and karaoke clubs to the open dance floor of the disco.[14]

Unlike the disco, the private rooms of these establishments limited who they interacted with and restricted the gaze of others to their immediate peers. More important, they also allowed hosts, with the aid of paid hostesses, to cater to the desires of their guests and clients more effectively. Most wealthy entrepreneurs contrasted these exclusive spaces with the public, uncontrolled spaces of the dance floor and bar, which they referred to as "chaotic" (*luan*) and the people who frequented them as "mixed up" (*za*, i.e., not belonging to any clearly defined social group.)[15] Nightlife for well-established entrepreneurs is

FIGURE 2.2. A mid-tier but pretentiously named karaoke (KTV) nightclub.

predicated on invisibility, secrecy, and control—control of both who interacts with your group and observes your activities and control over the means to satisfy the desires of the group.

The institutions of elite entertainment and leisure are also organized around a particular understanding of masculine pleasure and sexuality.[16] While teahouses, foot massage parlors, and saunas all serve their purpose in network building and leisure, karaoke clubs (from here on referred to as KTVs) are perhaps the archetypal entertainment venue in contemporary China.[17] Spatially, KTVs, nightclubs, and even teahouses are hierarchically arranged. Many nightclubs and discos offer a public hall (*dating*) where patrons can watch performances and dance on an open dance floor for a small entrance fee or with the purchase of drinks. Higher-paying customers, which included nearly all of my informants, however, usually rent private rooms (*baofang*) located away from the public areas, which are themselves differentially priced. Many of the top KTV nightclubs in Chengdu consist solely of these private rooms. The most expensive baofang are the largest and most lavishly decorated, and they frequently have their own bathrooms and even bedrooms, provide a dedicated attendant, and are auspiciously numbered or named (888 being a common number for the best room in a club.)

Many of the most luxurious KTVs in Chengdu are located in five-star hotels belonging to international chains, but some occupy several floors of an office building or entertainment complex. Near the end of my fieldwork I noticed the growth of entertainment complexes that featured teahouses, restaurants, massage parlors, saunas, karaoke, and sexual services under one roof. While some advertised themselves simply as "clubs" (*julebu*), many referred to themselves as "business clubs" (*shangwu huisuo*), suggesting that the enjoyments provided inside were not for leisure alone. My informants almost never lingered in the public spaces of KTVs or nightclubs. Even if they had no intention of singing or were out with a group of old friends, they would still rent a baofang.

Increasingly, singing karaoke seemed to be falling out of favor among my informants. Instead, they often selected the "disco" option on their karaoke computers. The TV monitor then displayed music videos that depicted scenes of fashionable young people dancing on crowded dance floors (much like the scene that was occurring just outside the doors to their private room), and the group would dance in the small space provided between the coffee table and the TV. Sometimes they spent the entire evening in a baofang just drinking, chatting, and listening to music.

Upon entering an upscale KTV nightclub, patrons are greeted by elegantly dressed young women who bow and shout out, "good evening" (*wanshang hao*). They are lead to their room by one of these greeters (*yingbin xiaojie*) or by a manager. If the patrons are regulars, the manager will personally escort them to their room and greet them by name. Depending on the establishment, they might also receive a visit from the madam, who assesses the wealth and status of the customers before sending in a lineup of hostesses (*xiaojie*). Again, if they are regulars, the madam might complain about how long it's been since she's seen them and how much she's missed them. The manager or madam then sends in a group of hostesses from which the patrons choose their "date" for the evening. If they are not satisfied with the group sent in by the madam, they can request a different group. Each member of the group chooses a hostess who will accompany him in singing, drinking, and potentially sex (off-site) for the rest of the evening.[18]

Hostesses play a variety of roles depending on the class of the club. In the lowest-end clubs, at the very least hostesses play drinking games with customers, most commonly a variation of "liar's dice," in which the loser of each round has to take a drink. Hostesses who don't drink at regular intervals are urged to do so by the evening's host. They are expected to be well versed in drinking protocol and to toast male guests with their glasses lowered as a sign of respect. Although they are supposed to focus on their assigned date, hostesses are also expected to toast other members of the group and any new arrivals. Most will sing upon request and serve as dance partners if necessary. More experienced (or more high-priced) hostesses usually flirt with customers through flattery and light caresses, sometimes referring to their clients as "husband" (*laogong*). All are expected to tolerate a considerable amount of groping, which generally increases along with the patrons' alcohol consumption.

The private rooms of KTVs (*baofang*) are lined with leather (or faux leather) couches that face a large television screen. In front of each couch is a long glass coffee table for placing drinks and playing dice games. Most tables also feature a rack for placing mobile phones and cigarettes to prevent them from getting wet in the drunken chaos that ensues in a typical evening. While the lighting in some upscale baofang resembles a comfortable bourgeois living room, most display the dim lighting and flashing colored lights of a disco.

In addition to a large-screen TV, each room features an elaborate sound system and a computerized karaoke system containing thousands of songs, which in upscale clubs is usually operated by a female attendant referred to as the "DJ." In the better clubs, the DJ pours guests their drinks, often kneeling on a pillow next to the table as she serves them. Typically a male server comes in to take drink orders, and the host of the group usually orders a bottle of liquor (or occasionally wine) accompanied by several bottles of mixers (the most common combination at the time of my research being Chivas Regal Scotch mixed with a popular brand of bottled, sweetened green tea).[19]

Unlike drinking in the West, which is organized by rounds, typically only one order is placed in an evening for an entire bottle, which can be kept at the club for the customer if unfinished at the end of the evening. Regular guests are usually also sent a complimentary plate of sliced fruit in acknowledgment of their VIP status. The size and style of the fruit plates vary with the class of the club and the status of the guest, with the most lavish fruit plates veering toward a form of fruit sculpture.

A hostess, server, or the private DJ then prepares drinks by pouring a modest amount of alcohol followed by a considerable amount of mixer into a pitcher of ice. The mixed cocktail is then poured out into individual glasses

FIGURE 2.3. A private room (*baofang*) in a KTV. Note the fruit plates that were sent to the VIP guests by the management.

in portions that can easily be consumed in one gulp. (Sometimes these individual portions are placed in a rack that resembles a rack of test tubes.) This individual portioning of drinks into shot-sized amounts is crucial to the socially oriented drinking that occurs. Unlike the affluent Westerners in the Chivas Regal television commercials on Chinese TV, who are depicted savoring their scotch on the rocks while they ice fish, wealthy Chinese businessmen in clubs rarely sip their Chivas in a leisurely manner. Drinking for them is fraught with strategy, power-plays, and etiquette. While drinking among friends tends to be more relaxed, it still bears the imprint of banquet propriety. One can never simply drink an alcoholic beverage without cursory toasts and pouring for others.

The flow of the drinking and entertainment depends on who is present. If government officials or business clients who are actively being courted are present, everything revolves around their needs and desires. Important clients and guests are offered first choice in hostesses and receive regular toasts (*jingjiu*) and flattery from the host, his allies, and, at the urging of the host, all of the hostesses. Toasts are accompanied by flattering statements (especially if they are uttered by hostesses), performative declarations about the relationship between the drinkers ("we'll be friends forever"), words of gratitude for a favor, offers of assistance, and invitations for future gatherings.

Important guests and government officials are encouraged to drink their fill but are seldom pressured to drink to levels of excess and discomfort in the way that is common among drinkers of similar status. A host would never challenge his guest to a drinking game, although two friends of roughly equal status might do so. Respect can be shown to a fellow drinker by toasting him and declaring, "You can drink as much as you like, but I'm going to down this glass" (*Ni suiyi, wo ganbei*).

Hostesses are expected to pressure clients and officials to drink (*quanjiu*) and to ensure that they drink their fill, sing frequently, and are generally at the center of attention. The hostesses' goal is to secure the guests' enjoyment for the benefit of the host—i.e., to lay the groundwork and create the context that allows for bonding between the male revelers. A pleased client, guest, partner, or official who "had a good time" (*wande kaixin*) more than anything marks an evening of entertaining as a success. Having a good time is evidenced by declarations of friendship and affection between the men present, displays of intense emotion such as shouting or group singing, and above all by doing away with the polite protocol with which the evening probably began.

Most evenings in KTVs do not have such a clear focus on securing a client's pleasure, but they have a purpose nonetheless. In order to clarify the mixture of interest, sentiment, and playfulness operating in any given evening it is necessary to differentiate between different types of entertaining.

Types of Entertaining: *Goudui, Yingchou,* and *Wan*

Many of the late nights my informants and I spent in KTVs were understood by them to have an instrumental function. My informants most often used a term from the Sichuan dialect, *goudui*, to describe the instrumental cultivation of a relationship. While Everett Zhang (2001: 238) understands the term to refer only to entrepreneurs' entertaining of government officials, residents of Chengdu and Chongqing used it to refer to any form of socializing or entertaining with a specific goal in mind.[20] Unlike yingchou, which suggested the maintenance of an established relationship, goudui usually referred to the early stage of getting to know someone, usually for some utilitarian purpose. Goudui literally refers to adjusting the level of alcohol in the process of liquor distillation, but in its everyday use, in many contexts "charm," "court," or even "seduce" could be substituted in its place. As Zhang argues, the techniques of goudui aim to transform a distant or casual relationship into a "thicker" bond held together with sentiment and mutual interest (238).

I first encountered the concept of goudui when I was working for a Chinese television show. My colleagues would often take me along to assist in their efforts to convince a local company or business to sponsor our show or to win the patronage of a local official. This often involved drinking and chatting with a potential sponsor over dinner. Sometimes, if my colleagues felt that I had done my goudui work well, they would urge me to personally call the sponsor the next day, insisting, "He likes you. You can convince him to help us." Thus I came to understand goudui as a kind of courtship in which the suitor tries to cultivate affection in the courted (for the suitor) that will serve as the basis for a future relationship of trust, cooperation, and mutual aid.

In their history of the Sicilian mafia, Jane and Peter Schneider (2003: 118) describe how members of the mafia "self-consciously condition" members of the elite by "constructing webs of mutual reciprocity that go beyond any narrow instrumentality." They explain, "In conditioning outsiders, Mafiosi are less concerned to establish quid pro quo exchanges than to cultivate 'many-stranded relationships' of intertwined interest and affect" (123). This notion of conditioning, with its deliberate mixing of interest and affect, nicely captures the logic of goudui.

In interviews, entrepreneurs frequently commented on and assessed their own goudui abilities (*goudui shuiping*) and those of others. Mr. Zhao, the owner of a travel agency that arranged publicly funded "investigation" trips (*kaocha*) abroad for government officials, bragged to me about his goudui skills. "I can go from unknown to known, to being friends with important people (*lingdao*) faster than most guys" (*cong burenshi dao renshi dao pengyou*). Ms. Liu, a mining boss, felt that her goudui ability was still at a "primary school level" (*xiaoxue shuiping*). She didn't like to play mahjong, and as a woman, she was excluded from full participation in many forms of business entertainment. When treating a group of clients or officials to a night on the town she was expected to pay for hostesses for the group, but when hostesses joined the party she was expected to leave and allow the men to enjoy themselves. Because most of her mining business took place in rural areas where the officials were known to be, in her words, particularly "dark" (*hei'an*) and of poor quality (*suzhi hendi*) and therefore especially demanding of all the illicit pleasures of nightlife, she "subcontracted" her goudui work out to local men familiar with the area whenever possible.

Evenings of goudui were marked (initially) by tight adherence to protocol. Toasting was sure to reflect proper status hierarchies. Activities were all oriented toward ensuring the pleasure of one's guest and eliciting good will and warmth toward the host. Mr. Wu, a government contractor, understood goudui as necessary precisely because of the ubiquity of bribery: "Even if you're a just a county head (*xianzhang*), there are literally thousands of businessmen lining up at your door to give you money. That's why relationships are so important. Nowadays you don't just need the right price or the right relationship to make money. You need both." Goudui entertaining can be understood as an attempt to inject sentiment into what initially is a relationship of cold calculation.

Scholars have contrasted the instrumental, material quality of vertical patron-client ties in China with more horizontal ties built on sentiment (Yang 1994; Davis 2000). Mr. Wu's words reveal that, in the context of increasing market competition and banquet saturation, only those who can successfully "condition" (*goudui*) an official or client to offer his patronage have a distinct advantage. While commodified forms of expenditure—dinners, bribes, gifts, and the like—are available to all, only those who can successfully marshal these objects in service of deepening ties have succeeded in goudui.[21]

Despite the instrumental purpose of goudui, the goal of successful goudui is precisely to transcend the interested nature of the relationship. My informants hoped that an official or client's cooperation was rooted more in their affection for the entrepreneur than in their self-interest since this would provide the foundation for a more stable, secure, and long-lasting relationship. Entrepreneurs bragged about their goudui skills and connections not in terms of notions of debt or lavish expenditure, but in the language of relationships (*renqing*) and sentiment (*ganqing*) (though sometimes the affection was one-sided). Mr. Li referred to his official connections as his "good friends" (*haopengyou*), bragging that he counted a few provincial department heads (*tingzhang*) among his close buddies. He explained to me, "They like me, so they'll help me out with things. If you want to do business in China, I can introduce you to them too."

Most evenings in KTVs, however, do not have such a clear instrumental function. A few friends or business associates might gather in a KTV after dinner and gradually invite more people to join them. Unfamiliar associates are introduced to each other and exchange business cards. Occasionally these introductions evolve into discussions of possible business cooperation.

To illustrate the open-ended nature of most entertaining, I recount below a typical evening that fell somewhere between the cyclical entertaining referred to as yingchou and a group of friends and business associates simply looking to unwind and "play" (*wan*). Whether the evening qualified as yingchou or wan depended on who was present. Yingchou typically was used to refer to the periodic entertaining of clients or business partners through dinner and fun in restaurants, KTVs, and massage parlors, whereas going out with friends with whom one had no business relationship were clearly considered just "play" (*wan*).

The clearest instances of yingchou occur around the Chinese New Year, when entrepreneurs often invite out all their important clients, partners, and official patrons to a formal banquet (*tuannianfan*) in a restaurant and then to a KTV. I understood such events to signify the yearly ritual constitution of the members of one's social network. Because yingchou involved the periodic maintenance and reconstitution of relationships important to entrepreneurs' business ventures, ignoring a partner's invitations for too long or failing to periodically invite a client out for dinner and drinking in a KTV might incur their disfavor. Ms. Liu told me that one of her customers complained about her behind her back because she rarely spent the evening playing cards or mahjong with him, and she worried about the effect her failure to socialize might have on her business.

Since most entrepreneurs in Chengdu did business with their friends, most evenings could loosely be considered yingchou. Evenings that began as yingchou often evolved into wan, and vice versa. Many entrepreneurs would invite clients and associates to join already established groups of carousers as an economical and efficient way of getting a yingchou obligation out of the way. This was a strategy I quickly adopted myself in entertaining the many people who had helped me with my research.

After an informant friend, Mr. Liao, treated me to dinner several times, I invited him out to eat barbecue. Mr. Liao was a Chinese entrepreneur a few years returned from New Zealand. I had met Mr. Liao when he opened a bar in Chengdu; another entrepreneur introduced me to him as a possible candidate to serve as the bar's DJ and as someone who could bring foreign customers to his bar. But after only nine months, the bar had closed, and Mr. Liao had gone into the liquor distribution business. For me, part of the purpose of the dinner was to smooth over any lingering negative feelings he might have toward me after I had declined to be his bar's DJ (and failed to find a suitable candidate to replace me). I met him at a nearby restaurant that featured "Brazilian-style" barbeque, and he showed up with a young woman I had never seen him with before. He introduced me to her but did not elaborate on the nature of their relationship. We drank beer with dinner, toasting each other frequently, and he talked about his current business ventures. During dinner he suggested that we go out afterwards to a KTV. It would be his treat, and he would invite some of his colleagues and the regional boss of the liquor company that made the neon-hued flavored malt beverages his company was distributing. He told me that it would be a good opportunity to meet people useful to my "career."

After dinner Mr. Liao whispered something to the woman, and she thanked me and left. We drove to a club with which Mr. Liao's company had recently signed a contract to distribute their drink, where we met up with a few of Mr. Liao's employees and partners. Once we were shown to a private room, an assistant manager came to greet Mr. Liao and his colleagues and then exchanged business cards with me, after prompting by Mr. Liao. I was told by the manager to bring my friends to the club anytime, and I would be given an excellent room. The manager assured me that any friend of Mr. Liao's would be treated well.

Mr. Liao then urged his colleagues to invite some of their company's female employees, and I was urged repeatedly to call and invite any girls that I knew, especially foreign ones. I sent a text message to a university student to whom I had recently been introduced by another businessman to help her with her applications to universities in America. I also invited a Spanish man I knew who was interested in distributing Spanish wines in China and who I thought would like to meet this group.

My two invitees showed up, and the Spanish businessman swapped business cards with everyone in the room. The boss of the liquor company showed up last and ordered a twelve-pack of his company's flavored malt beverage product, known as Tango, in assorted flavors. I deferentially toasted the boss by lowering my glass and complimented him on his company's product, declaring that I liked the orange "whiskey" flavor the best. (Little did I know that it would leave me with a brutal headache the next day.)

Mr. Liao sat next to the university student and offered her advice about whether to go abroad or stay in China and tips on looking for a job after graduation. I was encouraged repeatedly to drink with a female employee of Mr. Liao's company, Ms. Wang, and was asked at the end of the evening by Mr. Liao and his colleagues if I was going to call her again. Mr. Liao's employees grilled the Spanish man on his business plans and toasted him repeatedly with each flavor of Tango. Mr. Liao and his employees toasted the boss of Tango at regular intervals with small, test tube–like glasses of the company's product.

There was no clear goal for the evening. Each actor had his or her own agenda, which ranged from the sexual to the professional to the scholarly. Mr. Liao probably was both giving and gaining face (*mianzi*) by entertaining a few foreigners in the presence of the boss of Tango. I was hoping to deepen my relationship with him so that he would continue to help me with my research. Mr. Liao was probably also hoping to impress the university student with his knowledge of business and life overseas and harbored the hope of starting a sexual relationship with her. The student was interested in gaining some practical advice about studying overseas and getting a job after graduation, and she knew that Mr. Liao and his associates would be more than eager to help her. Mr. Liao was also trying to solidify his relationship with me by introducing me to a woman from his company, Ms. Wang.

Similarly Mr. Liao's employees cultivated more ganqing with both Mr. Liao and the boss of Tango by drinking with them (despite the fact that their attendance that evening was in some sense mandatory). Finally, Mr. Liao's company laid the groundwork for a potential partnership with the man dealing Spanish wines. But in no way could one reduce the "work" of the evening and the cumulative effect of these interactions to these multiple intentions and projects.

From Banquets to KTV

A great deal of scholarly literature has focused on the etiquette and art of social relationships in China (e.g., Fei 1992; Hwang 1987; King 1991; Yang 1994; Yan 1996; Kipnis 1997). It has depicted in considerable detail the various ways that Chinese use principles of hierarchy, reciprocity, and sentiment to navigate social relationships, from the near to the far, the familiar to the strange. Like banqueting and gift giving, KTV entertaining is one of the key sites for cultivating relationships. While banqueting was perhaps the dominant form of entertaining in the 1980s and early 1990s, I would argue that KTV nightlife is *the* central component to entrepreneurial courtship of clients and officialdom in contemporary China.

Most evenings begin in a restaurant over a banquet-style meal and usually end in a KTV or sauna; entrepreneurs stressed that it was in these sites where the really important work was done. Although successful banquets help to foster sentiment between participants that transcends their social ranks and roles, in the current milieu of "banquet saturation" they are less effective. Entrepreneurs stressed that this added venue was necessary to accomplish their goudui, i.e. "conditioning." The highly gendered and sexualized space of the KTV baofang also differentiates it from that of the private banquet room. In the baofang, new forms of play are possible, and the stakes of this play are also raised.

Banquets, however, still provide the basic template for etiquette in elite entertaining. In courting a government official, client, or business partner, entrepreneurs adhere closely to banquet protocol. However, the goal of a successful banquet or evening in a KTV is precisely to do away with protocol, to end the evening bonded together as friends (*pengyou*) or even fictive kinship brothers (*xiongdi*) through shared experiences of pleasure. Kipnis summarizes the ways in which drinking generates ganqing (sentiment):

> Perhaps most centrally, toasting generates ganqing. Drinking together works at several levels. The giving and receiving of toasts signifies a mutual respect and acceptance. The consumption of alcohol lowers defense mechanisms, making the guest more vulnerable to the ganqing manipulations of the host. As a consequence, a willingness to get drunk signifies trust. (Kipnis 2002: 88)

More significantly, Kipnis, drawing on Anne Allison's work on Tokyo hostess clubs, emphasizes how "such socializing in the long term transforms the subjectivities of the participants, constructing desires that never once existed" (2002: 89).[22]

Toasting patterns mirror this movement. Early toasts over dinner tend to reflect hierarchy. Juniors usually initiate toasting with seniors by deferentially holding their glass lower when they clink together and by filling both empty glasses after the toast. But by the end of the evening, toasting is likely to be freer flowing. The production of sentiment and intimacy at the core of banquet drinking underlies most forms of KTV entertaining as well. Despite the fact that some entrepreneurs conceptualized certain types of entertaining as an instrumental form of courtship or goudui, they understood very clearly that the production of "irrational" sentimental attachment rather than simple reciprocity or mutual interest was essential to their efforts. Entrepreneurs understood that memories of shared pleasure and intimacy in KTVs were key to this production of affect, and hence sought to provide as much pleasure as possible in all its forms.

Xin Liu (2002: 63) notes that the entrepreneurs he studied in Beihai referred to the wining and dining of officials as a form of "production" rather than "consumption." He interprets the scene of the entrepreneur, official, and *xiaojie* (hostess/sex worker) drinking together in a private room as effecting a breakdown of status differences between the two men. By singing, drinking, and groping hostesses, both men are reduced to mere "customers." Following Allison, I would add that drinking, singing, and carousing with hostesses enables patrons and clients, officials, and entrepreneurs to be reduced to not just customers but desiring *men*, comrades in the enjoyment of good food and booze, confidants in singing songs of love lost, and lechers in their pursuit of young women (Allison 1994: 4). These shared experiences of pleasure serve as the pretext and context for forms of homosocial intimacy. When "having a good time" was successfully achieved, evenings would often end with declarations of friendship and affection, plans for future forms of entertainment, and offers of mutual aid.

Other anthropologists analyzing the interactions between entrepreneurs, officials, and hostesses in Chinese nightclubs have generated different interpretations. Tiantian Zheng (2006) interprets interactions between entrepreneurs and hostesses as a test of potential business partners' behavior and trustworthiness. For her, sex consumption is a microcosm of the business world. Entrepreneurs watch their partners' interactions with hostesses to see if they can control themselves and negotiate for the kinds of services they want, and whether or not they are taken advantage of by savvy hostesses. She rightly highlights the anxiety surrounding making deals and doing business in China.

Zheng, following Wank (1999), points to the importance of establishing trust in the context of China's poorly developed legal system, in which contracts are difficult to enforce.

Entrepreneurs I accompanied often did observe and analyze the characters of their partners through shared participation in leisure (especially through gambling), but this evaluation constituted only one aspect of elite nightlife. Many of the businessmen with whom I worked in fact echoed Zheng's explanation and interpreted their constant wining and dining as a form of building trust. Yet, reflecting on their experiences further, most mentioned that this building of trust was difficult to achieve in a short amount of time. One evening in a KTV might be enough to size up a partner, but it took many nights to form the storehouse of incommensurable, embodied experiences that served as the foundation for trust. I would emphasize that, in addition to functioning as a kind of covert job interview, in KTV entertaining entrepreneurs manipulate male concerns with sexuality and status to generate affective ties between each other.

Another anthropologist, Everett Zhang (2001), reads the drama of the KTV baofang in psychoanalytic terms. For Zhang, the entertaining of officials by entrepreneurs is "fraught with hidden psychological conflict with the state apparatus and the symbolic order" (237). He posits a deep-rooted sense of castration among entrepreneurs brought by their experiences at the hands of the Chinese party-state. Entrepreneurs seek to reclaim their lost masculinity by controlling the bodies of hostesses and treating state officials to entertainment that they could not afford on their own (legitimate) salaries. Zhang emphasizes that by entertaining officials, entrepreneurs temporarily reverse the power hierarchy between bureaucrat and businessman. As Zhang understands it, as host of the evening's events, the entrepreneur "runs the show" for the official and has an opportunity to flash his wealth in the face of the official, showing him up in status for the evening (240). This desire for recognition by the state compels entrepreneurs to keep entertaining officials despite the fact that the acknowledgment they seek is "forever elusive" (252). Because entrepreneurs can never fully overcome their sense of inferiority wrought by state power, they endlessly repeat their ritual entertainment.

The analyses of Zheng and Zhang highlight some of the anxieties that permeate the realm of elite entertaining, but they neglect the lingering effects of entertaining and relationship building on both entrepreneurs and on government officials. Bonds rooted in sentiment formed during these evenings of entertaining create very real obligations for government officials that, as Zhang recognizes, are at odds with official state ideology and laws. Although lost masculinity and repressed sexuality were common themes of literature from the 1980s and 1990s, by the time of my fieldwork around 2004, few entrepreneurs openly expressed a psychic chip on their shoulder or a resentment of the power of government officials. At official levels and in the popular imagination, entrepreneurs' status was continually on the rise. In fact, I would argue that the status divide between officials and entrepreneurs has diminished. Former officials frequently enter business, and entrepreneurs are increasingly bestowed with government positions and unofficial state perks. Along with government officials, they constitute an elite network whose power cannot be rooted in either the state or the market. For this reason, unlike Zhang (2001: 236), who uses the term "entrepreneurial masculinity" to refer to the gendered subjectivities of businessmen castrated by the state, I use the term "elite masculinity" to capture the convergence of the practices and ideologies of entrepreneurs and government officials.[23]

Far from resenting the status of government officials, at times entrepreneurs even pitied the circumspection with which officials approached their entertaining and womanizing, which entrepreneurs could indulge in openly and freely. While in the popular imagination government officials are drinking, gambling, and cavorting with prostitutes nightly (spending either illicit income or public money), most officials cannot engage in these activities lightly or in the company of just anybody.

Although the types of exchanges between officials and entrepreneurs outlined above are ubiquitous among government officials in China, they remain illegal, and thus officials cannot allow themselves to be too visible in their dealings with entrepreneurs. To accept a dinner invitation or spend the evening drinking in a KTV is to recognize and confer legitimate status on a relationship with an entrepreneur "client." To engage in anything illegal in the presence of an outsider implies a degree of trust. Thus entrepreneurs fervently hope that officials or their clients indulge their deepest, darkest desires in their presence, for this implies that they have succeeded in their attempts at goudui.

My informants and many women I interviewed understood this scene as men letting loose and being themselves, or simply being men. But I would argue that this performance of selfhood and desire in these spaces is highly circumscribed and tightly governed by the codes of elite masculinity. KTV entertaining is highly scripted; it demands a particular performance of the self and gender and an articulation of specific desires in need of satisfying. In this sense, participants' "real" desires matter little in these encounters. Ironically, KTV play, which is often understood to entail dropping pretenses and "being oneself," is laden with vulnerability and anxiety and requires a great deal of conformity and aware-ness of the gaze of others. Play among business partners rarely departed from the conventional forms of banqueting, drinking, singing, and sex consumption.

When higher-status bosses and officials were being entertained, their pre-ferred forms of play became the standard of enjoyment for all present.[24] If the boss wants to dance with naked hostesses, everyone present must oblige him and participate. To refuse to participate in an official or client's preferred forms of play is to risk passing judgment on him and undermines the goal of fostering male solidarity. Among acquaintances, this refusal could also be interpreted as an unwillingness to deepen the relationship between them. Among more intimate associates, refusal to participate in these forms of play often lead to (usually lighthearted) accusations of being henpecked (*pataitai*) rather than jokes about homosexuality or femininity that a similar situation would likely generate in a North American context.

The majority of entrepreneurs I knew complained about being forced to participate in constant business entertaining. Although most of them enjoyed banqueting, drinking, and cavorting with hostesses on their own, they resented being obligated to entertain clients, partners, and officials whose company they did not enjoy and the considerable amount of time, money, and energy con-sumed by this entertaining. As I explain in Chapter Four, many saw constant drinking in KTVs and a fondness for hostesses as the very sign of being an uncultured nouveau riche, and some looked down on clients and officials who demanded this form of entertaining. Many insisted that they could rely on their own talent, charisma, and intelligence to attract patrons and clients and de-picted KTVs as a networking tool of the incapable and uncultured.

Despite their desire to live, in their terms, a "healthier lifestyle" (*geng jiankangde shenghuo*) and let their talents speak for themselves, they often still found themselves obligated to host and attend banquets and evenings in night-clubs. This was especially true when cultivating networks outside China's major cities, in areas where KTV entertaining was (and still is) the hegemonic elite form.

Despite the growing disdain for this form of nightlife, refusal to participate in these rituals of alliance building can have very material consequences for entre-preneurs and white-collar workers. An informant friend, Mr. Hou, worked in the distribution department of a national magazine for nearly eight years. Having joined the magazine during its fledgling years and helped it establish a national circulation network, he was nevertheless fired from his job. Although the reason given was that he was simply no longer needed, he attributed his firing to his fail-ure to cultivate a good relationship with his superiors through participation in shared forms of male play. During business trips, his bosses and coworkers had often collectively visited KTVs and brothels, sometimes having sex simultane-ously with a group of sex workers in their hotel room. Mr. Hou felt that having sex in a group under the gaze of his superiors and colleagues was somewhat "perverted" (*biantai*). While he occasionally patronized saunas and sex workers by himself, he preferred not to visit them in the company of his coworkers.

Mr. Hou's experience highlights the consequences for violating the codes of elite masculinity and emphasizes the role of types of male play in the pro-duction of reproduction of gendered relations of power. The forms of sexual relationships that permeated elite nightlife, which I turn to in the next section, perhaps best exemplify the kinds of performances required of elite men.

Wives, Mistresses, and Sex Workers: New-Rich Men's Sexual Worlds

Unlike the competitive "scoring" model of masculine sexuality, with its atten-dant victories and defeats familiar to American youth and portrayed in count-less beer and body spray commercials, the businessmen I knew in Chengdu operated according to a different underlying equation of sexuality, status, and masculinity. In the American model, heterosexual men accrue status through the sheer number and diversity of their sexual conquests, but in China, only certain types of sexual relationships with particular kinds of women project status onto elite Chinese men.

Many entrepreneurs asked me about the competitive "pick-up" culture that they saw depicted in Hollywood films and at Chengdu bars popular with for-eigners. While they understood the logic of the "open market" sexuality of the bar and dance floor, they were ambivalent about this type of masculine performance. They assumed that any unaccompanied women in these estab-lishments were most likely either sex workers or in some way morally tainted and physically unattractive. Otherwise, my friends assumed, these women wouldn't be there in the first place. Because of the presumed low status of the women who frequented pick-up bars, my Chinese informant friends did not view seducing women in these establishments as in any way confirming their virility, sexual attractiveness, or status (unless, that is, they succeeded in se-ducing foreign women, which is an issue too complex to be dealt with briefly here). Furthermore, for business-oriented entertaining this risk-laden field of "scoring" would be highly detrimental to building relationships with other men. Hosts would never dare risk the potential humiliation and loss of face to their guests (often older government officials) by leaving them to their own charms and devices on the dance floor or sitting at a bar. This would generate a hierarchy of winners and losers that would threaten the group's solidarity.

During instrumental, goudui-type entertaining, hosts make every effort to ensure that their "guests" receive their choice of women and that they are provided with whatever sexual services they require.[25] Thus, KTV entertainment is organized to guarantee control over sexual outcomes. This control is essential to ensuring that status hierarchies are adequately respected, guests are satisfied, and no one's masculinity is called into question. Properly orchestrated, an evening in a KTV or sauna renders fellow businessmen deserving of their status as elite men and capable of enjoying the same pleasures and luxuries.

Given the role of young women in forging ties between men, elite entertainment on the surface resembles a classic case of the "traffic in women," in which men form alliances through the exchange of objectified women.[26] As Gayle Rubin argues in her classic essay, gender roles and conventions of sexuality are "constituted by the imperatives" of a system of social organization (Rubin 1975: 179).[27] Similarly, in business entertaining, men attempt to harness and appropriate women's sexuality as a way of enhancing their own status and building ties with other men. As will be shown below, this particular traffic in women depends on the women being recognized as subjects with their own desires rather than as objects to be exchanged or transparently purchased. While nearly all of the men I worked with paid for sexual services, and sex workers played a key role in entertaining, paid sex ranked lowest among their many different kinds of sexual relationships. Some well-established bosses I knew insisted that they never paid for sex and that young women were attracted to them for their power and reputation (see also Zheng 2006).

In her ethnography of Tokyo hostess clubs, Allison outlines a dynamic that is in many ways similar to that of Chinese KTVs. She argues that Japanese hostesses project an idealized masculinity onto their clients. This ego massage helps smooth relations between coworkers and gives clients an exaggerated sense of masculinity, which is then sutured to their jobs. The activities that these men engage in in hostess clubs—drinking, talking about themselves, making sexual jokes—are not sex in any conventional sense. Through flattery, pouring drinks, and attentive listening, these hostesses serve as mediums through which men can construct themselves as ideal male subjects (Allison 1994: 22). What the companies of these businessmen are paying for is the recognition provided by the hostesses that they are attractive, funny, and masculine. According to Allison, this results in a kind of subjectivity that makes for good and committed workers—self-assured and with their ego oriented more toward work than toward home (202). The fact that the recognition provided by these women is paid for and therefore inauthentic is mitigated by the hope that the fake, commodified relationship with the hostess will evolve into a real love relationship. Stories of "real" love affairs between clients and hostesses serve to feed this hope. In fact, the most financially successful hostesses are those who most convincingly give the impression of genuine interest in a client without actually delivering on the promise of a real sex-love relationship (194).

Hostesses in Chinese karaoke clubs employ many of the same techniques to project an idealized masculinity on their clients. They flatter them with compliments about their singing and appearance and pretend to enjoy the endless dice games that accompany drinking. When drinking, they deferentially lower their glass and pour drinks for their clients before pouring for themselves. They address their clients either as "husband" (laogong) or as "handsome guy" (shuaige). Unlike the hostesses described by Allison, however, the majority of hostesses in Chinese KTVs are available for sex at the right price. Chinese hostesses do not need to employ the promise of a "real" romantic relationship to keep their clients returning, since it is usually understood that sexual services can be obtained for those willing to pay. For this reason, patronage of and sexual relationships with hostesses confer very little status on elite men in Chengdu.

While Allison posited a direct correspondence between the price and class of the hostess and the status of her male patron, this equation does not hold true in the Chinese context, as will be seen below. While hostess clubs in Japan help ease tensions generated by workplace hierarchies, for entrepreneurs in China hostesses help to secure the enjoyment and pleasure of their guests, thereby helping to cultivate affection for the evening's host. Just as bonds are formed over the shared enjoyment of good food and booze, these men are drawn closer over the shared pleasure of "illicit" sex, and this "shared transgression" and mutual enjoyment provide the basis for their intimacy (Cameron and Kulick 2003). These embodied memories of shared enjoyment lay the foundation for affective ties between business associates.

Despite the potential for shared pleasure and intimacy, the performance of elite masculinity required in KTVs generates its own set of anxieties. In her history of prostitution in Shanghai, Gail Hershatter (1997: 8) notes that prerevolutionary men's guidebooks were filled with advice on how to avoid being taken advantage of by wily courtesans. These guides, which Hershatter refers to as "primers for the production of elite masculinity," spoke to what appears to be a profound anxiety on the part of men that they would either be duped out of their money or engage in behavior that would call into question their elite status. In the contemporary context, Tiantian Zheng (2006) echoes this point, interpreting entrepreneurs' interactions with hostesses as above all a test of their sophistication and emotional control. Hershatter argues that in early twentieth-century Shanghai the ultimate goal of many of the men who patronized courtesans was not sex, but, through their own sophistication and status displays, to mold themselves into a courtesan's object of affection and reverse the vector of desire.

Similarly, many of my research subjects understood the ability to attract beautiful women, without directly and transparently paying, as the ultimate confirmation of their virility and status.[28] They hoped to transform a relationship founded on money into one rooted in mutual affection. Many elite men framed payments to mistresses or hostesses as gifts—as tokens of a concern for their well-being and happiness rather than as payments for time and services rendered. According this imaginary, only country bumpkins or old, ugly men actually needed to compensate women to overcome their "natural" lack of charm and desirability.

Among well-established and successful entrepreneurs, paid hostesses were a convenient means of securing a client's enjoyment, but they were not the preferred means. Men who only cavorted with paid hostesses and sex workers were often suspected of being nouveau-riche bumpkins new to the world of elite entertainment. Many well-established men of means instead called on networks of younger women who were not professional hostesses or sex workers to accompany them in KTVs. These networks included mistresses' friends and classmates, junior employees of their companies, and occasionally female business associates.

One strategy for securing a meeting or winning the favor of a hard-to-reach official or businessman was to promise to introduce him to an attractive young woman who might potentially serve as his girlfriend or mistress. Simply paying a hostess to sleep with a client or official, while often seen as necessary to ensure that he enjoyed himself fully, implied a distance in the relationship and generated less *ganqing* (sentiment) than organizing a date with a "beauty" (*meinü*). If one of these introductions succeeded, then the official would be "indebted" to the entrepreneur. My informants took obvious pleasure in pointing out the mistress-patron relationships in which they had played matchmaker. But even the introduction alone already enhances the official or client's status by implying that he is the kind of man capable of attracting and associating with beautiful women.

Among Chengdu men, the qualities of women who conferred the most status onto their male companions were well established and almost universally recognized. They included youth (under 30 at least, under 25 preferred), purity (evidenced by virginity or a low number of previous sexual partners), beauty, artistic cultivation (singing or dancing ability), education, and high "quality" (*suzhi*), which was often indicated by a combination of educational level, perceived morality, urban upbringing, and family background.

The most available women—hostesses—were usually the least desirable because of their low levels of education, perceived "dirtiness," and rural backgrounds. Hostesses, however, were well aware of this ideology and often played into customers' desires by claiming to be down-on-their-luck university students temporarily forced to work in KTVs and by disguising or denying their rural backgrounds. Ironically, real university students and women from wealthy families were more inclined to demonstrate their sophistication by wearing revealing clothes and exhibiting a more open sexuality. Chengdu men often joked that in Chengdu all the proper girls (*liangjiafunü*) dressed like prostitutes and all the prostitutes dressed like university students.

Nearly all of the male entrepreneurs I worked with were married, and virtually all of them engaged in some form of extramarital sex. Nearly all patronized saunas that offered sexual services and slept with hostesses, and the majority also had girlfriends on the side. They often differentiated between the types of emotions, desires, and financial transactions specific to their different sexual relationships (Zelizer 2005). Lovers (*qingren*), girlfriends (*nüpengyou*), and mistresses (*qingfu*) were the most idealized objects of desire. Lovers, more than wives, were seen to reflect a man's current status and the state of his finances. By examining entrepreneurs' different typologies of women and their corresponding sexual relationships, we can understand the different value attached to each type of relationship and the role status, sexuality, and money play in each.

Wives

The gendering of space associated with traditional Chinese society can be summarized by the phrase "men control the outside; women manage the inside" (*nan zhu wai; nü zhu nei*). A similar gendered separation undergirded the lives

of the elite men I worked with in Chengdu. While they were expected to perform certain normative roles associated with the domestic sphere—father, son,
husband—and the failure to fulfill these roles could result in condemnation by
their families and peers, the bulk of their time and energy was devoted to relationships associated with the "outside" world of career and business, which was
the primary source of an elite man's status (Uretsky 2007: 127).

Like the *sarariiman* studied by Anne Allison in *Nightwork*, over time the
identities, desires, and relationships associated with the outside world of society (*shehui*) came to overshadow my informants' domestic selves, often leading
to a sense of estrangement from home (1994: 199). In her study of masculine
sexual culture in Yunnan, Elanah Uretsky (2007: 128) notes that both female
and male informants often emphasized to her that "an unsuccessful man goes
home after work, mildly successful men go out after carousing, while the most
successful rarely go home." In this context, sexual relationships associated with
the outside world were far more important to men's status and the construction
of elite masculinity than their relationships with their wives.

Many entrepreneurs who had married before their rise to prosperity viewed
their wives as relics of the past and representative of a poorer and less sophisticated period both in their lives and in China as a whole. The derogatory phrase
for older wives, "coarse grain wives" (*zaokangzhiqi*), indicated both the harsher
times they had suffered through with their wives and their "coarser" appearance.

In fact, many Chinese I interviewed interpreted extramarital affairs as representing a temporal disconnect between successful entrepreneurs and their wives.
According to this interpretation, while entrepreneurs spent most of their time in
the outside world of society (*waimian*) "developing" with the times, their wives
were confined to the domestic sphere (*jiali*), limiting the scope of their knowledge and concerns to children and household chores. Thus wives were often understood to be incapable of understanding the complex social world navigated
by their husbands and to lack the social graces and cultural sophistication to
accompany their husbands while entertaining. Few of the entrepreneurs' wives
worked, especially if they were younger and thereby more at risk of seduction
and pollution in the "outside" world of business.[29]

Regardless of whether they worked outside the home, wives were almost
never present during evenings of entertaining. After dinner one evening,
Mr. Liao once apologized to me profusely in front of his wife for her insistence
on coming along with us to a KTV. "I'm so sorry you won't be able to have any
fun," he told me repeatedly.

Even at banquets or teahouses and other forms of entertainment that did not involve hostesses, girlfriends and mistresses were the preferred companions. Several entrepreneurs told me they would have felt embarrassed to bring their wife along to an evening of yingchou, especially if all of their peers were accompanied by mistresses or hostesses. Entrepreneurs often deliberately kept their business lives and connections separate from their wives and their wives' social circles. On the few occasions in which I met my informants' wives they often remarked how rarely they had a chance to meet their husbands' friends. Entrepreneurs also exploited their wives' apparent ignorance of their business ventures to hide their other romantic activities. "Taking care of a client" (*pei kehu*) and "business entertaining" (*yingchou*) were the most common excuses for late nights out or even vacations with girlfriends or mistresses.

For these men, the domestic (*jiali*) was a realm of responsibility. But this responsibility was measured not by "quality time" and fidelity, but by the conditions their families lived under—such as their houses, their children's schools, and their wives' cars. They felt that once their financial obligations to their families were satisfied, as evidenced by the material comfort in which they lived, they had a license to enjoy the fruits of their labor and the pleasures offered in the outside world of business entertaining. According to their logic, the more time they spent in the outside world of society cultivating relationships, the better their chances of business success and thus the better they could provide for their family and thus fulfill their responsibilities. Besides, they told me, successful men have a stressful life (*huode henlei*) and deserve to enjoy themselves every now and then.

This ideology of enjoying the pleasures of the outside, while keeping their domestic relationships intact, is best summarized by a saying frequently quoted to me, "Outside flags of many colors flutter about, but at home the red flag is never taken down" (*Waimian caiqi piaopiao, jiali hongqi budao*).[30]

Mistresses and Lovers

Local interpretations of Valentine's Day reflected the division between wives and lovers. In Chinese, Valentine's Day is rendered as "Lover's Day" (*Qingren Jie*), and many older, less cosmopolitan entrepreneurs interpreted this holiday quite literally. They understood it as the day to treat their mistresses and girlfriends (not their wives) to dinner, shower them with gifts, and be seen out with them in upscale Western-style restaurants. (Many young people, who were more familiar with the significance of Valentine's Day in America, found this local interpretation of the holiday rather amusing.)

When I asked one older businessman if his wife got upset if he didn't take her out on Valentine's Day, he replied that she probably only had a vague idea that such a holiday even existed. Whether this was true or not, it reflected the strong division between the domestic realm of responsibility and the outside world of romance and pleasure, from which their wives were mostly excluded.

Christmas was another Western holiday (*yangjie*) in which it was important to be seen out with a young, attractive lover in an upscale restaurant, hotel, or bar. Jealous, cash-strapped male university students complained to me that on Christmas Eve Mercedes Benzes and BMWs of rich men lined up at their school gates to pick up female students for Christmas dates. While entrepreneurs' wives accompanied them for any traditional Chinese holidays, such as the family reunion dinners (*tuannianfan*) around Chinese New Year, mistresses were seen as the only suitable partners for the new "Western" holidays promoted by high-end leisure establishments.

The most highly desired mistresses were those with backgrounds in the arts and entertainment, preferably with some nascent fame. In practice, however, mistresses were frequently drawn from the ranks of entrepreneurs' own companies. Secretaries were often expected to sleep with bosses and would risk being fired by refusing their bosses' advances. Lovers were also plucked from the staff of elite entertainment venues and other businesses that catered to the new rich. A manager of a newly opened five-star hotel in Chengdu confided in me that the hotel faced a significant staff turnover problem. Desiring to create a luxurious environment and meet the service standards for elite men, the hotel hired young, well-educated, and attractive female employees. These employees were all too often poached by wealthy businessmen who promised them better positions in their own companies or a life of leisure as a full-time mistress.

In the late 1990s, the foreign and domestic press abounded with stories of so-called second wives (*ernai*) in the more economically robust areas of China, and in Guangdong in particular. Ethnic Chinese businessmen from Hong Kong, Taiwan, and Singapore were the first to seek de facto second wives in areas where they were doing business. They took advantage of the stark contrast in wages and living standards between overseas Chinese and mainlanders at the time to attract young women abandoned by the state sector and with limited avenues for success in the new market economy. Cities such as Guangzhou and Shenzhen, which attracted many investors from Hong

Kong and Taiwan, even saw the rise of "second-wife villages" (*ernai cun*) in areas of the city. By 2004, however, most of my informants in Chengdu viewed the institution of *ernai* with disdain. They understood taking a second wife to be a more "feudal" (*fengjian*) mode of expressing elite male status more appropriate to newly rich peasants (*baofahu*) than to sophisticated, urban entrepreneurs.

I believe that their attitude was largely due to the blatant transactional nature of the relationship. The verb used in conjunction with *ernai*, *bao* (to rent or contain) is the same verb used in *baofang*, to rent out a private room. It connotes exclusive access and complete, although temporary, control. A "bao" relationship is in essence a contract. It is founded on a transaction and contains no connotation of emotion or nonmaterial interest. Sex workers could be paid for particular services or could be "rented" (*bao*) for a particular period of time.

A favorite topic of conversation among my male research subjects involved quoting the monthly rates to bao current female models, actresses, or pop stars and speculating on the rates that up-and-coming stars could fetch.[31] Presumably all one needed to bao someone was the right amount of cash. The price paid however, was not only a reflection of the value of the mistress—i.e., her youth, purity, beauty, or fame. Older, less attractive, and less cultured elite men were expected to pay more. Just as beautiful, cultivated women fetched a higher price, ugly, old, and uncultured men were "fined" for their unappealing qualities. Thus "renting" a woman was seen by many entrepreneurs I knew as a technique of necessity for the newly wealthy and presumably old, fat, ugly, and uncouth as well. Men who resorted to bao lacked the charm, sophistication, status, and reputation to elicit "authentic" affection and desire in women.

My informants used a different verb, *yang*, to categorize their relationship with girlfriends and mistresses.[32] *Yang* means "to provide for or take care of," and is most commonly used to describe parents' care for their children and later, children's care for their parents in old age. For wealthy businessmen, caring for their mistresses meant providing them with a monthly stipend, an apartment, and, if they were truly wealthy, a car as well, but it also involved caring for their general well-being and helping them solve any difficulties they faced. An entrepreneur might provide other forms of support depending on their mistress's circumstances. He might help her start a business or find work for her friends and relatives (especially her ne'er-do-well brother). I encountered several female university students in Chengdu who had their tuition and living expenses paid by wealthy, older male patrons.

Providing for multiple dependents, be they mistresses or fellow business-men, indicated elite masculine status. The desirability of the woman "provided for" directly reflected the wealth, reputation, and status of her male patron. In other words, only mistresses or lovers were seen as effective indicators of the noncommodifiable qualities (charm, sophistication, and appearance) of their male patrons.[33]

Despite the apparent material foundations of the relationship, my infor-mant friends often spoke of their lovers in idealized romantic terms and un-derstood their relationships to be primarily composed of affect. A journalist I interviewed from a popular Chengdu newspaper understood mistresses as providing overstressed businessmen with an emotional and spiritual confidant: "You foreigners can go to church, but in China a rich man has only his mis-tress to pour his heart out to" (qingsu). Several informants echoed this notion that mistresses served as spiritual and emotional confidants in ways that wives could not. Mistresses were purported to understand the pressures faced by an entrepreneur because they were part of the outside world of social relationships and deal making, unlike wives, who only understood domestic affairs.

In an interview I asked Mr. Wu what compensation he provided for his mistresses and whether the material interest of young women bothered him. I explained that many Americans felt that material interest tainted the emo-tional purity of a romantic relationship. Rich men in the West sometimes wor-ried that women "were only after their money" as represented by the popular figure of the young female gold digger. Mr. Wu replied that it did not bother him that women were initially attracted by his money: "I think it's normal for them to be like that. In fact, I hope that they put money first. That makes it easier for people like me." (Mr. Wu considered himself to be overweight and ugly and thus only able to attract beautiful women because he had money.) I explained that Americans felt that material interest did not provide a very solid foundation for a relationship. He responded that if two people are together for long enough, affection (ganqing) will develop naturally between them, espe-cially if they take care of each other.

In fact, providing tangible evidence of one's feelings in the form of comfort-able apartments and nice clothes was seen as a more effective demonstration of affection than mere romantic rhetoric. Young women even criticized men who made declarations of feelings and romantic gestures without backing them up with tangible actions and gifts.[34] Mr. Wu understood providing for his mistresses as the foundation of their affection for him, but not its only basis. Similarly, many elite entrepreneurs in Chengdu, along with their mistresses, wives, and subordinates understood human relationships, be they between husband and wife, parent and child, or patron and client, to be composed of varying degrees of interest and affect. But for them this was no "dirty secret" that induced anxiety or denial.

While entrepreneurs idealized their relationships in terms of taking care of dependent young women, both entrepreneurs and their lovers manipulated this social field to achieve more limited social, economic, and sexual goals. The men promised cars, jobs, apartments, and all the perks of full-fledged mistress status to their lovers, but these more substantial items seldom materialized. Most of my informants would string along young women with gifts of mobile phones and Louis Vuitton handbags until, from their perspective, the woman became too demanding of goods, money, or favors (thereby revealing her purely material interest) or their relationship evolved into one of increasingly plausible authentic affection. Relationships also ended when mistresses were deemed too old, which generally meant over 30, or when they pushed too hard for marriage. Some entrepreneurs do divorce their wives to marry their mistresses, but this was not common among the entrepreneurs I knew in Chengdu, who mostly subscribed to the "colored flag, red flag" ideology mentioned above.

Mistress affairs sometimes ended with a "buyout," whereby a wealthy patron would provide his mistress with an apartment, a lump sum of money, or a business to run to guarantee her long-term income. Young women often singled out and praised men who "took responsibility" (*fuzeren*) in their extramarital affairs. One well-known real estate developer in Chengdu was often commended as a model patron. He was known to have provided each of his past mistresses with a villa (*bieshu*) of her own before he moved on to a new, younger mistress.

Just as in their relationships with other men, wealthy men and government officials strive to cultivate relationships of patronage with their mistresses and lovers. Elite men gain status from being the provider for multiple dependents, be they aspiring entrepreneurs or college co-eds. And just as officials hand out capital and licenses that guarantee success for entrepreneurs, elite men provide the easy street to enjoyment of the fruits of the market economy for young women. For elite men, status derives above all from being able to deliver the goods—favors and connections, houses and handbags—to grateful dependents.

These practices of patronage are central to the "boss-patron" imaginary that informs the practices of many elite Chinese. Underlying these forms of patronage is a mechanism of control. In the minds of rich men, the financial dependence of mistresses ensures their fidelity. Similarly, officials know that when they are the only line of defense between a businessman and a predatory tax bureau they will never be short of dinner invitations.

Paid and Unpaid Sex

Entrepreneurs understood sex workers and hostesses as good for little more than enjoying oneself, entertaining clients, and for providing a sexual release. Several informant friends, both male and female, understood the role of sex workers to be merely that of "solving the problem" (*jiejue wenti*)—that is, taking care of men's basic physical needs (*nanren shentishangde xuyao*).

For an entrepreneur, falling for a sex worker or even a hostess not normally available for sex would likely incur the ridicule of his peers, for these women lacked most of the qualities desired by a man of status. Similarly, men who let their affairs go too far were also criticized. While divorce was understood and rarely condemned, divorce of a proper and decent wife merely for a younger, more attractive woman of dubious moral character was usually criticized as revealing a lack of responsibility (*zerengan*) to his family.

Allison (1994), in her study of Japanese hostess clubs, found that the ability to pay for sex directly corresponded to a man's status; but among the groups of entrepreneurs I knew in Chengdu, sex with sex workers occupied a more precarious position. Paid sex was often described as highly pleasurable and sometimes contrasted with sex with mistresses (who, because of their perceived purity, were often characterized as inexperienced and lacking in technique) and with wives (who were viewed as beyond their sexual prime and almost desexualized). But commercial sex even in the most high-end saunas did little to enhance men's status. Instead it was viewed as an essential component of entertaining and an occasional necessity to help them take a break from the pressures of business.

Some elite men even expressed an aversion to any form of blatant commercial sex. Others portrayed themselves as being forced to pay for sex because they were unable to attract women with their looks and charm. When I asked a married entrepreneur, Mr. Zhou, about his love life he responded, "Not so good. No girlfriends, only prostitutes."

The first night I met Brother Fatty, a local boss of a mafia-like brotherhood (*heishehui*), he insisted to me that he never pays money for sex: "I refuse to pay money, and I don't need to pay" (*Wo bugei qian, buxuyao gei qian*). His ideal sex partners were those who, in recognition of his greatness and power, willingly offered themselves to him (or at least expressed their sincerity and lack of venality convincingly). As evidence of the type of beauty he could attract without paying, he dropped the names of several second-tier actresses who (he claimed) were his former mistresses. Although he would offer his guests their choice of hostesses at his nightclub, I rarely witnessed him interacting with hostesses at his club or at others. Instead he surrounded himself with young female students, actresses, and dancers introduced to him by his business associates.

Never paying reflected Fatty's self-understanding as a man with enough face (*mianzi*) to transcend commodified relationships, and it was a principle that he extended to many other facets of his life. He understood that the power of his relationships and reputation allowed him to transcend most crude transactions. Twice (once at a carwash, and once at a restaurant) at establishments run by associates who were under his protection he was mistakenly given the bill. Somewhat embarrassed by their lack of deference to him in my presence, he told the clueless cashiers, "I don't have to pay here."

Given his wealth, power, and extensive network of influential friends, businessmen and underlings frequently sought to win Fatty's favor by introducing him to younger women. In negotiating these offers he was concerned first about the women's features—their age and the quality of their skin in particular—but above all he was interested in their motives for wanting to be with him. Once while I was riding in his Mercedes he received a call from an acquaintance offering to introduce him to a "virgin" university student who was eager to meet him. Fatty was very interested, but he was concerned that the girl was only after money or gifts, and asked his friend, "Are you sure that she just doesn't want a mobile phone?" He was uninterested in women looking for a mobile phone or a shopping spree; he wanted women to want him and for their desire to spring from an awareness and recognition of his fame and power. Only these authentic forms of desire effectively confirmed and reflected his status.

Conclusion:
Sexuality, Status, and Alliances Among the New Rich

Elite men in Chengdu clearly preferred meeting and forming relationships with women who most closely possessed the qualities described above—youth, purity, beauty, and class. They would often sweeten their dinner invitations to colleagues and officials with the promise of an introduction to a "beauty" (*meinü*). Some entrepreneurs used such promises to secure a meeting with a hard-to-meet high-ranking official or businessman. It was assumed that men who already possessed significant amounts of money and power could still be tempted by sex, especially less blatantly commercial forms.

Many entrepreneurs I worked with encouraged their girlfriends to bring their friends along during evenings of entertaining to provide potential dates for their associates. From a distance, this behavior quite closely resembles a "traffic in women" in which men seek to secure alliances with each other through the "exchange" of young women. However, the effectiveness of this exchange depends on an understanding of the women involved as not objects, but as subjects, with their own motivations and desires that men can only hope to influence. In fact, it is the noncommodifiable and autonomous nature of these women's desire that served as the source of their value in mirroring men's status and mediating relationships between men. This process resembles objectification less than exploitation in the Marxist sense—the extraction and appropriation of the value produced (or performed) by young women's desire for the purpose of building ties and mirroring status among elite men.

Furthermore, seldom did this traffic take the form of a reciprocal exchange but was instead bound to the hierarchy of host/guest and patron/client relationships. Introductions to beauties were most often understood as prestations (gifts or exchanges that establish or reinforce a social relationship) to powerful men that reflected (or enhanced) the men's status and virility. These presentations were most effective when the woman "presented" seemed to harbor an authentic desire for the official or client. Simply treating a client or official to sexual services often reflected a distance in the relationship between the two men, and nothing augmented an elite man's masculinity more than having a young beauty (*meinü*) fall for him (or at least give a convincing performance of falling for him). This outcome, however, depended on the desires of young beauties, which entrepreneurs attempted to influence with stipends, apartments, and gifts but disavowed "purchasing" entirely. Despite their fantasies of control, they could only hope that the young women they called upon to aid in their alliance-making succumbed to the temptations of luxury and opted to "take the shortcut" (*zou jiejing*) by serving as the mistress to a wealthy man.[35]

For elite men in Chengdu, merely paying for sex or to bao a second wife represented lower-status forms of sex consumption. More successful and wealthy men such as Fatty felt that real status was indicated not by the price paid but by less transparently commodified forms of value—their fame, connections, and reputation. The possession of these qualities was confirmed by the authenticity of the affections of their high-class girlfriends and the depth of their ties to other elite men.

In many ways entrepreneurs faced similar dilemmas in their relationships with mistresses and with other elite men. Creating relationships of financial dependency might bring about a degree of fidelity and trustworthiness, but only deep bonds based on sentiment will bring long-term loyalty and control. While instrumental motives such as gaining the patronage of a powerful official or winning a contract often serve as the basis for the initial invitation for a night of banqueting, drinking, and carousing, the goal of a successful evening of entertaining is precisely to transcend agendas and interest and create a lasting bond out of shared experiences of pleasure. In the context of banquet saturation, where countless businessmen are offering bribes and dinner invitations, only entrepreneurs skilled in the arts of goudui "courtship" have a distinct advantage.

Elite nightlife constitutes the primary arena in which entrepreneurs' consumption, social networks, and sexualities are on display to their peers, but male play in KTVs is not merely a gendered performance. Here relationships between men are made that structure politics and business. Whether for the more instrumental purposes of goudui or simply a night carousing with friends, the subjectivities generated and the networks produced in these encounters cannot be reduced to a "hypermasculinity" surging forth after decades of repression. Instead they create networks governed by their own codes of honor (*yiqi*), face, and brotherhood. As will be shown in the next chapter, these networks constitute powerful, "informal" institutions that transcend state, society, and market in China.

3

"RELATIONSHIPS ARE THE LAW"

Elite Networks and Corruption in Contemporary China

Early on during my fieldwork in Chengdu, China, I met two wealthy business-men in a bar popular with English-speaking white-collar workers. Normally men like them would never be found in this kind of place, but they had been brought there by one of the men's girlfriends, an entrepreneur who exported rare mushrooms from the highlands of western Sichuan to Japan.

After treating them to a round of drinks, I explained to the two business-men why I was in Chengdu and described my research, hoping they might offer to be of assistance. One of them, who I later came to know as (Elder) Brother Chen (*Chen Ge*), kept offering to introduce me to a side of society that I would not be able to access on my own (*ni jinrubuliaode quanzi*). Not understanding his implied meaning I explained that I had been in Chengdu for a while and claimed that I knew people at all levels of Chengdu society. He continued to hint at the nature of this group: secret, closed, not open to all. Slowly I realized he was talking about what ordinary Chinese referred to as the *heishehui* (liter-ally, "black society"), and understood by most outsiders as the underworld of organized crime.

After that meeting, Mr. Chen called me the next day and invited me to see his furniture company's showroom. This was one of his many businesses, which also included nightclubs, smuggling, and protection rackets. (They exported a great deal of their furniture to America, and he proudly proclaimed that Wal-Mart was one of their biggest clients.) When I arrived at his store, several junior members of his organization, referred to as *xiongdi* (brothers), were lounging around playing the card game sweeping southwest China at the time, "struggle against the landlord" (*doudizhu*). Mr. Chen showed me some of his company's furniture and asked if their products suited the tastes of American consumers.

After we had sat around watching his xiongdi play cards for a while, Mr. Chen invited me to dinner, and I was eager to accept, but I had already made plans for that evening. As Chen walked me out of his store to a place where I could get a taxi, he mentioned that one day he would like to introduce me to his group's *jiaofu*, using the Chinese translation of the English term "godfather." He explained to me, "Meeting and getting to know the godfather is more valuable than getting to know the mayor (*shizhang*). You know, in China there is no law. Relationships are the law (*renqing jiushi falü*)."[1] He told me that winning the favor of the "godfather" would be great for my future career and would guarantee me prosperity. Brother Chen explained that he liked me and would do whatever he could to help me out. His sudden expression of affection for me and interest in my well-being was unsettling.

Thinking back to my anthropological education on reciprocity, I interpreted his gesture as a deliberate strategy to put me into a relationship of indebtedness to him, and I immediately became anxious about potentially being approached for favors by a powerful criminal boss. When I meekly replied that I wished I could do something for him in return, but I'm just a poor graduate student, he laughed and told me, "Don't worry, we [i.e., his organization] are not that calculating" (*women meiyou name xianshi*).

The comment by Mr. Chen that "relationships are the law" captures a particular imaginary of power, one in which an informal structure of relationships, reputations, and sentiments dominates the official formal structure of bureaucracy, titles, and law. But what is this "law" that Mr. Chen is referring to, and what is so compelling about these relationships and their associated ethics that they can come to substitute for "law"?

The particular economic and political conditions of reform period China, in which state officials and entrepreneurs (both the legitimate and the illegitimate types) have become increasingly dependent upon each other both to achieve state goals and to enrich themselves, has contributed to the evolution and institutionalization of informal networks as a means of consolidating power and appropriating both public and private resources among the elite. As He Qinglian (1998) has argued, while the transformations in China's economy during the reform era have largely been interpreted under the rubric of privatization and the spread of markets, the "privatization" of state enterprises and land has rarely proceeded according to an idealized market logic. Nor has privatization and the retreat of the state resulted simply in the "liberation" of entrepreneurial forces and "powers of the self" (Zhang and Ong 2008: 2). Rather, the insider transfer of state assets into private hands during the reform period has in large part followed the dictates of moral economies based on kinship (both real—in the case of the princelings [*taizidang*]—and fictive), bureaucratic hierarchies, and ideals of interpersonal morality such as brotherhood and mutual aid. Even entrepreneurs who made their initial fortunes independent of state connections and assistance eventually end up enmeshed in official networks in order to maintain their enterprises and ensure their political survival.

Writing about the increasing collusion between the bureaucratic and entrepreneurial elite during the 1990s, He Qinglian highlights the centrality of relationships and morality to their business dealings:

> It goes without saying that the situation involving rent-seeking activity in China is deeply rooted in our nation's traditional culture. In Chinese culture the tendency is to ignore the public good altogether and concentrate solely on personal relationships and the all-important network of personal connections. Throughout Chinese history personal ties are created by "cementing relationships with gifts" [*lishang wanglai*], an action that ensures that virtually every profitable exchange in any human relationship carries some moral overtones. (He 2001: 56)

What I take from this statement is not simply that "traditional Chinese culture" serves as a template for organizing relations among the elite, but rather that members of the elite have strategically employed guanxi techniques of relationship building in their political and economic projects, transforming the cultural idioms of guanxi in the process. In the midst of what some observers have seen as a wave of privatization and neoliberalism, well-connected businessmen and state officials employ modes of exchange and distribution that organize "the market" to their advantage.[2] These modes of exchange and the informal networks on which they rely are key to the consolidation of power and the "private" appropriation of state resources during the reform period. He Qinglian goes on to argue:

> The fact is that what has emerged in China is a system for distributing resources that is rooted in neither a purely planned nor a market-based economy. Instead, rent-seeking activities that lead to acquisition of capital and other forms of wealth rely on a highly elaborate and informal network or web of social con-

nections. . . . Informal networks of social relationships are, in short, a major resource, in that they are the key mechanism for mobilizing and directing the flow
of wealth, making them not just of great economic significance, but also critical
to the way in which China goes about handling its raw materials and other such
social resources. (He 2001: 53)

For He Qinglian, an economist with faith in the inherent efficiency of un-
hindered market forces, these networks represent a distortion of the proper
workings of market mechanisms. Rather than creating wealth, they lead to
"enormous waste and squandering of resources" (He 2001: 60). According to He,
the wealth they do generate is purely the product of rent-seeking or the manipulation of personal and kin relationships. Echoing Brother Chen, but with a different moral valence, she critiques the current system in China as a "legal state
ruled by men" (*renzhide fazhi shehui*) as opposed to a "legal state ruled by law"
(*fazhide fazhi shehui*) (56).

While underground hierarchical brotherhoods such as Brother Chen's represent the most organized and explicit version of informal networks for appropriating and distributing the spoils of the market and the state-owned economy
in contemporary China, similar networks can be found at many levels of Chinese society structuring several aspects of politics and business to their competitive advantage. Many of these networks draw from the highly gendered
field of kinship as their moral template.

As Maoist collectivist ethics have lost their power over people's moral
worldviews, gendered notions of interpersonal morality and authority, rooted
in kinship and *renqing* (human sentiments), have increasingly served to legitimate everyday forms of power and ethics. Elite men, be they bureaucrats,
businessmen, or underworld bosses, strive to forge lasting networks of mutual
aid with each other by invoking these notions—ideals of brotherhood, paternalism, mutual aid, and *yiqi* (sense of honor and obligation in personal relationships). For most of these men, informal networks rooted in ideologies of
male solidarity are an integral part of their business ventures and central to
their elite status.

Because they are constantly engaging in new ventures, entrepreneurs are
continuously establishing new ties with needed businessmen and officials and
expanding the reach of other networks. (Not every real estate developer has
an uncle or a cousin in the concrete business, for example.) As I observed
in Chapter Two, much of the work that constitutes being an entrepreneur in
urban China consists of maintaining and expanding these networks through

favors, entertaining, and generating business opportunities and wealth for one's fictive kinship "brothers."

Mr. Chen's statement highlights the institutionality of these networks in China. For Mr. Chen and for the heishehui, the compelling, lawlike force of such networks is taken for granted—it is the very precondition for the existence of their organization. However, despite the moral rhetoric of brotherhood and reciprocity, most of these informal networks, held together by shifting bonds of morality, desire, and interest, are highly fragile and contingent. There is constant suspicion of the intentions and interests of others and a pervasive fear of being taken advantage of. Informal networks that involve corrupt officials are continuously threatened by anti-corruption campaigns and exposure in the Chinese media, which often incite the public outrage that spurs the state to take action against them.[3]

Despite Mr. Chen's assertion that "relationships are the law," deals and alliances between government officials and businessmen, and even within the heishehui itself, are constantly threatened by venality, narrow personal interests, and deception. Thus, these alliances should not be read as mechanistic manifestations of a stable, traditional moral economy, but rather as strategic, fragile, ad hoc structures that invoke and draw on a closed, moral frame of distribution as a means of gaining an advantage in China's economy and that are constantly under threat by other modes of power, distributional logics, and personal loyalties. These networks have proved to be a powerful tool of the elite in appropriating public resources and in generating wealth in China's reform economy, but their formation and maintenance is always tentative. And they often fail to realize their internal ethics in practice.

The previous chapter described the formation of elite networks through shared experiences of leisure in China's new entertainment venues. This chapter widens the analytic scope to examine the operation of these networks in the overlapping worlds of officialdom and business, looking at how state power and resources, in addition to private wealth and informal power, flow through these networks.

In this chapter I examine the workings of three of these networks and their associated moral economies: the "unwritten rules of officialdom" (*guanchangde qianguize*) as narrated by a corrupt official; the organizational ideology of a criminal brotherhood (*heishehui*) in Chengdu; and the networks of entrepreneurs, bureaucrats, and gangsters that underlie real estate development in urban China.

My analysis of the heishehui derives primarily from my experience accompanying members of a local heishehui organization in their daily lives and evening entertainment and from interviews with their personal and business associates.[4] Because I was never formally initiated as a member, my knowledge of their rituals and business dealings was limited, but through discussion with them I was able to gain a sense of their organizational ethos and how they conceived of the source and reach of their power.

Although I frequently interacted with government officials during evenings of entertaining, I rarely had the chance to interview them either formally or informally given that many of my interests centered on their illicit activities. Thus, my second example, which looks at the moral economy of corruption, relies on textual sources, primarily a published interview with the former tax bureau chief of Hebei Province, Li Zhen, conducted before his execution for corruption.

My final example is drawn from the experience of an official turned entrepreneur, Mr. Wei, whose business practices and personal identity transcend "black" and "white" society (i.e., legal and illegal worlds).

Through a discussion of three examples of how these elite networks operate in practice, I show how they complicate any neat analytic division between state and civil society in contemporary China. The latter two examples, in particular, also exemplify what He Qinglian (2002: 45) describes as the "growing alliance between the social underground—'black society' [heishehui]—and the 'white' or legitimate organs of state authority."

Conceptualizing Corruption

Many of the practices described in this chapter form the basis of the broad social field described by scholarly and nonscholarly observers alike as corruption (fubai) in China.[5] Corruption, however, is a polysemic term that carries with it a great deal of moral baggage and thus often lacks analytical precision. The literature on corruption both within China and elsewhere is too vast to be dealt with in detail here, but the material in this chapter suggests some limitations of what is arguably the most widespread characterization of corruption—the failure of public institutions to curb the private desires of individuals. Jennifer Hasty summarizes the limitation of this approach as follows:

> [T]his normative scholarship on corruption tends to view the practices of corruption as alienated, self-interested acts by greedy public servants poaching on national resources and as selfish crimes of calculated desire in the absence of

public discipline. It is therefore assumed that a more pervasive public exercise of social discipline through state institutions will work to prevent corruption by stifling the selfish greed of individuals. What this corruption scholarship fails to recognize, however, is that forms of desire that fuel corruption are not merely selfish and private but profoundly social, shaped by larger sociocultural notions of power, privilege, and responsibility. (Hasty 2005: 271)

Following Hasty and others (Olivier de Sardan 1999; Yang 2002), I view corruption as a product of elite networks and their moral economies—as the dominance of an informal mode of power and distribution over the legally enshrined one.

In developing this approach, this chapter emphasizes a few points about corruption in China that challenge models of corruption which conceive of it either in terms of individual incentive structures or as a product of broad cultural tendencies.[6] First, corrupt activities are both highly risky and inherently social; that is, they involve the coordination and cooperation of several actors, and the success of their endeavors depends on trust among the many different individuals. Second, "relativist" approaches, which stress the cultural factors facilitating corruption, tend to operate with a simplistic model of culture. They often invoke dehistoricized or timeless cultural values or tendencies. In doing so they often neglect the political and economic institutional frameworks in which corruption takes place and the ways in which cultural institutions (such as *guanxi*) evolve along with them. Thus they fail to account for the different forms corruption takes in a single society and its corresponding distributional effects (Sun 2004: 203).

Furthermore, in taking a relativistic approach to corruption it is not enough to simply assume that what is considered corruption in one society might not be considered so in another. Instead one must be attuned to the ways that the same practices in any given society may be considered either corrupt or moral depending on how they are framed and interpreted by actors and observers (Smart and Hsu 2007). In other words, one person's concern for his nephew's business success might be another person's insider dealing. Or, to use the example above, the relationships Mr. Chen refers to as moral *renqing* would no doubt be perceived by most Chinese citizens as the highly immoral basis of corruption. This helps to explain why, to quote Daniel Jordan Smith's observation about corruption in Nigeria, ordinary Chinese are "paradoxically active participants in the social reproduction of corruption even as they are also its primary victims and principal critics" (2007:5).

Many scholars both within and outside of China have described corruption in reform-era China as the "privatization of the state" or "transactions in money for power" (*qianquan jiaoyi*) (e.g., Sun 2004). The material presented here suggests, however, that there are many other forms of value circulating in corrupt "transactions" besides money. In fact, the differing convertibility, visibility, and materiality of each form of value partly determines their strategic use by actors. Treating an official to sexual services, for example, creates an obligation that is difficult to trace or document, and female sexuality is understood to still elicit desire in an official whose pockets are already stuffed with cash.[7] Furthermore, in a context in which businessmen are lining up at officials' office doors to offer bribes, noncommodifiable ties of blood and sentiment are rendered even more significant and powerful (see Chapter Two).

Accounts of corruption that emphasize structural and institutional factors above all else tend to rely (usually implicitly) on a universal version of human nature that manifests under the right structural conditions. I argue in this chapter that official corruption, in most instances, is not merely a matter of individual incentives operating within a set of structural constraints, but of the contending *social* forces of morality, sentiment, status, and duty in a complex social field.

As much anthropological work done on corruption in Africa has noted, forms of official malfeasance are often grounded in local norms, ethics, and expectations from kin and other members of an official's social network (Olivier de Sardan 1999). In his essay on the moral economy of corruption in Africa, Jean-Pierre Olivier de Sardan depicts the "value systems and cultural codes, which permit a justification of corruption by those who practice it (and who do not necessarily consider it to be such—quite the contrary)" and seeks "to anchor corruption in ordinary everyday practice" (25–26). Rather than viewing corruption as evidence of moral decay or a lack of ethics, he argues that the practices of corruption are "standard practices deeply rooted in more general social relationships" (50). Josiah Heyman (1999: 1) argues that studying criminal practices more generally requires one to do away with the trite assumption that states always uphold the law and focus on how "state law and the evasion of state law" must be studied together. In certain contexts, alternative moral and ethical systems can be more compelling to state agents than those enshrined in law or bureaucratic procedure. Following Heyman and Caroline Humphrey (1999: 2), this chapter asks: "When formal law does not prove to be the exclusive embodiment of morality, then what competing mores do state actors and illegal networks mobilize?"

The lack of universal ethical principles or a transcendent legal-moral code internalized by officials has been a long-standing theme of Sinological literature and analyses of Chinese politics (see, e.g., Pye 1992, 1995). This position is perhaps most clearly and forcefully articulated by Fei Xiaotong in his classic essay on the nature of Chinese sociality, *Earthbound China* (*Xiangtu Zhongguo*). In his discussion of differences between Western and Chinese morality, Fei states:

> A society with a differential mode of association is composed of webs woven out of countless personal relationships. To each knot in these webs is attached a specific ethical principle. For this reason, the traditional moral system was incapable of producing a comprehensive moral concept. Therefore, all the standards of value in this system were incapable of transcending the differential personal relationships of the Chinese social structure.
>
> The degree to which Chinese ethics and law expand and contract depend on a particular context and how one fits into that context. I have heard quite a few friends denounce corruption, but when their own fathers stole from the public, they not only did not denounce them but even covered up the theft. Moreover, some went so far as to ask their fathers for some of the money made off the graft, even while denouncing corruption in others. When they themselves became corrupt, they can still find comfort in their "capabilities." In a society characterized by a differential mode of association, this kind of thinking is not contradictory. (Fei 1992: 78)

Fei views Chinese society as composed of multiple, categorically different relationships, each with its own situated ethical principles. Within this ethical framework, allegiance to an abstract public or body of law is not only "foreign" to Fei's Chinese subject but potentially *unethical* from the perspective of his or her other social relationships. Thus the moral value of any given act depends on the perspective of the observer—whether he or she stands inside or outside the actor's social network. Although one can question whether this is an adequate characterization of Chinese society as a whole, it clearly captures the contending and shifting ethical spheres of the networks in which members of the contemporary business elite, and government officials in particular, are enmeshed.

In his account of the history and origins of corruption in the Chinese Communist Party, Xiaobo Lü(2000) argues that the CCP failed both to establish a "modern" bureaucracy committed to formal rules and procedures and to maintain an inspired, loyal cadre core dedicated to the goals of "continuous revolution." He shows how many CCP policies, which promoted the goals of revolution over bureaucratization, undermined the establishment of an elite culture committed to formal bureaucratic rules and norms. Instead, the insecurity and uncertainty generated by constant political campaigns led officials to seek protection in interpersonal networks, thereby undermining the bureaucratic power of the state and strengthening informal networks, a process he calls "organizational involution."

Building on Lü's (2000) historical argument, I understand corruption primarily as a product of evolving informal formations of power in contemporary China. While there are no doubt many acts of simple theft and deception committed by self-interested individuals, corruption as a larger social phenomenon relies on the coordination and cooperation of others. In contemporary China, it is built on personalistic networks of mostly men bound together by overlapping ties of affect, interest, loyalty, and mutual obligation that permeate different levels of state and society.

The networks in which corrupt officials are enmeshed and through which they exert power and distribute favors include ties of kinship, native place, schooling, and colleagueship; increasingly they also include connections formed through evenings of entertaining and courtship. From an official's perspective, corruption often involves serving these personal "mini-publics" at the expense of the abstract public good (see Lü 2000: 43). In other words, corruption is less about the proliferation of rotten apples undermining a healthy organizational logic for their own "private" ends than it is about the spread of elite networks that distribute state resources according to their own logics.

Thus, an analysis of the practices I describe below from an ideal of Western bureaucracy or morality will necessarily frame them as a failure to conform to the Western model. Instead of beginning with the question, "Why can't China maintain a disciplined bureaucracy loyal to an abstract public good?," I examine corruption within the broader social field in which the CCP and its individual cadres operate. I view the practices associated with corruption as rooted in strategic alliances that contain their own forms of morality and transgression.

In this chapter I examine a few of the "mini-publics" that officials both manage and serve, and their concomitant social obligations. Given that these networks are largely composed of groups of elite men, how do ideologies of male solidarity inform official corruption and organized crime? In the case of corrupt officials, how do they negotiate contending spheres of value and obligation—state policies, professional ambitions, cultural ideologies of brotherhood and mutual aid, sentiment (*ganqing*), and their overall social reputations or face (*mianzi*)? How do these informal commitments and "power projects" (Schneider and Schneider 2003a) intersect with the "governance" of the state?

Despite the ways in which these practices can be interpreted as evidence of the weakness of state control, I argue that they are not inherently resistant to state power. Although illegal and corrupt practices might undermine the formal laws and institutions of the state, they do not necessarily undermine the reach and effectiveness of state governance.

In many Chinese cities and towns, the local government uses its connections to wealthy businessmen and crime bosses to manage the underground economy and its unruly actors, and even to achieve the aims of economic development. By cutting deals with mafia bosses over seafood banquets, the government is able to exploit the masculine solidarity of junior members of mafia groups, who imagine they are the embodiment of honor and loyalty (*yiqi*), to undertake tasks that would incite public outrage if carried out by organs of the state. These informal networks, which transcend state and society and legal and illegal realms, complicate any neat division between the state and civil society and blur the lines between official state organs and illicit forms of authority. In fact, the very power and effectiveness of these networks derives from their ability to draw upon multiple modes of power—from the bureaucratic power of the CCP leadership to the threats of a club-wielding junior gangster.

Finally, my account of corrupt practices also briefly examines the discourses that both observers and participants in China use to explain the widely acknowledged "social problem" of corruption—in particular the ideology of "temptation" (*youhuo*) and the presumed difficulty men have in resisting some of the perks of power, money, status, and, in particular, sex.

As I noted above, many scholarly accounts of corruption assume that it is largely the absence of constraining forces, be they organizational, legal, or ideological, that facilitates the proliferation of corruption. These accounts take for granted that unchecked and unconstrained individual desires lie at the root of corruption.[8] In fact, this is also how corruption is accounted for in official discourse in China: as the product of the failings of individuals who have lost their sense of belief, faith in the Party, or public morality and who fall prey to the temptations of money, social vanity, or sex.

Rather than presume an ahistorical, gendered "human nature" that rears its ugly head when not held in check, my account emphasizes that how actors conceive of and account for corruption (and whether particular actions are construed as such) varies considerably with the social context, the actor's perspective, and one's conception of "human nature."

Corruption Confessional: *At the Gates of Hell*

When it was published in 2004, *At the Gates of Hell* (*Diyu Menqian*) (Qiao 2004) caused quite a stir among the public for its frank and explicit discussion of corruption. It consists of an extended interview with Li Zhen, a former party secretary and tax bureau chief from Hebei, after he had been convicted of corruption and was awaiting execution for his crimes. Li recounts his fall into corrupt practices to a journalist, Qiao Yunhua. He describes in great detail his money-making schemes and the backdoor channels through which he wielded power, and he reflects on the factors, both personal and social, that led to his "fall."

In addition to recounting Li Zhen's rise from a city-level secretary to the head of the Hebei tax bureau, Qiao includes three additional chapters dealing with Li's understandings of the lust for power (*quan*), money (*qian*), and sex (*se*). The interview transcripts are interwoven with commentary by Qiao, who often references stories from ancient China and classical Chinese novels and histories to analyze and explain Li's thoughts and actions. In doing so, he frames many of Li's flaws as typical of a "backward" Chinese national character still awaiting modernization. He also includes interviews with many of Li's associates, some of whom have very different interpretations of the events described by Li.

Unlike many other detailed accounts of the activities of corrupt officials, which are most prevalent in loosely controlled websites, this account was unique in being published by an official state-owned publishing house, Xinhua. Given the sensitivity of the material, the entire work was given a didactic framing as a warning to other officials to avoid similar temptations.[9] The work as a whole, then, must be considered in light of its didactic aims as an official effort to curb corruption and illicit ties between the government, officials' personal networks, and private enterprise.

The preface, written by Liu Liying, the former assistant secretary to the head of the Central Disciplinary Committee of the Communist Party and the head of the special group investigating Li Zhen's case, frames the book as a strong "warning" to other officials. He encourages a "multitude of cadres to earnestly read it and think about it thoroughly" (Qiao 2004: 5). Liu Liying also insists,

"The corruption that has appeared during this stage of our country's history is absolutely not fundamental, systemic corruption. The phenomenon of corruption is fundamentally incompatible with the party's aims and the socialist system" (2).

As Carolyn Hsu (2001) has argued, the ways in which corruption is narrativized in China have shifted during the reform period. In the 1980s, dissident intellectuals invoked the traditionalist discourse of a dynasty in decline, viewing corruption as a symptom of the expired mandate of the Communist Party and blaming the regime for China's social problems. In the years following the Tiananmen Square protests, however, the Party reconstructed itself as a manager of economic issues and refigured itself as an agent fighting the war on corruption on behalf of Chinese citizens, rather than as its cause.

At the Gates of Hell, as it is framed by Liu Liying, partakes in this narrative as well. I would supplement Hsu's argument by adding that this shift in official discourse, in which the Party presents itself as an agent fighting the war on corruption, transfers the "causes" of corruption to individual behavior and motives. In official discourse, corruption has increasingly been portrayed as the result of moral and ethical failings of individuals rather than the product of a flawed political system or institutions in need of reform. In both official and unofficial narratives, it has come to be portrayed as the result of proliferating temptations in a morally decadent society that (primarily) men find very hard to resist. According to this narrative, elite men are particularly susceptible to these temptations, which are especially powerful in the context of a "loss of belief" seen to be afflicting Chinese society. Li Zhen tells Qiao Yunhua that the most important factor in his fall into corruption was his "loss of faith in the Party" (Qiao 2004: 147), which made him susceptible to "hedonism" (*xianglezhuyi*) and the "lust for power" (*tanquan*).

At the Gates of Hell is an inherently polysemic text that can be interpreted in conflicting ways. While framed as a warning to other officials about the temptations associated with power, it also offers an exposé of the inner workings of officialdom and the ways official power can be and is wielded for private ends. At times, both Qiao and Li point to Li's personal lack of belief, loss of faith, lack of cultivation, and shortage of public oriented morality to account for his actions; at other times, Li defends his actions by appealing to notions of interpersonal morality, face (*mianzi*), and honor (*yiqi*). This defense echoes other confessional and courtroom testimony by corrupt officials in which they appeal to notions of morality and sentiment in justifying their actions (Yu 2007).

In their testimonies, officials on trial may refer to the "unwritten rules of officialdom" (*guanchangde qianguize*), implying that negotiating "unofficial" demands and obligations to other officials and other members of the elite plays a significant role in determining the course of official careers. They cite the costs to their reputations (*mingyu*) if they were to deny favors to members of the various networks in which they are involved. Li Zhen defends himself by declaring, "If I didn't take gifts and offer favors to powerful people it would diminish their support for government work and affect my ability to get things done" (Qiao 2004: 247).

In reform-era China there are significant expectations of material and immaterial gain surrounding officialdom from both state officials themselves, their kin, and members of their personal networks. These expectations are often summed up by the phrase, "*Xiao pin buxiao tan*" (People laugh at you if you're poor, but they don't laugh at corruption).[10] Underlying this statement is the notion that the public will accord status to those who get rich no matter by what means. When I first heard this saying, a law student friend explained it in these terms: "If you don't get rich as an official, people assume you're inept (*meiyou nengli*), or there's something wrong with you."

In his interview, Li Zhen talks about going to a class reunion early in his career, before his rise to power, and being ignored by his classmates, while his classmates who had found success in government or business were surrounded by fawning favor-seekers and admirers. He found this experience humiliating and cites it as the first time that he really came to worry about the importance of face (*mianzi*) (Qiao 2004: 85). He began to realize that being an ordinary, upright official would never provide him with the means of gaining the recognition of his peers, and he abandoned his original aspiration of being an honest, self-sacrificing "Jiao Yulu type" official (149).[11] The book quotes his reflections on the career prospects of an "honest and clean" (*lianjie*) official:

> Honest and incorruptible [officials] have become the subjects of many jokes for people shooting the breeze. I saw the same phenomena and the same type of people when I was secretary and when I was director [of the tax bureau]: Because they're upright and honest, they not only can't improve their livelihood and achieve an important position in their work, but they also are subject to other people's ridicule and censure as well as often excluded and isolated [by their colleagues]. The typical upright official has become like an "ascetic monk" [*kuxingseng*]. Conversely, some corrupt officials, including me,

of course, [even though] we have a bad reputation [*koubei buhao*] and have had our illegal activities reported to superiors many times, time after time we're still able to evade investigation and punishment for our violations of Party discipline and national law. In fact, we're considered capable cadres [*you nenglide ganbu*]. . . . This kind of situation makes me wonder, do I have a problem, or is there a problem with others? Or is it that this society has a problem? . . . I came to the incorrect conclusion that "people laugh at the upright and honest but not the corrupt" [*xiao lian buxiao tan*] had become a universally accepted notion. (Qiao 2004: 164)

Li Zhen relied on a few well-placed "brothers" (*tiegemen'er*) to achieve his goals—in particular, the director of a state-owned cigarette factory, Li Guoting, the head of an import/export company, Zhang Tiemeng, and a former official turned businessman, Wu Qingwu. Li's career was closely intertwined with Wu's, who helped Li Zhen move up in official circles. Li Zhen explains that the first step of his fall into corruption was "getting to know and actively fawning on [*xianmei*] and flattering [*bajie*] Wu Qingwu" (Qiao 2004: 46).

Using some of the techniques described in Chapter Two, including banqueting and entertaining, Li Zhen sought to befriend Wu Qingwu by both inflating his sense of self and appealing to his ambitions. He also strove to create intimacy between the two by sharing privileged administrative information with Wu. According to Wu's interview, this involved Li Zhen giving him insider information on the inner workings of the Hebei provincial government when Wu had just arrived there from Henan.

In addition to gaining Wu's trust by helping his transition to Hebei, Li Zhen influenced Wu by claiming that his father was a former Red Army solider and a comrade-in-arms with a high-ranking central government official in Beijing; Li Zhen referred to this Beijing official as his "godfather" (*yifu*). (He even produced fake photos of his "godfather" with central government officials to back up his claim.) Li Zhen told Wu Qingwu that he was in Hebei merely doing grassroots training and that his real career and connections were based in Beijing (Qiao 2004: 47).

After gaining Wu Qingwu's trust and giving him the false impression that his unofficial ties rendered him more powerful than his low bureaucratic position would indicate, Li Zhen encouraged him to leave his official post to go into business, and when Wu Qingwu officially "jumped into the sea" (*xiahai;* i.e., left his state-run work unit to do business on the market economy), he recommended Li Zhen to replace him. Li Zhen recounts his conversation with Wu Qingwu as follows:

> After you "jump into the sea" if you need anything I'll support you. I'm in the official world; you're in the world of business. I'll take care of [your] matters with the government. If I need money, I'll ask you. If we coordinate well I'll keep rising up in the government ranks, and you'll be making more and more money in business.... I'm in the government, Zhang Tiemeng is in a [state] enterprise, Wu Qingwu is in business. We each have our advantages. All we need to do is help each other and our future is limitless. (Qiao 2004: 51)

Li Zhen surmises that on the surface Wu Qingwu left his government job because he was tired of the constant power struggles associated with an official career, but "objectively speaking, he ascertained my boldness and sense of *yiqi* (honor and loyalty in personal relationships) and had faith in my promises and my 'guanxi' network" (Qiao 2004: 51).

We can read Li Zhen's partnership with Wu Qingwu and Zhang Tiemeng as representative of the intermingling of affect and interest, morality, and deception involved in elite networks. Li Zhen deliberately presented himself as a man of yiqi and as well connected in order to solidify his network and ensure the loyalty of its members. Li Zhen begins by attempting to court Wu Qingwu by both appealing to his interest and presenting himself as a trustworthy confidant. He presents himself as an attractive partner by claiming connections to a fictitious powerful relative.

Li Zhen later uses his ties with Wu and Zhang to engineer a money-making scheme in which they exploit the discrepancy between the foreign currency exchange rate available to state enterprises ($1 = 6 RMB) and that available on the open market ($1 = 10 RMB) at that time. Using their ties to Li Guoting, the head of a state-owned cigarette company, they have Li request a loan for 5 million dollars to buy equipment for his company. Once the loan is approved, they transfer the money to Zhang Tiemeng's import company, who converts it to RMB on the open market, netting them a profit of 20 million RMB. After considerable shuffling around of the money in order to hide their actions, they finally split the profit between the three of them.

Li Zhen was referred to as "Hebei's Number One Secretary" (*Hebei Diyi Mi*) and an unofficial "*yibashou*" (a capable, powerful person) whose abilities and power far exceeded his official position. Before his promotion to the head of the provincial tax bureau, Li Zhen served as personal secretary (*mishu*) to the

Hebei Party secretary (*shuji*). Despite deriving no *de jure* formal power from his position, Li Zhen describes how his proximity to the leadership allowed him to wield a great deal of de facto power. Part of his power came from his control over the Party secretary's schedule. Heads of companies and government work units were constantly seeking ways to get Li Zhen to bring important leaders to visit them and voice their support. Qiao Yunhua describes this kind of official support as an "intangible asset" (*wuxing zichan*) to enterprises, one that cannot be purchased with cash alone (80).

Visits by government officials in the form of inspection tours are highly sought after and coveted by both private and state-owned companies. Company leaders view them as recognition of their achievements and a sign of symbolic and material support. These official visits are often meticulously documented with photographs, and government leaders are often asked to leave their signatures or compose inspirational slogans in calligraphy for the company. Such photos and official inscriptions are ubiquitous in companies' promotional literature and in the public areas of their offices. Entrepreneurs and company heads prominently display photos taken with important officials in their offices as tangible and visible evidence of their connections.[12] Because investors and business partners read these visits as signs of ongoing useful connections, visits and praise by the leadership can translate into bank loans, contracts, and tax breaks.

Li Zhen used his control over his superior's schedule and his access to secret internal discussions to gain leverage and win the favor of others. He made high-ranking officials' decisions on promotions appear to be the result of his influence. When he learned that someone was about to be promoted, he would tell the anxious candidate that it was the result of his own hard work on the candidate's behalf.

Through these means, his reputation spread, and an increasing number of promotion seekers came to Li Zhen for assistance. Because of his growing reputation and perceived power, officials, even those that outranked him, were reluctant to deny his requests for favors out of fear that he would work against them behind the scenes. He was able to translate his partly fictitious reputation into actual power over decision making.

Li Zhen interpreted his own power as partly "bestowed by the system" (*zhidu fuyude*), partly "tacitly consented to by the leadership" (*lingdao moxude*), but mostly developed and expanded (*kaipi tuokuan*) by himself.[13] He also attributed his power to his proximity to high-ranking cadres for many years, which, in addition to allowing him to gain their trust and friendship, gave him several opportunities to "whisper in their ears" (*chui erbian feng*) at opportune moments (Qiao 2004: 72). At times Li Zhen actively deceived the leaders he served by feeding them false information or presenting his own opinion as that of an official he served.

He explains how leaders also serve as their secretaries' protectors. Li describes how he would "play his boss's card" (*taichu lingdaode zhaopai*) in order to get something done or to get himself out of trouble (Qiao 2004: 82). He claimed that "the most frightening [aspect of corruption] that we should be most on guard against but is very difficult to prevent is the collusion between leaders and their secretaries. It renders power privatized and 'nepotized'" (*jiazuhua*) (81).

Face (*Mianzi*) and Other "Defects in the National Character"

Qiao's interview with Li proceeds from an account of his corrupt activities and how he was able to amass and exert his power to an analysis of the underlying causes and enabling factors of Li Zhen's activities.

Echoing the book's preface, Qiao reasserts that Li's behavior was not a product of the Chinese political system but rather of "long standing defects in the Chinese national character (*liegenxing*) which still remain to be rooted out of certain individuals and that stand in the way of China's modernization" (Qiao 2004: 83). He states, "Without the modernization of Chinese people's characters (*renxing*) and a modern national character there will be no true modernization in China, and it will be very difficult to realize the revival of the Chinese people" (83). He asks the reader whether Li Zhen's corrupt behavior exposes the flaws of human nature in general or simply the "bad congenital traits" of the Chinese people (84).

Li himself sees his primary flaw as a "lack of cultivation" (*xiuyang bugou*). Here Li Zhen references the Confucian notion that moral behavior and strength of character derive from the constant cultivation of the self. Despite one of the manifestations of *xiuyang* being a concern with others (Hu 1944: 49), here possessing xiuyang is deliberately contrasted with a hypersensitivity to the status concerns of face (*mianzi*). Hsien Chin Hu's classic essay on the two Chinese concepts of face, lian and mianzi, explains the moral ambiguity surrounding mianzi:

> Mien-tzŭ [*mianzi*] differs greatly from *lien* [*lian*] in that it can be borrowed, struggled for, added to, padded—all in terms indicating a gradual increase in volume. It is built up through initial high position, wealth, power, ability,

through cleverly establishing social ties to a number of prominent people, as well as through avoidance of acts that would cause unfavorable comment. The value that society attaches to *mien-tzŭ* is ambivalent. On the one hand, it refers to well-earned popularity which is called *ming-yü* [*mingyu*]—reputation in its best sense; on the other, it implies a desire for self-aggrandizement. While moral criteria are basic in evaluating a person's worth to his group, self-maximization is allowed as a motive for greater exertion. (Hu 1944: 61)

For Hu, while both lian and mianzi are based on how one is perceived by one's community, a person's lian is more a reflection of fundamental moral character than mianzi. Mianzi is based on a person's "surface" appearance and status achieved through professional endeavors, accumulated wealth, and so-cial connections. When concern with mianzi becomes the primary motivating factor in one's behavior, it undermines the interpersonal morality, concern for one's community, and self-policing associated with lian (see also Kipnis 1995).[14] While the press that covered Li's case often referred to him as "brazen and ar-rogant" (*kuang*), Li argues that is wasn't his unbridled ambition that did him in but rather his obsession with vanity (*xurong*) and face (*mianzi*). Echoing many of my interviewees' criticisms of wealthy businessmen as "living for the sake of others" (see the next chapter), Li Zhen states, "All of officialdom is fond of face [*haomianzi*]; it's not just me. Who hasn't suffered for the sake of face [*wei mianzi suolei*]?" (Qiao 2004: 84).

Li portrays face as the most important component of the "unwritten rules of officialdom." He talks about the absolute centrality of face in official circles, summarizing its importance with the phrase, "Matters of life and death are small, matters of face are big" (*Shengsi xiao shi, mianzi shi da*). For Li, mianzi becomes a currency that can be used to get things done in informal networks. He explains the progression of the symbolic economy of mianzi as such:

> When I started, I exchanged the mianzi of my position as secretary, after that it was my personal [*geren*] mianzi, and then it was just the mianzi of my name, Li Zhen. When I reached that stage, a phone call, a meal, a note, a name card, even mentioning my name had an effect. Basically I no longer needed to put forth anything else [*bufu shenme daijiale*]. (Qiao 2004: 90)

As one's reputation builds, one gradually gains power that transcends mate-rial and institutional foundations in wealth or bureaucratic position. Eventually Li Zhen no longer needs to exchange anything else (e.g., money, gifts, meals) to have favors granted. His relations with his clients transcend the level of a quid pro quo transaction. People grant him favors simply because of the symbolic weight of his name and in anticipation of an imagined future moment when Li Zhen might help them.

Face, however, is linked to wealth in complex ways. Although wealth adds to one's face, taking money for a favor or accepting bribes can diminish it. When someone with a great deal of face accepts money, others might infer that he is in need of it and therefore not as wealthy as he appears. His acceptance of money also plainly reveals that his motivation is rooted in self-interest rather than human sentiment (*renqing*), generosity, or personal loyalty (*yiqi*). When Brother Chen offered to introduce me to the "godfather" and I responded by implying that I would find a way to return the favor, Chen quickly replied, "we're not that opportunistic" as a way of denying the self-interestedness of his offer. In the story of Mr. Wei that I recount below, he refuses to accept bribe money early in his official career as a way of building his reputation. Li Zhen talks about the relationship between face and money as a compromise:

> That's right, in taking someone's money [in a bribe] you lose a little bit of face, especially when you've just started [accepting bribes.] But after a time you get used to it. Power and money are both the "hardware" [*yingjian*] of face. In other words, no matter how much power one has you will lose some of it one day. If you have no money, once you've lost your power are people going to give you face? Thus, even though it's a loss of face, one still hopes to get a little money. (Qiao 2004: 82)

Although the symbolic currency of reputation is at the core of face, it ultimately rests on the hardware of money and power. Because power diminishes as one gradually withdraws from professional life, one increasingly has to rely on money as the materialization of one's face; but to rely on money values entirely, to appear too interested in material gain, or to blindly pursue wealth is to risk damaging one's face.

In addition to blaming himself for his loss of beliefs, lack of cultivation, and obsession with face, Li also blames the "thoroughly servile" (*nuxing shizu*) spirit of the officials surrounding him for enabling his actions. Qiao comments that in addition to Li Zhen's overly developed sense of face, Li's actions reflects the remnants of another deeply rooted feudal trait of the Chinese people—the "servility" (*nuxing*) of subordinates (Qiao 1994: 91). Li thanks the few officials who attempted to stand in his way and uphold justice, but he angrily exclaims that if he weren't surrounded by so many favor-seekers and yes-men his corruption would not have gotten so out of hand (93).

Despite his condemnation of the servility of those around him, Li admits to having employed similar techniques of flattery, fawning, and appeasement when dealing with his superiors. He quotes a saying that was also repeated to me by many interviewees when discussing officialdom: "Officialdom is like a battlefield; being in the king's company is like living with a tiger" (*guanchang ru zhanchang, ban jun ru ban hu*) (Qiao 2004: 92). But he goes on to explain that with the right techniques (*dao*) an official career can be smooth sailing:

> Particularly important is dealing with your superiors. You just need to cater to their likes and you won't face any danger. It's like the tiger tamers in the circus. They spend their whole day with tigers, but the reason there's no danger is that they've figured out the tiger's temperament. Once you understand this principle, then you've gotten a taste of "using your connections to power to control others [*hujiahuwei*]." (Qiao 1994: 92)

Like the businessmen described in Chapter Two, Li employs techniques of entertaining, flattery, and gift giving to win the favor and affection of his superiors. As both the agent and the beneficiary of these techniques, he recalls that even bribe givers portrayed their offers to him as assistance extended out of concern for Li and his family's well-being. Lower-level officials and businessmen he didn't know would rack their brains to find pretexts for offering Li material assistance.

Some of his first bribes came when a favor-seeker found out that Li was planning to travel abroad. A state enterprise manager showed up at Li's house with an envelope of cash, explaining that he heard he was going on an "investigation" trip [*kaocha*] to America. The giver explained, "I have some dollars that I don't need, and I thought you might need some 'pocket money' [*linghuaqian*]" (Qiao 1994: 239).

Other forms of assistance offered by favor-seekers included: "tuition" for his wife going abroad to study; condolences while Li Zhen was hospitalized; and traditional gifts of money for his son during the Chinese New Year. Lower-ranking officials who wanted to "take the shortcut" (*zou jiejing*) would send him not only money, but all sorts of gifts, including Viagra, inscribed honorary swords (*peijian*), fortune tellers, and massage girls. Some even "offered" lovers and wives (Qiao 1994: 94).

When I asked research informants who had read *Gates of Hell* to tell me their reactions to the book, virtually all of them had the same response—that the book doesn't go far enough. As they did with other journalistic accounts of corruption, they complained that it tells only part of the story, and that the role of the higher-ranking leadership is suspiciously left out. Li Zhen provides many examples of using his superiors' unquestioned authority to accomplish tasks that added to his own face, but he either portrays himself as deceiving the leadership or refuses to answer questions dealing with their involvement.[15]

In Internet reports on the 2007 case of the underworld boss of Tangshan, Yang Shukuan, who rode around town in an armored military vehicle and whose organization controlled a large portion of the city's economy, several Chinese "netizens" expressed outrage that the highest-ranking official implicated in the case was only a department head (*kezhang*). One commenter argued that it was impossible for such a low-ranking official to possess the power to provide Yang Shukuan with the weapons and vehicles used by his organization and effectively serve as his protective umbrella (*baohusan*) for so many years. The writer argues that unless you believe the government is extremely weak, Yang must have been supported by a far-reaching guanxi network to be able to so openly flaunt his power in a major city just over 100 miles from Beijing (Xian 2007).

Li Zhen's narrative offers insight into how the practices, relationships, and desires surrounding corruption are organized. Despite the attempt by Qiao to portray Li Zhen as a rotten apple who embodies Chinese character flaws left over from the feudal era, Li actually describes a social field in which officials are enmeshed in networks of obligation that well exceed formal regulations and contain their own "unwritten rules," strategies for advancement and enrichment, and modes of power. Rather than viewing these unofficial rules as a threat that undermines formal bureaucracy, Li Zhen's case demonstrates how formal bureaucratic hierarchies enable and support informal networks. Li relied on the authority of the leadership over subordinates to intimidate others, protect himself, and achieve his goals. In particular, the top-down, secretive system of promotion enabled many of Li's activities.

The next two examples elaborate further on this intermingling of official with unofficial, legitimate with criminal, and formal with informal worlds.

Meeting the "Godfather"

A few weeks after Brother Chen offered to help out my career by introducing me to the godfather, he finally gave me the mobile phone number of an individual he referred to as "Boss Cai." After I called a few times without receiving an answer, Chen gave me another number and told me to try calling within a specified period of time. I called and left a message and soon received a call from a raspy-voiced man with a thick rural accent, who apologized for the difficulty I had getting a hold of him and invited me to join him for dinner that evening. He explained that I would have to take a long taxi ride to meet him but that he would cover all the costs.

I found a taxi and rode for almost forty minutes out of the city to an area that was mostly farmland. The driver was unfamiliar with the area, and he had me repeatedly call Boss Cai to clarify the directions. Cai told me to look for his car, a black Mercedes S500 with an auspiciously numbered license plate from a provincial-level government work unit, parked by the side of the road. When I exited the taxi and attempted to pay, Cai's driver leaped out of the car and paid my fare. He then drove me in Cai's Mercedes the final half-mile down a dirt road to the restaurant.

A group of about thirty men, mostly in their early twenties with shaved heads and leather jackets, occupied a few private rooms in the back of the restaurant. Boss Cai explained to me that their organization has to get together in these out-of-the-way places because the police don't like them assembling in the city as a large group. The restaurant, though rural and spartan, was famous for its spicy loaches (*niqiu*), a small eel-like fish popular in the rural areas around Chengdu. Although I had braced myself for banquet-style drinking, I was relieved to find dinner very casual and the toasting light and perfunctory.

After dinner I rode with Cai in his Mercedes to a nightclub he owned in the center of Chengdu, which consisted entirely of private rooms for singing karaoke, drinking, and illicit drug use, for which the club had a reputation. I sat next to him while his *xiongdi* (junior members of his organization) ritually toasted both him and me. Midway through the evening one of his bodyguards came into the room and handed him a mobile phone.[16] Cai explained that he had a meeting with a boss at another nearby club, but he invited me to accompany him.

When we arrived at the club, a manager greeted us at the door and led us down a hallway and into a small room behind a curtain. He then asked for proof of Cai's membership. Cai produced an oversized key, and the manager nodded in acceptance. When the manager entered a password on a digital keypad, what I had assumed to be a wall slid open to reveal an even more lavish wing of the club reserved for members only. We entered a large *baofang* (private room in a restaurant or club) filled with middle-aged men accompanied by several hostesses. A male DJ was playing music in the corner of the room.

Cai explained to me that these visitors were from Guangdong, and he proceeded to have a private discussion with one of the men. During the discussion, he leaned over to me and asked, "Can you get them a letter of invitation to come to America?" I gave a noncommittal answer, explaining that I was not the representative of any American company, but I could try. The visitors then introduced a young woman to Cai, and she accompanied us when we left.

We returned to his club, where I toasted everyone one last time and prepared to leave. As I drank with Cai once again, he told me to call him "Big Brother Fatty" (*Pang Ge*), clarifying, "People call me that because I'm fat." He then leaned over to ask me if I wanted to become one of his xiongdi.

From the beginning of my time with Fatty's group I had reservations about being a researcher among them. I also worried about my outsider status: for me to understand this group with any degree of depth I would have to observe more than their interactions with outsiders; to acquire knowledge about their business practices, relationships with the state, and rituals I would need to become a formal member, one of Fatty's xiongdi. But becoming a xiongdi required a set of obligations that I was both unwilling and unable to fulfill.

I also became concerned about the risks of accompanying criminals who routinely engaged in violence. However, my inquiries into the risks of associating with this group among entrepreneurs and other research informants were all met with similar responses.[17] They insisted that high-ranking heishehui members would never "do anything rash" (*buhui luanlai*) and were men who "adhered to principles" (*henjiang daoli*). In fact, many emphasized that because their success was built on their reputations, they were even less likely than the average entrepreneur to cheat or endanger me in some way.[18] But many told me to watch out for the junior members of these organizations, who were viewed by most people as uneducated, violent thugs.

When students or colleagues learn that I conducted research with underground criminal bosses, they are often impressed that I was able to "access" such a seemingly closed and secretive group. My chance meeting with Brother Chen no doubt gave me a point of entry, but once I was introduced to Fatty, my problem quickly became not how to deepen my relationship with Fatty's group but precisely the opposite—how to maintain distance.

Fatty, Chen, and their xiongdi were masters of a type of relationship building referred to in the Sichuan dialect as *goudui*, which can be understood as a form of courtship for some instrumental purpose. They were constantly inviting me to dinner, offering me gifts and introductions to women, and presenting me with business opportunities. At a nightclub, if I got up to use the restroom, I would be personally escorted by one of their bodyguards, who would wait outside the restroom door and escort me back to the table. When I returned to the United States for the holidays, Fatty called me minutes after my plane landed to inquire whether I had had a safe trip. A few days later, on Christmas morning, he called to wish me and my family a "Merry Christmas." Faced with this onslaught of goudui techniques, I was at some pain to maintain distance in a way that didn't threaten to undermine our relationship.

At the time I met him, Brother Fatty was a permanent resident of the United States and spent six months of every year in New York to maintain his residency status. After my first few weeks of meeting with this group, Fatty's associates began to hint and suggest that my role was going to be to help out Brother Fatty in America and that this was one of the reasons for their "court-ship" of me. His underlings often joked that the only English phrase Fatty knew was "I love you."

Fatty told me that because of his limited English he had to depend on others to get by in America, or he had to be creative. He explained that when dining in America he ordered milk by placing his fingers on top of his head in the shape of horns and then making a squeezing motion next to his chest. He complained that during the Chinese New Year he sat alone at his house out-side of New York City, which he described as being in a wealthy *white* neigh-borhood, "not a Chinatown." Most of his stories were related to his feelings of loneliness and isolation in America, but he frequently retold a story about having his hair cut in Flushing, a neighborhood in Queens, New York, with a large Chinese community. While chatting with the barber he mentioned that he was known as "Brother Fatty." The barber replied, "*The* Brother Fatty, from Sichuan?" When Fatty confirmed that he was indeed the one, the barber re-fused to accept money for the haircut.

Knowing that Fatty would soon be leaving for America, I dodged the issue of formally becoming a xiongdi as long as I could. In the end, United States permanent residency regulations resolved my growing anxiety—Fatty left to spend six months in the U.S., and I stayed in China to finish my research. And by the time he returned to China, I was preparing to return to the U.S. My anxi-eties about reciprocity and indebtedness also diminished somewhat, however, as it became clear that Fatty and Chen felt as if they gained face by having an American in their entourage, especially one who spoke Chinese and acknowl-edged their organizational hierarchy.

Their associates were often surprised and impressed when I appeared with Fatty's group, and both Fatty and Chen hoped that my presence would indicate to outsiders that their group possessed "international" connections and a "global" reputation, however imaginary those were. While they never explicitly asked me to pose as someone else (as many other entrepreneurs I worked with did), they often asked that I try to conceal my student status. When introducing me to others, Fatty would explain, "He's going to help me in America," or "He's going to teach me English," as a way of explaining my role in their organization. After a few months with Fatty, however, he started talking about setting me up in a business in Chengdu, explaining that he would provide all the necessary startup capital. Both he and Chen suggested that I start a Western restaurant, which I inferred would serve to help them launder money.

Despite the excitement and possible danger associated with hanging out with an underworld organization, the bulk of the time I spent with them consisted of engaging in their ritualized leisure: gambling and holding court in clubs. Staving off boredom during my time with this group became a challenge.

During the day they would usually play the card game "struggle against the landlord" (*doudizhu*) in teahouses, and I lacked both the skill and disposable income to gamble with them. Thus my only option was often to chat with members who were taking a break from gambling, or with drivers and bodyguards, who seemed to view me with a mixture of suspicion and disdain given my unearned and instant high-status as a foreigner. When higher-ranking members took a break from their card playing to discuss business, I was usually asked to sit at another table. Sometimes, however, they asked me about aspects of life or business in America and pitched business ideas to me.

In the evening, most of the time I spent with Brother Fatty and Brother Chen was in the private rooms of clubs they personally owned or "managed" (*guanli*) (i.e., extorted for protection money). Their behavior in clubs differed markedly from that of the more lively and playful "legitimate" entrepreneurs I accompanied. These evenings became boring and repetitious to me because they were mostly opportunities for the mafia leadership to "hold court" by ritually constituting their organizational hierarchy through deferential toasting. Occasionally they entertained associates from outside their organization, who were most often police officers, entrepreneurs under their protection, or members of other criminal groups allied with them.

Most of the group would sit around on leather sofas drinking and smoking, rarely interacting with each other, other than to make toasts. Some used the drug ketamine as well, and danced with the hostesses.[19] Frequently, the higher-ranking members danced in a circle, holding hands with the hostesses and each other. Drivers, bodyguards, and junior-ranking members toasted their superiors but never interacted with hostesses while in the presence of their bosses. Junior members also served as gophers and bodyguards. They lit cigarettes for their big brothers and escorted them to and from the restroom (if there was no private bathroom in the room) or on errands, such as picking up or greeting guests arriving at the club or buying cigarettes. Little substantive business seemed to be discussed during these evenings.

In the evenings spent in clubs, Brother Fatty would sit in the center of the U-shaped leather sofas of club baofangs. In recognition of my "special guest" status, as a personal friend of Fatty and a foreigner of undetermined rank, I was usually expected to sit next to him. Higher-ranking men usually sat closer to him, and the youngest xiongdi, bodyguards, and drivers sat on edges of the sofas farthest from him. When the group was large, the bodyguards sometimes waited outside the door or went to a separate baofang.

Throughout the evening his xiongdi would toast (*jingjiu*) Fatty and the other leaders at regular intervals.[20] When Brother Fatty was seated, the xiongdi stood, bowed their heads, and held their glasses with two hands (one on the bottom of the glass, the other on the side) and downed their drinks in one gulp. The lower-status xiongdi who initiated the toasting would then refill the glass of the person being toasted before refilling his own. Because of my location next to Brother Fatty, I was deferentially toasted as well.

Given my outsider status, I was uncertain whether I should allow others to toast me, symbolically figuring me as a superior. I often lowered my glass at the last minute as a sign of modesty, but I was never certain if this action achieved its intended effect.[21] When toasting the higher-ranking members I always lowered my glass. To relieve my boredom, I sometimes circulated among the group, toasting people and trying to chat with them.

Brother Fatty's Organization

Brother Fatty's organization was cellular, and I spent most of my time with Brother Chen's "cell" and that of another Elder Brother (*dage*), Brother Zhang. Each cell had a leader at the top who was addressed as "Big Brother" and a one syllable name, which was usually different from his surname (such as Chen Ge), to distinguish him from their true "elder brother" (*dage*), Brother Fatty. Below this cell leader would be the cell's "Second Brother" (*erge*) and Third Brother (*sange*), who would be referred to as such.

I occasionally met with other cells, but I only saw all of them come together once, during a massive banquet hosted by Brother Chen and attended by over 200 people during the Chinese New Year. Each cell sat at their own table, and I saw xiongdi ranging in age from their late teens to early fifties.

The vast majority of xiongdi were from small towns and rural areas around Chengdu, including Fatty himself. This form of organization, in which xiongdi are loyal first to their more proximate big brother and second to their "big brother's big brother," constantly threatens the solidarity of the entire group. Jane and Peter Schneider make a similar argument about the Sicilian mafia. They describe it as

> an engine of insecurity, its order-enhancing structures and solidarity-building rituals frequently distorted by rivalries and provocations. . . . [A]lthough initiation rituals induct novices into a collectivist fraternity, they also express each novice's quasi-feudal relationship to a particular sponsor bent on developing his own power base. (Schneider and Schneider 2003b: 82)

Despite the whole purpose of informal networks being to provide security and protection in a context of uncertainty, they are constantly threatened by their own forces of dissolution, many of which are inherent to their organizational logic.

Many entrepreneurs I worked with had heard of Brother Fatty, but there seemed to be a consensus that although he was one of the biggest heishehui bosses in the city, his power and influence were declining in Chengdu. He had made his initial fortune producing and selling counterfeit famous-brand liquor, but seemed to generate most of his wealth during my research from his share of the revenue from his underlings' enterprises, which consisted primarily of protection rackets, high-interest loans, debt collection, and underground gambling. In the late 1990s he had come under police investigation, and part of the reason he sought permanent residency in America was to have an "escape hatch" if the police decided to pursue him again.

Several entrepreneurs and police also suggested to me that his power and influence were in decline, and the kinds of activities he could engage in now were limited. They saw him largely as a broker of face, able to use the reputation and connections won from his past activities to help out those allied to him. As one businessman put it, "Lots of people owe their wealth and success to him, so they still give him face, but deep down lots of his xiongdi feel that they are bigger than he is."

This seemed to be the case with Brother Chen, who on several occasions hinted to me that he was now wealthier and more powerful than Fatty. At the New Year's banquet described above, Chen rather ostentatiously and in view of most of the xiongdi present handed Fatty a large bag of 100 RMB bills as a New Year's present. This conspicuous gift served both to perform his deference to Fatty but also to show the rest of Fatty's group that he was doing quite well.

Brother Chen stood out not only for being a true Chengdu native, but also for having worked as a policeman in another province. In private conversations with me, he expressed some ambivalence about his relationship with the organization, complaining that he did not like the constant *yingchou* (ritualized entertaining) associated with his lifestyle.

I was surprised by the distance and strong boundary he maintained between his private life and the world of his xiongdi. When he invited me to his house, he explained that none of his xiongdi, other than his driver, even knew where he lived. He complained that too many relationships with his friends and associates were complicated by overlapping and conflicting *liyi* (interests). When I asked him why he didn't do something else, he replied "*mei banfa*" (there's no way [out]), which is also how many entrepreneurs explained why they did so much entertaining. When I left the field to return to the United States, he told me that we needed to keep in touch, declaring, "We're true friends; there's no interest [or angle] between us" (*Women shi chuncuide pengyou, meiyou liyi*).

Jing Fei Yi Jia—"Police and Thieves Are All One Family"

Brother Fatty frequently alluded to or boasted about his connections with state agencies. On several occasions, he boasted about having dinner with public security department leaders (equivalent to the police) during which he negotiated with them over his organization's permissible activities. Police were sometimes present on evenings when Fatty and his group held court, and some introduced themselves to me as members of the police, making no attempt to hide their status. Brother Chen referred to a few of his organization's members as "secret police" (*mimi jingcha*), the exact meaning of which remained obscure to me.

Like most underworld organization bosses, Fatty had many official patrons who tipped him off about anti-crime campaigns and helped him avoid prosecution.[22] He referred to these patrons as his "protection umbrellas" (baohusan). He explained that these official patrons frequently made requests (e.g., to tone down certain activities or to move them elsewhere) and asked for favors.

Fatty's organization was a key source of income for the police and other officials connected to them, but through their connections with Fatty they were also able to "govern" the underground economy and the activities and individuals associated with it. The ideologies of loyalty, brotherhood, and sub-servience to hierarchy that organized Fatty's group ensured that most actions of Fatty's underlings were subject to Fatty's command, and thus a large num-ber of potentially "ungovernable" subjects were rendered governable through him. He explained that although there were several competing organizations in Chengdu, they rarely fought with each other over territory, choosing instead to negotiate disputes over banquets whenever possible. With the exception of a notorious gang of young rural migrants from Suining, they all, according to Brother Chen, "adhered to principles" (jiang daoli).

I asked interviewees and other informants why the police or the military do not crack down on organizations like Fatty's. Their existence, membership, and activities seem to be an open secret. In response, people usually cited two rea-sons. First, they explained, shutting them down entailed costs. There were the considerable resources required to launch an investigation and amass evidence, but there were also the social costs of disrupting a large sector of the informal economy and the risk of causing hundreds, if not thousands, of undereducated young men with a propensity to violence to lose their livelihoods.

These observations point to a second reason—the heishehui are able to provide effective forms of governance beyond the formal reach of the state.[23] Not only do they regulate forms of vice—such as drugs and prostitution—and generate considerable revenue for the police, but they also govern one of urban China's most dangerous and difficult-to-control demographic groups—the aforementioned young, undereducated bachelors who have left their rural hometowns for cities.[24] The story of the rise of Fatty and his organization can be read in terms of a potentially dangerous, underground group's co-optation and domestication at the hands of the state.

Fatty presented himself as a generous man of ability whose sole purpose was to help those around him. Never once did he or any of his xiongdi refer to their group as heishehui. In an extended monologue at a dinner banquet in the most upscale hotel in his hometown, Brother Fatty explained to the attendees (which included the hotel's owners), "People always talk about the heishehui in

China, but as far as I'm concerned there is no heishehui. Sure you have people copying what they see in Hong Kong movies and pretending to be gangsters, but they're not heishehui. . . . As for me, I'm just a guy who can get things done; we're a group that can help people get things done."

From Official to Elder Brother: The Case of Mr. Wei

Let me end this chapter with an example of how these networks operate in shaping the career of an individual, Mr. Wei, a government official turned entrepreneur.

Mr. Wei's case demonstrates clearly how elite networks allow for the mobilization of different forms of power, each grounded in different economies of value, and how the coordination of these different institutions is an integral component of capitalist expansion and the consolidation of elite power in China. As this example shows, the reorganization of state power during the reform period should be understood as resulting in the interplay of multiple modes of power rather than simply as an expansion of the market and retreat of the state. This example also demonstrates some of the techniques elites use to forge ties with other elites, described by Li Zhen: acts of sacrifice and demonstrations of loyalty. Among my informants, it was agreed that such acts were far more effective in creating relationships of mutual aid than entertaining, flattery, gift giving, or bribes alone could accomplish.

Mr. Wei claimed to be a self-made man who had prospered from hard work and a good reputation; but Mr. Wei also came from a politically connected family. Originally from Jiangsu, his parents were members of the Red Army and were later assigned to government jobs in Sichuan.

Mr. Wei himself became an official at a young age, working for the city construction and planning bureau. He explained to me that during his time in the construction bureau, in order to accomplish his official tasks he had to interact and do business "with all kinds of people" including, in his words, "*shehuishangde ren*" or "men of society," referring to people with expansive social networks that included members of the underworld. He said that he did many favors for people at the time but refused to take any money from them. In this way, he claimed, he was able to earn people's respect and gain a reputation.

Early in his career his superiors were investigated for corruption, which Mr. Wei thought was unfair given that, in his view, his superiors were merely interpreting policy to suit the local conditions of Chengdu. He considered this typical of the organization of the Communist Party:

> They give you an order and tell you there will be serious consequences if you don't get it done, but they don't tell you how to go about getting it done. Of course they [lower-level officials] are going to try anything to get the job done, and they're also going to find a way [to do it] that best serves their interests [*dui tamen you liyi*].

During the investigation Mr. Wei was questioned by anti-corruption investigators but refused to provide any information about his superiors. He was kept in detention for several weeks. During that time he felt that his family and friends turned their backs on him, and his wife nearly divorced him.

Finally he was released from custody but stripped of his official position. Temporarily estranged from his family and former friends, he borrowed some startup capital from an underworld friend and went into business. Naturally, he chose a career closely related to the work of the construction bureau—the demolition business.[25] His act of sacrifice and loyalty to high-ranking construction bureau officials all but ensured Mr. Wei's business success.

Because of this demonstration of loyalty, Mr. Wei won the respect and trust of many powerful officials in the construction and land bureaus; these were the very people who decided which neighborhoods would be torn down to make way for new developments. He explained that this act of sacrifice demonstrated that he was a man who could be trusted, who understood the value of yiqi and the importance of relationships.

In addition to hiring Mr. Wei to demolish old neighborhoods, local government agencies subcontracted the negotiation of compensation for displaced residents to his company, and he commanded a gang of young thugs to scare away residents reluctant to leave their homes. He also acted as a broker with the government bureaus involved in real estate, helping his friends, both new and old, acquire land marked for development. Countless entrepreneurs courted him for his access to inside information about land auctions, zoning, and development plans.

His business grew very quickly, and he not only commanded an important position in the legitimate world of real estate, but became an underworld boss (a self-described *laoda*) to several younger followers, his "little brothers," who helped carry out some of the less savory aspects of his business.

Mr. Wei thus had many faces. When dining with other entrepreneurs outside his circle of friends, he presented himself as a modern businessman, launching into monologues about the latest business strategy and management techniques. When alone with me or with his circle of friends he focused on his roles as the "boss" (*laoda*) of the demolition world and paternal "big brother" (*dage*) to his "little brothers" (*xiongdi*).[26] Mr. Wei characterized his relationship with his xiongdi as follows:[27]

> My xiongdi look to me as a god. They don't have much education or good family backgrounds, so I provide for them and teach them how to achieve success in today's society. They come to me with business ideas, and I help them get started with advice and money. Sometimes they try to cheat me, but I can always see through them. They also come to me with personal problems. Sometimes they even cry in front of me. Without me they would be lost.

Mr. Wei frequently held gatherings of his xiongdi and was constantly on the phone with them giving orders and advice. When I first met him he was helping his xiongdi establish a debt collection agency. Occasionally, legitimate entrepreneurs used heishehui to help collect debts, protect them from other extralegal predators, and threaten and intimidate their competitors.[28] Mr. Liao, the liquor distributor, for example, felt that he needed to associate with heishehui because he was worried that people would take advantage of or pick on (*qifu*) him, especially given that nightclubs were his biggest customers. Before the establishment of their debt collection business, Mr. Wei's xiongdi generated most of their income from showing up en masse at businesses, providing either protection or intimidation, for which they charged an "appearance fee" (*chuchang fei*).

When I left Chengdu in 2006, Mr. Wei declared that he was already the *laoda* (boss) of the demolition business and soon he would be the laoda of the city. I asked him whether, now that he was becoming well known, and given his previous experiences with anti-corruption officials, he was worried about falling out of the state's favor and having his business activities investigated. But Mr. Wei explained to me, "The government needs people like me. I can accomplish things that the police and the government cannot do or that are not convenient for them to do."

The activities that Mr. Wei refers to are the more violent aspects of China's privatization of formerly collective or state-owned property. It is the younger brothers at the bottom of the underworld organizations who are sent to scare away or inflict violence on residents who refuse to leave housing pegged for redevelopment or who protest their often paltry or skimmed compensation funds. The implied or actual threat of violence is also used to persuade residents to accept below-market prices for their housing and land rights. These "little brothers" also quite often appear in newspaper accounts as the "armed thugs" who are brought in to clash with protestors and intimidate their organizers in instances of rural and urban unrest.

The use of young men, who see themselves as the embodiment of cool and righteous masculinity, to do the dirty work of the state is illustrated in the 2006 Jia Zhangke movie, *Still Life* (*San Xiao Hao Ren*). Set in a small city in the process of being demolished and evacuated before being submerged by the reservoir created by the Three Gorges Dam, the film depicts a gang who spends their days hanging out at the local government's "demolition and relocation team" (*chaiqian ban*) office. Their laoda is a former soldier turned entrepreneur, who also happens to be having an affair with the real estate developer building the new city across the river. When one of their members returns to the office after being beaten, they all stop their mahjong games, grab machetes, and run off to avenge their injured brother.

Although we never see their victims, they are presumably ordinary townspeople resisting relocation. Jia shows one of the gang members constantly watching Chow Yun-fat (Zhou Runfa) films and mimicking his every move, from lighting a cigarette with a hundred dollar bill (which he does with a plain piece of paper) to his iconic thumbs-up gesture.[29] Despite the near-innocence and youthful exuberance with which they perform Hong Kong cool and gangster masculinity, the more violent side of state power is refracted through them, with tragic consequences both for them and for their fellow townfolk.

Conclusion:
Elite Networks as Powerful Institutions

Since the beginning of China's reform period in the late 1970s, there have been many well-publicized incidents in which state institutions were completely co-opted by networks of entrepreneurial criminals and state officials. Perhaps the most famous of these incidents was the Yuanhua case in Fujian in the late 1990s.[30]

Lai Changxing, the head of the Yuanhua group, and his personal network were able to take over the entire customs administration of Fujian province such that it not only gave them preferential treatment, but the agency's bureaucracy functioned as an extension of the Yuanhua firm. Lai had final say in all personnel decisions, and the chief customs official answered to him. From 1996 to 1999, Lai and his company were able to smuggle about 10 billion dollars worth of goods into China, which included primarily refined oil, automobiles, and cigarettes (Wank 2002).

He reinvested his profits from smuggling not only into legitimate businesses but also into expanding and consolidating his network of protection through gifts of luxury cars and villas, expenses for mistresses, gambling subsidies, and children's educational expenses. Lai also built a pleasure palace referred to as the "Red Mansion" (*honglou*), where he entertained countless officials with lavish banquets, karaoke, and sexual services provided by a staff of young women (August 2007). Lai was so successful in commandeering the bureaucracy for the benefit of his own company and network that customs agents referred to him as the "underground director" of the customs house (Wank 2002: 8).

More recently, the 2009 mafia crackdown in Chongqing revealed the ways in which criminal organizations, police, and justice administrations are often densely intertwined. As a result of the campaign, more than a thousand people were arrested, including more than fifty public officials (Jacobs 2009). The highest-ranking official prosecuted in the sweep was Wen Qiang, the head of the Chongqing justice bureau itself, who acted as a protective umbrella (*baohusan*) for the organized criminal groups of a region of 30 million people.

Police and thieves were not only "one family" in this instance, but one and the same person. Wen's sister-in-law, referred to as the "godmother" of Chongqing, ran an underground casino across the street from the provincial courthouse, one of thirty she operated in the city. The Party secretary of Chongqing at the time, Bo Xilai, even commissioned a four-volume official history of the campaign and a film version (Tatlow 2011). Tellingly, Wang Lijun, the police chief of Chongqing who ran the crackdown, instructed the writers to portray Wen Qiang as "not all bad," suggesting that many of his actions were perceived by members of Wen's network as stemming from his generosity and concern.

These two cases, along with the other examples provided in this chapter, illustrate the two different trajectories of elite power in contemporary China: the privatization of the state—the appropriation of state resources by nonstate elites; and the official penetration and co-optation of informal modes of power such as the masculine solidarity of underworld gangs.

These two trajectories (both of which depart from the almost complete state monopoly on power in the Maoist years) have not led to an increasing separation between "state" and "society" but rather have generated networks, the nodes of which extend through multiple modes of power and forms of authority. These elite networks provide protection and opportunities for the accumulation of wealth and status for both state and nonstate elites, and they are also the networks through which the state-driven goals of economic development are achieved.

While entrepreneurs and underworld leaders cultivate relationships with members of the state to provide them with protection, insider access, and government privileges, state officials rely on underground forms of force to achieve the aims of development, and they depend on unofficial incomes to support the extra-bureaucratic "face" appropriate for a powerful official in the reform period. Furthermore, local governments, especially in poorer areas, often rely on the revenue received from land sales to private developers to fund development and infrastructure projects that are essential to impressing higher levels of government and advancing local officials' careers (in addition to allowing them to personally profit). In such a context, elite men such as Fatty, Li Zhen, and Mr. Wei, in addition to being "beyond" the law, conceive of themselves as "above" both state and society and capable of mobilizing the resources of both. In short, these networks governed by their ideologies of face, reputation, and predatory accumulation are becoming significant institutions in their own right. They support forms of distribution that undermine official state hierarchies and organize the market economy to their advantage.

In anthropological work on contemporary China, much ink has been spilled over whether guanxi, broadly understood as social connections, are increasing or decreasing in importance as China has become more integrated with the global economy and more subject to the institutional controls of global capitalism. From her perspective studying guanxi in the early 1980s, Mayfair Yang (1994) saw the potential for a Chinese minjian (civil society) to form from the techniques and values of guanxi, a development that would help resist the dehumanizing, rational force of state power. However, since the early 1990s, as Mayfair Yang (2002) and He Qinglian (1998) have more recently emphasized, many guanxi techniques instead have flourished among the new elite and helped to consolidate their power while channeling vast amounts of public property into private hands. In other words, rather than assuming a zero-sum game between the gift economy of guanxi, the legal-rationalist regime of the state, and the market economy, it is more productive to examine the complex ways in which they are interwoven with and feed on each other.

Moreover, by highlighting network building and the conditioning of state officials as a form of work involving the production of affect, I hope to stress that the social field of corruption is not merely a "market" in direct exchanges of power for money but relies on and operates through multiple modes of power and forms of value.

4

FROM FRUIT PLATES

TO LICENSE PLATES

Consumption, Status, and Recognition Among Chengdu's Elite

Who's Living the Right Way?

Wang Jianjun was his own boss. Despite being just over 40, he was the chairman of the board (*dongshizhang*) of a company that owned a chain of mid-range hotels. "Being a boss" was an important indicator of status for people in Chengdu who distinguished between those who worked for others (*gei bieren dagong*), who were seen as always limited by their relationships with their superiors, and those who were independent entrepreneurs, who in theory at least, controlled their own destiny.

Jianjun began to make his fortune in the mid-1990s. He started in the late 1980s as a purchaser for a state-owned factory, and he was able to meet many early entrepreneurs in the burgeoning market economy through the orders he placed for the factory. After a few years, he had amassed enough connections in the business world that he decided to leave his job at the factory, borrow some money, and set up his own electronics trading company. His company grew quickly, and he used his earnings to buy land and start several new businesses, one of which was a hotel that later became his primary focus.

Wang Jianjun owned a "villa" (*bieshu*) in one of the oldest (built in the mid-1990s) and most prestigious luxury real estate developments in the southern part of Chengdu. He prided himself on being able to avoid most of the *yingchou* (entertaining) associated with building up a business, although he still occasionally dined with people important to his company: mostly bank managers and officials overseeing property development. On most evenings he ate dinner at home with his wife and two children (cooked by one of his two domestic servants) and follow his meal with a serving of expensive *wulong* tea and imported cigars. When the weather was warm he often strolled around his housing complex smoking his cigar or took his children swimming in the compound's pool. Frequently I joined join him for tea and cigars, and he would talk about the habits of his friends and his impressions of elite lifestyles in the many countries he had visited. He half-jokingly talked about spending time in the evenings with his family as very "American." The joke among his friends was that only the promise of introductions to pretty girls, especially foreign ones, could bring him out on the town.

Mr. Pan, an old acquaintance of Wang's, was a former police officer turned real estate entrepreneur. He had been instrumental in obtaining access to cheap land for Wang's company's hotels, and the two considered each other good friends despite an increasing divergence in their lifestyles and social circles. Mr. Pan frequently held his company's parties and ceremonies at Wang's hotels, and the two still occasionally dined together.

Shortly after Wang introduced me to him, I told Pan about my research and shared some of my thoughts about the lives of Chengdu's elite. Knowing that I had been spending a lot of time with Mr. Wang, he pointed out to me, "He's got a lot of money, but look at his lifestyle. It's no different from a laid-off factory worker's (*xiagang gongren*). He stays home every night smoking cigars and drinking tea. He might drink top-grade *wulong* tea and smoke imported cigars, but his lifestyle is basically the same." It turns out this was not just Mr. Pan's private opinion but a view that he had expressed to Mr. Wang directly.

Rather than being proud of the fact that he, unlike most of his peers, had the time and resources to relax (*xiuxi*) and avoid the stresses associated with business and constant entertaining, Wang was angered by others' depiction of his life as leisured (*xiuxian*) but not luxurious (*shechi*). Apparently Mr. Pan's comment caused a temporary rift between the two, and I found myself caught in the middle of their squabble. When I was out with Mr. Pan, I couldn't invite Wang to join us and vice versa, and Wang frequently made disparaging comments about Pan's aspirations to be an underworld-type boss and his unhealthy lifestyle. In his own defense, Wang made the following rebuttal, reflecting on Pan's leisure time:

> Look at Lao Pan, he's spent so much time in a KTV *baofang* [private room] that's all he knows. He can't go home at night to his family. Even when he doesn't have any yingchou he just sits in a baofang drinking whiskey, surrounding himself

with hostesses, and dealing with his *xiongdi*.[1] He doesn't know how to live a normal life [*zhengchangde shenghuo*] anymore.

Ironically, Mr. Pan, while sitting in a baofang, often described to me the lives of wealthy bosses he knew who, from his perspective, didn't know how to live "normal lives" anymore either. He told me about his own "boss" (*laoda*) a well-known heishehui leader who had made his fortune through violence and deception. Mr. Pan understood this experience as inducing a kind of paranoia about social relations:

> Now our laoda just sits in a baofang in a high-end club all night and drinks whiskey with hostesses. He doesn't want to see anyone or entertain anyone because he's afraid of being cheated. That's how he made his reputation so that's how he thinks everyone is. His underlings handle all his affairs now. At the end of the night he might go home with a prostitute, but he's still very lonely.

With the exception of a few minor differences, this could have been a description of Mr. Pan's life. In the evenings he would often call or send me a text message inviting me to drink scotch with him in the baofang of an upscale club. He usually frequented two clubs, both of which were owned by a close friend of his.

Most often I met him in a nightclub in the basement of a five-star hotel operated by an international chain. Pan's former mistress was a dancer in the club's floorshow, and he was known by name to the entire club staff.[2] He estimated that he spent between 2 and 3 million RMB per year in this club, and given that his nightly bill was often several thousand dollars, I believe his estimate.[3] He claimed that this expenditure was worth it for the recognition he received from the hotel and nightclub staff. In his words, "Everyone from the foreign managers to the bathroom attendants greets me by name." He contrasted this situation with that of many of his friends who had lost similar amounts of money gambling in Macau: "Once you walk away from the table, the dealer forgets who you are, and you've gained nothing."

I usually met him after dinner and found him alone or with a nonbusiness friend. Like many of the businessmen I knew, he carried several mobile phones. Although he frequently handled business on his phones, he rarely drank with his employees, with xiongdi, or with business associates during these evenings. I think he enjoyed having me around precisely because I wasn't involved in his business and at first knew relatively little about his past or current affairs. He often complained to me about the stresses of his work, the incompetence of his staff, and the particular problems of doing business in China, contrasting the complex (*fuza*) nature of Chinese society with the simplicity and transparency that he imagined characterized commerce in the West.

Occasionally one of his xiongdi would stop by briefly and chat privately with Mr. Pan, but they never stayed to drink or sing. Sometimes he invited some younger women he knew to join us, or he simply arranged for hostesses from the club to drink with us and play dice games.

I learned from the manager at his other favorite nightclub that he always came alone and sat in the same VIP baofang. He kept his own crystal decanter and glass set at the club, and all the staff addressed him by name. On nights when he was in a good mood he would invite several hostesses to drink and play dice games with just him, which was precisely how he described the average, unhealthy night of his "boss."

When our conversations shifted into a more formal interview register, Mr. Pan presented a very different conception of himself. He insisted that everything he did was for his own personal happiness or for the benefit of those around him. Echoing many of my interviewees, he described most wealthy Chinese as "lost" (*mishi*): "They blindly pursue luxury and lack any individuality in their consumption. They think they are enjoying their life, but they're really being used by money" (*beiqiansuoyong*). According to Mr. Pan, nearly all the bosses one saw in KTVs or at the mahjong table thought they were enjoying themselves and tasting the fruits of their success, but they were simply putting on a performance of success and happiness for the benefit of others: "They pursue a kind of luxury, but they cheat themselves. They consciously think they are happy, but deep down inside they're actually miserable."

As Mr. Pan understood it, they lacked a framework of belief or values to orient their consumption, and they had even lost touch with their inner selves and personal desires. Thus, even luxury purchases and hedonistic indulgences brought them little satisfaction. He contrasted this predicament with his understanding of America, where he believed consumption is oriented toward the satisfaction of individual desire:

> In America, if you want a sports car, you work hard for a period of time until you have enough money for a sports car and then you enjoy it for a while. China's not like that. People think that a certain amount of money will make them happy, but they don't know how to spend it, so they just follow others in their social

circle. After you eat the best, wear the best, live the best, what do you spend your money on if you don't have any beliefs or hobbies?

To distinguish himself from those who are used by money in their blind pursuit of more wealth and who have lost themselves, Mr. Pan described how taking care of his relatives and his employees provided the impetus for his drive to get rich. In these interviews he asserted that he derived happiness from helping others in his social network: "My power has its limits, but I can help those around me. So I might hire a friend or relative even though they might not be the most qualified employee, but this way I'm helping someone out who needs my help." Despite his constant complaints about the pressures of doing business in China and the unhealthy lifestyle it generates, he always insisted that he, unlike his peers, made money serve his personal happiness.

The Wang-Pan squabble and the contrasting tendencies the two exemplify contain many of the elements that are key to understanding how status and wealth are negotiated and interpreted by wealthy Chinese and the effect social networks have on their consumption practices and ideologies of taste. The wealthy entrepreneurs and businesspeople I worked with in Chengdu operated in an environment of constant scrutiny. They criticized their peers incessantly, sometimes as a class, sometimes singling out individuals I knew, citing aspects of personal biography, habits, and character traits as evidence of an imperfect and suspect elite identity. Informing these critiques were notions of a proper and normal elite life that was usually lived in other countries and understood to be difficult to achieve in China given the "complex" (fuza) nature of doing business and spending money there.

While their ideas about how the wealthy lived in Europe and North America informed this imaginary, "the West" was not simply held up as a model to be emulated, and perceived hyperconformity to foreign tastes could lead to accusations of cultural betrayal. In short, claims to elite status for many new-rich Chinese rest on constantly shifting and contested grounds.

Distinction and Recognition

Pierre Bourdieu's classic work on taste and social distinction in France, *Distinction* (1984), stands as perhaps the most influential work on consumption and social class. On the surface, the process I am describing in China lends itself to a Bourdieuian analysis. China's new rich strive to create naturalized social distinctions out of economic capital; they seek to transform quantitative differences in money into qualitative social differences. Although Bourdieu's model offers a useful starting point, it ultimately obscures more than it reveals about the complex process of class formation in China.

Bourdieu's work on France is most concerned with revealing how economic capital enables, but is often obscured by, other forms of cultural, social, and symbolic capital. His goal is to reveal the power relations and forms of domination that elite consumption practices in France serve to obscure and deny (1987: 242). This is why he was so concerned with exposing the interest, domination, and economic power at the heart of "pure" and "disinterested" aesthetics and taste (Bourdieu 1984).

Bourdieu's model provides an awkward fit with contemporary China for two reasons. First, for wealthy Chengduers, the whole purpose of consumption is to make one's economic, social, and cultural capital as transparent and legible as possible to the widest audience. Thus, attempts to conceal economic capital (unless one is concealing it from tax collectors or anti-corruption investigators) in rare and obscure tastes work against the primary goal of consumption for the new rich—to let everyone know they're wealthy and well-connected (even if they're not). Second, Bourdieu's notion of different forms of capital suggests a seamless convertibility between money (economic capital) and social recognition (cultural or symbolic capital) that fails to capture the dilemmas faced by nouveau-riche Chinese entrepreneurs, operating in tightly bound social networks, when they attempt these conversions in practice.

Bourdieu (1987) labels the process in which economic capital is converted into forms of social, cultural, and symbolic capital "capital conversions," and while he acknowledges the risks inherent in capital conversions, his theory of capital cannot fully account for the anxieties and risks associated with rendering economic wealth into forms of prestige, including fears that it might dissipate, be rendered illegible, or, to use Bourdieu's language "poorly invested."[4]

Thus, I understand elite identity for many wealthy Chinese to be rooted in a notion of "recognition" rather than "distinction." I distinguish between these two terms in order to call attention to the fraught process of claiming elite status for many nouveau-riche Chinese in which their economic capital by no means automatically translates into social or cultural capital. With "distinction," I am following Bourdieu's (1984) use of the term: as a way of converting economic capital into forms of social prestige that appear to be rooted in noneconomic qualities: good taste, refinement, "class," etc. With "recognition"

I mean to highlight the fundamentally social origins of status for China's new rich.[5] Because status is conferred by others, being recognized as belonging to a particular group—the elite or just another *baofahu* (literally, a "suddenly rich person")—is dependent on the precarious and fickle perceptions of and relationships with both proximate and distant others.[6]

Managing these perceptions of others cannot be achieved with money (or capital conversions) alone. Many Chinese hoped to possess symbols and trappings of wealth that would be acknowledged both by their peers and by elites around the globe. Entrepreneurs I knew employed what could be called an "audience-based theory of consumption" in which different goods are valuable precisely because they are legible and recognized as such by different groups. Instead of a notion of taste and connoisseurship in which lower-status groups might acknowledge the superiority of a cultural object but lack the cultural capital to appreciate it, entrepreneurs in Chengdu consider the best status-conferring goods to be those that are the most widely recognized, famous, and whose exchange value (price) would be the most readily apparent to all.

This connection between consumption, status, and audience was clearly illustrated by Mr. Lin, a government contractor who depended entirely on connections to make his fortune. He distinguished between cigarettes you could smoke with your friends, those you could put on the table during dinner with a woman, and those you could smoke when you were entertaining for business (*yingchou*), the latter being the most expensive and well-known brand.[7]

In her comparative study of the upper middle classes of France and the United States, Michele Lamont (1992) argues that societies characterized by high mobility (like present-day China) generate a "more dynamic [status] system made up of a number of partly overlapping spheres of competition and comparison" (183). In addition to challenging Bourdieu's (1984) emphasis on taste as the primary mechanism of distinction, she critiques his dismissal of status divisions based on moral differences as merely tools for those lacking other forms of capital. While Bourdieu argues that those who draw social distinctions based on morality do so because it is their only resource and they must, in his language, "make a virtue of necessity," Lamont's research suggests that other spheres of comparison, such as morality and ethics, play a more important role than Bourdieu allows for and that he overemphasizes the importance of culture as the primary field of social distinction. Among the entrepreneurs I worked with, divisions of morality, personal quality (*suzhi*), education, family background, and even how one made money could all be invoked to draw status distinctions.[8] Furthermore because forms of spending and outward status displays were often understood to be obligatory and necessary and part of a calculated performance, their utility as an index of personal qualities was limited.

Further complicating the Bourdieuian model of distinction was the "boss-patron" (*laoda*) ideal that many Chengduers strove for in their business dealings and networks. The boss is defined above all by his pivotal position in a social network as a provider for multiple dependents and a dispenser of favors, wisdom, and opportunities, and this affords him the recognition of society and his peers (*shehui renke*). This recognition is maintained through public displays of generosity and shared conviviality that leave little time for the self-cultivation through consumption idealized by many wealthy Chinese.

Through an analysis of several interviews with wealthy Chengduers, this chapter examines many of the contradictions and anxieties generated by the "boss" status ideal when confronted with competing understandings of how to be elite, ideals that are in many ways informed by the imaginary of consumer individualism. Many Chinese imagine the achievement of bosshood as a key to independence: no longer must one suffer through long nights of drinking and singing and flatter officials and big bosses to achieve success. However, powerful bosses by definition attract a legion of clients, favor-seekers, and flatterers hoping to advance through the boss's patronage.

Ironically, wealthy Chengduers' valorization of independence and autonomy, often expressed as "living for oneself" rather than "living for others," results in a distancing from the very social networks upon which their prestige rests. Indulging in individual pursuits and forms of social distinction, which is understood by many Chengduers as the hallmark of elite status in the West, leads to a kind of social invisibility that undermines the very foundations of their "boss" status. This contradiction is perhaps best revealed in the domain of consumption, where elite Chinese I encountered exhibited an alternating tendency toward extreme legibility and paranoid secrecy. Instead of the "chase and flight" model (McCracken 1988: 94–103) in which the upper classes constantly move on to newer and better goods and tastes and the middle classes try in vain to keep up, elite consumption in Chengdu exhibits an inherent conservativism and conformity.

Thus, the dispute between Mr. Pan and Mr. Wang can in many ways be understood as a consequence of tension between the paternal "boss" status ideal exhibited by Mr. Pan and more cosmopolitan understandings of how to be elite referenced by Mr. Wang. While Wang's ideal is rooted in notions of personal autonomy and private consumer pleasure, Mr. Pan's patron-provider, boss ideal references kinship values, *jianghu* culture, and Hong Kong gangster movies, among other sources.

Contemporary urban China is awash with newly rich entrepreneurs from a variety of social and economic backgrounds. Unlike their counterparts in the West, this group lacks an established old bourgeoisie to emulate, as well as access to many forms of symbolic and cultural capital accumulation employed by elites elsewhere, such as charity and patronage of the arts, which, while emerging, lack many of the state and institutional supports they enjoy in the West. Although there is no "old rich" for the new rich to contend with, state officials, the sole elite class remaining from the Maoist era, are still a presence in most of their financial endeavors and social lives and still inform many aspects of the boss imaginary. Moreover, not only are ties to officialdom key to business success in many fields, but they also enable a particular form of conspicuous consumption—the acquisition of state privileges such as government license plates from patrons in the government. This form of consumption serves as a means of displaying one's social capital and indexing the power and reach of one's connections. It constitutes, I would argue, a form of consumption uniquely suited to the boss imaginary.

Above all else, the maintenance and formation of relationships both with other elites and with state agents orients most forms of elite consumption. For wealthy Chinese, consumption is not simply an arena of status display, but a form of social practice through which relationships with other elites are forged. Because of the crucial role consumption plays in network building, elites must draw on other practices and domains in order to establish boundaries and distinctions between themselves and other Chinese, including personal quality (*suzhi*), morality, family background, level of education, and forms of money-making.

Conceptions of how rich people live and behave outside of China and how market economies function elsewhere also inform many critiques of the new rich. Many Chinese view their current political and economic milieu as either transitional or pathological and therefore see the success of most new rich in this context as unearned and undeserved. Given the contending models and spheres of value used to measure status, no one can be secure in the belief they have truly made it in reform-era China.

Making and Signifying *Guanxi* in Urban China

For the 40th birthday party of a wealthy entrepreneur the host of the party had rented out the largest private suite in one of the most exclusive karaoke clubs in Chengdu. The suite featured multiple rooms, several TV monitors playing music videos, an elaborate sound system, and leather couches lining every wall.

With little fanfare, the manager of the club brought out the biggest fruit plate (*guopan*) I had ever seen; but it dominated the room and exercised a gravitational force on a portion of the party. It was five feet long and consisted of three tiers, each tier featuring elaborately carved watermelon rind serving both as garnish and as a container for other types of fruit. I had previously encountered fruit plates during fieldwork in the nightclubs of Chengdu accompanying wealthy entrepreneurs as they entertained clients, state officials, and business partners, but this gargantuan fruit plate led me to ponder their significance for the first time.

A few months later I myself was the recipient of a fruit plate. I brought a group of friends to a club where the manager had seen me on previous occasions with groups of businessmen. Soon after we sat down and ordered some drinks, the manager came to our table, greeted me, and called over a server to bring us a fruit plate at no charge. It was a modest, one-tier affair, but an important gesture nonetheless.

On many other occasions thereafter at bars or nightclubs, upon meeting the manager or establishing my connection to the club, I was sent a free plate of fruit. Bars and nightclubs frequently offered fruit plates as a perk that came with the issuance of a VIP card, of which I collected several during the course of my fieldwork. As I came to understand it, these slices of watermelon and orange signified that my status was already above that of a mere anonymous customer; I was familiar, and the member of a social network. Returning customers and high-status VIPs were always given free fruit plates.

While giving away plates of fruit might be read as a calculated form of customer relations, I argue that the gesture accomplishes a more fundamental task. The presentation of a fruit plate is above all an act of recognition, an acknowledgment that you are a friend, a member of a particular social network, and distinct from the undifferentiated other customers. Fruit plates are crystallized social capital of a kind not simply for sale to all who can afford it. They embody the dynamics of recognition and status characteristic of contemporary urban China.

The seemingly mundane fruit plate points to an important aspect of consumption among the new rich in China. Fruit plates both make and signify relationships, and in China relationships (*guanxi*) are fundamental to elite power. The structure of elite networks in China gives new meaning and function to what has been called "conspicuous consumption." I argue that consumption practices among the new rich in China challenge classic notions of bourgeois conspicuous consumption and distinction, and problematize the convertibility of various forms of capital, and even whether the notion of "capital" is entirely adequate for conceptualizing the source of their social power. As Bourdieu (1984) argued, consumption serves to reify social power by signifying and naturalizing divisions between groups. But in the context of contemporary China, consumption is more than a marker of elite status or an expression of habitus: the shared consumption of conventional luxury objects—liquor, tobacco, and food—serves to make social relationships among the elite. One extends one's influence, reputation, and name through experiences of conviviality and acts of consumption.

In Chapter Two I described the forging and maintaining of networks of businessmen and government officials through shared experiences of increasingly lavish consumer pleasure: eating, drinking, massage, and sexual services. Membership in these powerful networks is indicated by a few highly conventional status objects: famous-brand (*mingpai*) liquor, cigarettes, clothing, and imported luxury cars. For many entrepreneurs, consumption is less about revealing the personal qualities or cultural capital of the consumer than about signifying, establishing, and maintaining accumulated and condensed social capital. In other words, it is less about naturalizing personal power than about creating and maintaining the types of networks through which power and status can be expressed. In this context consumption becomes highly conventionalized and ritualized. Many entrepreneurs conceived of consumption as a necessary performance they enacted for others that bore little relationship to their "personal" desires or tastes.

After I completed my fieldwork, Wang Jianjun came to visit me in Chicago. Since most of his previous trips to America had been with tour groups, and he had seen little of America other than, in his words, "airport, hotel, shopping, casino, Disneyland," I took him to my hometown in suburban Middle America. A childhood friend of mine joined us for dinner, and the two of them got along well. Before Wang left to go back to China, my friend, who makes custom jewelry and accessories, gave him a wallet crafted from stingray skin. Wang accepted the wallet and thanked my friend, but later told me, "You know I really like this wallet, but I'll never use it. If I started using it all my friends in China would think I had lost all my money." For Wang to use a wallet other than his Louis Vuitton would violate the symbolic order of his network. His custom-made stingray skin wallet was illegible to his peers.

Wang Jianjun's comment also points to the overwhelming importance of price in turning a good into a status object. When showing me a new purchase, entrepreneurs seldom commented on the quality of the good or its features; they merely quoted the price. Quoting price ensured that anyone, even a pedicab driver unfamiliar with Louis Vuitton, Gucci, or Cartier, could recognize an object's value and that one didn't have to draw on a potentially unfamiliar ideology of taste or aesthetics.

An entrepreneur I had met at a local gym invited me to visit a hot spring in a small city outside of Chengdu. He was closely connected to some bureaucrats from the city where the hot spring was located, and they had offered to pay for our hotel, meals, and hot spring entrance fees. When these officials later went to Chengdu, the entrepreneur, Mr. Zhao, would in turn cover all of their expenses. While he ultimately "paid" for this trip by treating his government friends when they came to Chengdu, this reciprocal arrangement allowed him to gain face as a man who, owing to the strength of his connections, has transcended the status of a mere customer and, like Brother Fatty in Chapter Two, "doesn't pay." Furthermore, by bringing a few of his friends along he was able to demonstrate his degree of connectedness to power and the strength of his guanxi, about which he boasted frequently.

Although at dinner the previous evening Mr. Zhao's car had displayed the license plates of an ordinary citizen, when we set off on our trip, his Audi A4 now sported government license plates that exempted him from paying highway tolls and allowed him to disregard whatever traffic regulations he deemed inconvenient, which, given my experience in the backseat, felt like all of them. Along with his government plates, he displayed a permit in his car window that allowed him to use a police horn and loudspeaker, which he used repeatedly when driving through streets crowded with bicyclists, pedicabs, and peddlers, barking at them to clear the way.

Mr. Zhao, however, had no official connection to the government or Communist Party. He was an entrepreneur who frequently undertook government construction contracts and who was rumored by many to be connected with one or more local criminal organizations (*heishehui*). State agents had bestowed these privileges on Mr. Zhao as a sign of their close guanxi with him. Like many entrepreneurs, he had earned his perks through countless evenings lavishly entertaining state officials in upscale restaurants, karaoke clubs, and foot massage parlors.

Among other new rich I encountered, these elite privileges also included the granting of other police and even military privileges.[9] One entrepreneur I knew who was well connected with officials in the city Public Security Bureau had an official police identification and a licensed gun even though he distributed Chinese wines for a living and had never spent a day in the police academy or a police station.

Beyond being indicative of the privatization of state controlled powers and privileges, this entrepreneurial appropriation of government privileges suggests a convergence in the lifestyles and increasing integration of China's economic and political elite.

Consumption and Power, Visibility and Invisibility

These relationships between businessmen and officials are forged during long nights of entertaining that consist primarily of shared experiences of bodily pleasure. The forms of elite consumption partaken of by the new rich in these venues, though highly conventionalized, are subject to the dynamic of inflation described in Chapter Two.[10]

An evening's entertainment usually began with a banquet in the private room of an expensive restaurant. Hosts usually ordered far more dishes than could possibly be consumed, and the meat of rare and exotic animals was sometimes served as well. But eating was less central to these banquets than drinking and the ritual toasting that accompanied it. Toasts offered an opportunity to flatter officials and make declarations about the relationship between the entrepreneur and his official patron. Banquets were usually followed by other activities, the most common of which was singing in karaoke clubs that provide young female hostesses to accompany male guests. Other popular venues included massage parlors, foot massage parlors, saunas, bars, and teahouses that offered spaces for gambling.[11]

In my interviews with entrepreneurs, they constantly complained about these incessant evenings of entertaining (*yingchou*). Many entrepreneurs had obligations five nights out of the week and longed for leisure time that "truly belonged to them" (*shuyu zijide shijian*), when they would be able to do, or consume, as they pleased. Many even characterized *yingchou* as their true work, and it was a major source of anxiety for these entrepreneurs. Refusing an invitation or failing to maintain a relationship through periodic evenings of entertaining had real social and financial consequences. Similarly if one's choices of venue, food, and alcohol were insufficiently lavish or if the government official, state enterprise manager, or client didn't have a good time (*meiyou wande kaixin*), one risked damaging the relationship and the loss of all the privileges afforded by that relationship. Thus many entrepreneurs emphasized their guest's evident enjoyment as the mark of successful *yingchou* and the establishment of a successful relationship.

The forms of courtship through consumption outlined above generate different anxieties for entrepreneurs and state agents, and the flow of wealth from "market" to businessman and businessman to bureaucrat also generates contrasting modes of consumption. Although the type of networking described here is ubiquitous among government officials in China, it remains illegal, and therefore officials cannot allow themselves to be too visible in their dealings with entrepreneurs. Officials are subject to periodic anti-corruption purges, and any evidence of illicit income or even income with an "unclear source" (*caiyuan buming*) can be used as evidence against them in an anti-corruption sweep.

Several entrepreneurs explained to me that officials are in a difficult bind. It is almost too easy for them to generate illicit money, but it is rather difficult to transform this illicit income into the kinds of assets that are commensurate with their status, such as a large house or an imported car. These forms of conspicuous consumption are likely to attract too much negative attention. A bureaucrat's social and political capital, while easily converted into economic capital, cannot lead to accumulation. Many entrepreneurs claimed that this is why government officials spend so much on perishable forms of consumption of the "wine, women, and song" variety, and why the vast majority keep mistresses, who are a favorite outlet for their illicit income and are often useful in hiding wealth. Just as their illicit income comes easily, it goes easily as well. It cannot be converted into all the forms of conspicuous display available to entrepreneurs.

The entrepreneur faces a different dilemma. Every one of his possessions, from his pen to his car, is likely to be scrutinized by his business associates for signs that he might not really be "one of them." Is he successful enough to afford an extravagant lifestyle, or is he putting on a performance in order to trick us into doing business with him? When entertaining, his choices are even more risky. For example, if he chooses a brand of whiskey unfamiliar to his guests, he risks, on the one hand, being seen as an unsophisticated bumpkin (*tubaozi*) who is unfamiliar with the established brand hierarchy. On the other hand, if he chooses a brand that's expensive but unfamiliar to his guest, he risks embarrassing the official or client by revealing his guest's lack of sophistication.

These considerations lead to an inherent conservatism in entrepreneurial consumption practices, what Buckley (1999: 227) has termed "conspicuous conformity," which is characterized by "an underlying impulse to demonstrate a person's belonging to a certain status group, a new moneyed elite, that is still unsure of its social boundaries and its relations with the rest of Chinese society." Unlike the dynamic of distinction outlined by Bourdieu (1984), in which the elite emphasize refinement, distance, and rarity in their consumption choices, new-rich entrepreneurs favored legibility, price (the higher the better), and famous brands (*mingpai*). Some admitted privately to me that they preferred a particular brand of scotch, but come time to entertain they always opted for Chivas Regal Royal Salute for its certain recognizability and fame.

Although entrepreneurs don't face the kind of scrutiny of their wealth that officials do, there was a widespread sense among entrepreneurs that their wealth could be taken away by the state at any time. Mr. Wang considered himself an honest taxpayer, an exception among his peers, but he explained to me, "I pay my taxes, but it still doesn't matter. If they want to come after me (*zheng wo*) they'll find a reason for doing so. Even if I've tried to do everything by the rules, they can always find some violation from the past," which is part of the reason that he still felt the need to entertain bureaucrats even though his business no longer depended on them. Similarly, Mr. Wei talked about how "the word fear" (*yige pa zi*) is always in the back of the mind of most businesspeople, and some feel the need to keep growing just to mitigate future uncertainty.

Ostentation among one's peers was seen as necessary, and one was expected to spend lavishly for the benefit of government officials and clients, but wealthy Chengduers were considerably wary of publicly visible forms of expenditure. Organized forms of charity and philanthropy were viewed as particularly problematic because they not only attracted the attention of various state agencies but were also believed to attract even more seekers of handouts and favors.

As many scholars of China have noted, secrecy and privacy have long been privileges of the wealthy and powerful (Y. Yan 2003: 136). Remaining hidden from the gaze of voyeuristic commoners was in itself a form of distinction.[12]

Partly because of the conventionalized nature of many other status objects, place and space play a key role in drawing divisions among the new rich (see also Zhang 2010). Controlling the gaze of others and limiting interactions to a select audience serve as important means of drawing boundaries in one's social network and of maintaining a privileged invisibility and distance from outsiders.

This role of place is exemplified most clearly by the preference for private rooms (*baofang*) in nightclubs and restaurants described in Chapter Two. Private clubs, with exorbitant membership fees and a rigorous application process are also rising in popularity among the new rich. Because the social backgrounds (education levels, rural vs. urban background, etc.) and wealth (both amounts and sources) of members is verified in advance, these clubs are viewed as places where one can safely network without fear of being deceived or cheated by others "pretending" to be elite.

Living for Others or Living for Oneself: Autonomy as a Form of Distinction

The tendency toward conservativism and conformity among the new rich extended beyond clothing, tobacco, and drinks to forms of leisure, lifestyle, and ethics. Ms. Gao, the owner of a public relations company, explained to me that in her social circle (*quanzi*) if she were to "go against the group" (*bu hequn*) and their preferred activities, her friends would consider her an "alien" (*waixingren*) or an "eccentric" (*guaiwu*). She expressed boredom with the incessant routine of banquets, drinking, and karaoke, often visiting with three or four different groups of officials, clients, and associates in one evening. Ms. Gao longed for what she described as "personal time" (*shuyu zijide shijian*) but explained that participating in this entertaining was essential to expanding her business.

Autonomy and Dependency

Virtually all entrepreneurs with whom I worked complained about the monotony of entertaining and the toll it took on their health. Ms. Long, a businesswoman in her late thirties, described the unhealthy lifestyles that many of her friends led as indicative of a loss of personal autonomy. Businessmen, she asserted, "are at the beck and call of their friends. Whatever their friends do, that's what they have to do to maintain their guanxi. They don't know how to live their

lives. They just follow others." Their wives, she added, despite lacking the financial imperative to network, also exhibited the tendency to follow others' lead.
"The wives play mahjong all night and go shopping during the day."

After a good friend of hers, whom she characterized as very successful
but a workaholic, died of cancer, her perspective on the lives of those around
her changed. "I saw that everyone around me was living for others. They were
blindly making money, and they didn't know for what purpose anymore."
Ms. Long began taking classes on healthier living and eventually opened up
a healthy lifestyle clinic of her own. She sold off businesses that required too
much attention and found subordinates to do most of her management work
in the businesses she still maintained. She attempted to realize the fantasy of
autonomy that she felt was the privilege of the financially successful.

Ms. Long felt that entrepreneurs' family background and level of education exerted a strong influence in determining their lifestyles and modes of
consumption. She articulated a critique heard frequently from the women
entrepreneurs I interviewed that highlighted the "deception" inherent in elite
consumption. This critique privileged the cultivation of self over cultivation of
relationships with others as the mark of a true elite. She characterized the typical nouveau riche (*baofahu*) as from a more rural, poorer, and less-educated
background and more likely to be concerned with appearances. They were the
ones, she claimed, who "madly pursue famous brand names" (*fengkuangde
zhuiqiu mingpai*), and she gave an example of a friend who exclusively wore
Prada brand clothing, down to his underwear and socks. To Ms. Long, this
concern with appearances betrayed a loss of sense of self and a loss of direction (*mimang*). (She also suspected that someone so obsessed with appearances
probably lacked the ability to distinguish fake from real luxury goods.) Despite
their wealth and status, they are little more than puppets of those who surround them: "They basically live for others, not themselves. They live how they
think that others want them to they live."

While there was a practical component to entrepreneurs' flashy but highly
conventionalized consumption in that they needed to look the part to impress
and attract more business partners, Ms. Long understood their obsession with
appearances as indicative of their being trapped in a particular social circle and
unable to "find themselves" (*qiu ziji*). Citing the experience of her friend who
passed away, she explained that the influence of the web of their connections
over their daily lives leads them to sacrifice their bodies and families for the
sake of their social networks. Summing up their situation she stated, "These are

the ones you find at teahouses sitting at a mahjong table all night. Their bodies are unhealthy and their family lives are unhappy."

She contrasted the "low-quality" (*di suzhi*) nouveau-riche obsession with external displays of wealth and the opinions of others with the concern of the super-rich with "internal" (*neimian*) cultivation.[13] She gave the example of an extremely wealthy friend of hers ("wealthy beyond our imaginations") who devoted a lot of his time to philanthropic activities.[14] She differentiated his low-key, private forms of charity from the more common form in China—media events sponsored by companies. More remarkable, however, was his ability to pull himself away from his network and business concerns.

As an example of his autonomy, he was able to turn off his cell phone for *fifteen* days and take off traveling abroad. Yet, according to Ms. Long, looking at him one would never know that he is super-rich because he dresses rather plainly. She explained that this class of individuals also focuses on bettering themselves by taking training classes that help them achieve even greater success, such as Top Human and NLP (Neuro-Linguistic Programming). These courses offer methods for overcoming personal weaknesses and realizing one's full potential in both professional and personal domains. She understood these programs as a way of improving and cultivating personal quality (*suzhi peixun*). Members of the new rich demonstrated their "high quality" (*gao suzhi*) through forms of self-improvement such as sports, healthy hobbies, travel, and education.

Those who depend entirely on guanxi to make money, she explained, fare the worst. They have to spend all of their time flattering some government official or business partner. They are forced to drink and ruin their health just to please someone else. Even if they want to improve themselves, they lack the time, energy, and autonomy to do so.

Now that Ms. Long was relatively successful, she proudly proclaimed that she no longer depended on anyone to make money. She wasn't beholden to any big bosses or high-ranking officials because she no longer feared the rejection of her business ideas or loss of face from people refusing to help her (*meiyou deshixin*). She contrasted her mindset with that of most of those around her, who were trapped in their social networks by a blind desire for wealth: "When doing business, the more you show that you're desperate for something the more the cadres control you."

Like many other entrepreneurs I interviewed, Ms. Long felt that her success derived from the power of her ideas and the value that her business proposals created (*shili*) rather than the strength of her connections or family background. She saw herself as "lifestyle pioneer" who served as a model for others and offered guidance to many of her mostly female friends and business associates. Ms. Long saw her primary mission as teaching them to worry less about how they were perceived by others.

This emphasis on earning one's wealth as opposed to obtaining it on the basis of family background or through guanxi was particularly prevalent in the self-narratives of female entrepreneurs. It is no surprise that female entrepreneurs were the ones who articulated this notion of the "unearned wealth" of the nouveau riche most clearly and forcefully. Their marginal position in a masculine business world in which deals and partnerships often took the form of fictive brotherhoods led them to view many of their peers' nepotistic practices as distortions of a meritocratic market.[15]

Wealth, Earned and Unearned

In assessing her autonomy in comparison with that of those around her, Ms. Gao echoed many of Ms. Long's themes. As a measure of her success, she bragged to me that she didn't depend on others in her business dealings and had no need to seek the patronage of big bosses: "*Wo keyi buqiuren*" [I don't need to ask for help]. Having become financially successful and her own boss, she hoped to "experience the greatness in an ordinary life [*tihui panfandangzhongde weida*]." She contrasted her attitude with that of most of her PR company's clients:

> A lot of men in their forties and fifties really suffer for the sake of face [*weile mianzi er huode henlei*]. You see lots of rich men and they throw around their money everywhere, but they're really just playing with the bank's money. If it were really their own hard-earned money they wouldn't be so generous.

In differentiating herself from the "big bosses" (*da laoban*) she encountered daily in her business, she emphasized that her wealth was the product of her ability and hard work, unlike the flashy bosses who had struck it rich through family background, *guanxi*, or dumb luck. She explained that Chinese society, however, rarely rewards those who merely possess talent and ability (*benshi*). "In this society having ability is not enough; you've got to have money to cultivate relationships and court people (*goudui*). On top of that you need to find the right people [to serve as your patrons]."

Ms. Gao came from a very humble, small-town background but was able to attend the central arts academy in Beijing, where she studied singing. After winning several national singing competitions, she was on the verge of becoming a pop star when she had to return to Sichuan for family reasons. Despite, in her own assessment, having more talent than many established stars, she lacked the financial and social capital to move up in the entertainment business. "If I had had money, I would have been famous long ago."

Underlying these statements is an ideology about earned and unearned wealth. According to this ideology, only those who possess ability (*benshi*) or have a business idea that creates value (*shili*) have truly earned their money. Others are just manipulators—of opportunities, of power, and of people. According to Ms. Gao and many other rich Chengduers I interviewed, most *baofahu* are just taking advantage of "gaps" (*kongzi*) in China's development, whether loopholes in the law or market opportunities created by the speed and scale of China's growth. They happened to be in the right place at the right time, and anyone with open eyes and a little effort could have made a fortune in their place. Because they simply exploited an existing condition, they needed no personal ability to succeed, and their success does not reflect or confirm their quality, education, or cultivation. With the right combination of social and financial capital, their success was virtually guaranteed. The sons and daughters of wealthy entrepreneurs (*fuerdai*) and government officials were often spoken about in these terms. Their success was guaranteed by their family backgrounds (*beijing*) and the strength of their parents' connections; it bore no relationship to their actual ability.

Corrupt officials and well-connected gangsters represented the most extreme form of this means of leveraging social capital for financial capital. Wang Jianjun referred to the businesses of many of the neighbors at his housing complex as falling into the category of "tricking banks out of their money" (*pian yinhangde qian*). They used their guanxi with bank officials to secure loans and then leaned on that same guanxi to ensure that they would never have to be repaid. One of Wang's neighbors, a well-known underworld figure from western China, accumulated his initial fortune by securing bank loans from bank directors he was closely associated with (and by offering them a cut of the money). His subsequent marriage to the daughter of a high-ranking official ensured that forcing him to repay would be very difficult.

Ms. Gao and Ms. Long asserted that uncultivated baofahu often created their own undoing through their ignorance and lack of sophistication. According to the two women, while some baofahu had the sense to hire capable managers and surround themselves with people who could steer their business ventures and continue their success, the majority wasted their money on the four occupations of the nouveau-riche man: banqueting, drinking, gambling, and womanizing.

As most entrepreneurs understood it, when faced with an actual competitive market rather than the fortuitous conditions that had brought their initial success, most baofahu lost their fortunes. According to this imaginary, some newly rich entrepreneurs from poor, rural backgrounds who had the sense to better themselves through forms of suzhi education adapted with the times, but the majority who didn't eventually exposed the ephemeral foundations of their fortunes.

Most Chinese understood China's evolution toward a fully competitive market system as inevitable, and according to this imaginary, undeserving baofahu and the spoiled children of well-connected cadres would gradually be eliminated by real competition. Many entrepreneurs, as well as ordinary Chinese I spoke with, predicted that the increasingly globalized, meritocratic market will eventually confirm who is truly a person of quality and ability and who is just a flash in the pan riding the tide of China's explosive growth.[16]

These analyses of new-rich lifestyles point to a fundamental contradiction. Ms. Long's model of a successful, cultivated elite individual was defined primarily by his or her autonomy and independence from others. She understood this autonomy as creating a space for the cultivation of inner selves rather than flashy exteriors and for the satisfaction of personal desires rather than the wishes of one's peers. But this distancing from social networks creates a kind of invisibility, which undermines the very foundations of their status and "face." Interestingly, despite Ms. Long's claims of being an independent lifestyle pioneer, virtually every time I saw her she was accompanied by what she described as a new "follower" (*tudi*). Ms. Long proudly explained to me that they were learning from her how to break out of their social circles. They were adherents of Ms. Long's "zero-distance theory" (*lingdian lilun*), which advocates that an entrepreneur only make enough money to satisfy personal desires. Instead of allowing the gazes and opinions of others to direct one's lifestyle, Ms. Long claimed to offer a path to autonomy and authentic personal happiness.

The Search for Standards, Models, and Beliefs

Early on in my fieldwork, a friend asked if I was interested in giving a talk on Western manners to a group of women described to me as "entrepreneurs and white-collar women" as part of an International Women's Day celebration at an upscale department store. Thinking this would be an interesting form of cultural exchange and hoping it would give me a chance to make some connections for my research, I agreed.

In my presentation, I reviewed basic Western table manners (the details of which I was somewhat foggy about and had to verify online) and presented some examples of conversation topics that might be offensive to Americans, such as direct questions about age and income. After talking with some of the attendees and with the organizers of the celebration, it became clear to me that very few of these women had a real need for this knowledge. Almost none of them spoke English or had traveled outside of China, and even fewer had had any interaction with foreigners. The purpose of the workshop that afternoon was to instill in these women an awareness and deference to a standard (*biaozhun*). The "standard" by default could not emanate from China, but resided elsewhere and was most authentically represented and explained by an actual foreigner. The assumption underlying the workshop, which was titled "Essential Knowledge for the Successful Woman," was that elite women should possess an awareness and deference to standards even though they might never need to employ them.

The talk that followed mine, given by a Chinese woman who had studied cosmetology in America, made the ideology that informed our presentations even more apparent. She worked as a professional image consultant and sold a well-known brand of American hair care products to her customers. She demonstrated different techniques for applying makeup to different face types and skin tones. She urged her audience not to wear the same outfit more than once a week and to wear clothes that radiated professionalism.

In her talk, which focused on addressing the perceived lapses in urban Chinese women's beauty education, she constantly invoked "international standards" (*guoji biaozhun*). There were standards for the skirt length of a white-collar woman, for ways of sitting in a chair, and for appropriate bodily deportment when exiting a car. During her discussion of the proper seating hierarchy when riding in a car with one's (implicitly male) boss, she turned to me for validation, asking me where rich men from the West who are driven by chauffeurs sit in a car. After I responded correctly she explained, "In Western countries the boss sits in the back seat on the right hand side. He doesn't sit behind the driver like many of you might have seen your bosses do. A lot of Chinese bosses and officials don't sit in the right seat."

This notion that there is an "international standard" for everything is echoed at many levels of Chinese society, from central government campaigns to store clerk sales pitches. Advertisements for products claim that their level of quality meets international standards or employs foreign technology.[17] Interior decorators advertise experience abroad as proof of familiarity with the tastes of a global elite. Foreign fast-food chains imply that their menus are based on an international nutritional and taste consensus. Many businessmen showed me the tags on their clothing and asked if a particular brand of clothing was popular in the United States and how much it cost there.

Knowledge and mastery of international standards is crucial not only to the Chinese elites' project of global recognition but to the Chinese state's as well. Given the assumption that China's economy is moving toward more rational forms of economic organization and integration with the global economy, many businessmen asserted that the "Chinese way" of doing business would gradually decline and that they would need to "get on the global track" (*yuguoji jiegui*).

This assumption of the ever-encroaching tide of global standards for economic and social formations provided the backdrop for critiques of business practices, tastes, and ethics. Furthermore it was intertwined with a claim, articulated at many levels of Chinese society, that Chinese people lack the beliefs (*xinyang*) to anchor and guide a modern, "civilized" society. This problem was seen to be particularly acute among the elite, who were supposed to serve as the role models for the rest of China and were often the face of "the new China" abroad. International standards were seen as one possible way to fill this gap and provide a foundation for establishing a proper, more globally recognized way of being elite.

Mr. Zhu, the editor of *First Class* (*Toudengcang*), a Chengdu-based publication with a national circulation, started his magazine as a way of introducing proper ways of being wealthy and living the good life to China's new rich. In its introductory issues, *First Class* distinguishes between class in the sense that it's been used for most of modern Chinese history, as a scientific category of social analysis (*jieji*), and the notion of class as something that can only be achieved, as a sense of cultivation and refinement (Jiu Yue 2004).

In his introduction to the magazine, Mr. Zhu, writing under a pen name, quotes a French proverb, "Paris may give rise to ten nouveau riche every day, but in ten years it won't necessarily give birth to a single aristocrat" (Yi Hui 2004). Mr. Zhu felt that this phrase captured the problematic of wealth in contemporary China: that people with money are everywhere, but few are able to convert their wealth into the forms of cultural capital that would provide the foundations for a globally recognizable Chinese elite. In Chengdu in particular, the rich were too caught up in local tastes (hot pot and green tea), local forms of leisure (mahjong and foot massages), and local ways of doing business (entertaining and cultivating guanxi) to turn themselves into nationally and globally recognizable "aristocrats" (*guizu*).

Mr. Zhu explained to me that Chengdu lagged behind other Chinese cities such as Shanghai and Beijing in its level of cultural sophistication and taste, characterizing Chengdu's elite culture as "backward" (*luohou*). He illustrated Chengduers' lack of taste with the example of a wealthy man who drives his Mercedes Benz to the outskirts of town for a bowl of noodles at a rural "hole in the wall" restaurant (*cangying guanzi*). He then painted an image of the man squatting by the side of the road next to his Benz slurping his bowl of noodles. "This is what rich people in Chengdu are like. Their wealth and tastes lack harmony; they don't match. They understand luxury, but they don't understand quality of life" (*Tamen dong shechi, danshi budong shenghuo pinzhi*).

Mr. Zhu also criticized Chengdu's elite for being insufficiently international (*guojihua*). As an example, he decried the lack of house parties and dinner parties (like the elite have in Europe) in Chengdu and devoted an issue of *First Class* to promoting such a custom. Chengdu was also missing a cigar culture among its cigarette-smoking elite, which he sought to remedy with his magazine's monthly cigar column. Chengdu's upper crust also lacked an appreciation for the arts, preferring to spend their money on recognizable famous- brand status goods rather than unique works of art. He critiqued the propensity of the local elite for engaging in unproductive leisure, stating, "Enjoying [one's wealth] doesn't create [anything of value]" (*xiangshou bushi chuangzao*).

In short, Mr. Zhu's critique of Chengdu's wealthy echoed Mr. Pan's insult of Mr. Wang: the rich in Chengdu might eat better hot pot, smoke better cigarettes, and play high-stakes mahjong on automatic mahjong tables in the private rooms of exclusive teahouses, but their leisure practices and tastes were ultimately no different from those of retired grandmothers and laid-off factory workers who played mahjong on street corners while sitting on bamboo chairs. They simply lived in more comfortable houses, wore nicer clothes, and ate, drank, and smoked better.

As part of its project to instill international standards of taste in Chengdu's new elite, *First Class* organized forums on wine, food, and fashion and sponsored cocktail and dinner parties. The commercial nature of these events was often blatant. At one event meant to emulate a Western cocktail party, men were required to wear suits and women cocktail dresses. Partygoers drank wine and conversed in the lobby of a high-end real estate showroom. The theme of the party was classical music appreciation, but instead of a live performance, attendees were required to watch an hour-long video of a concert by the London Symphony, which allowed one of the party's sponsors, a manufacturer of high-end stereo equipment, to showcase its products.

I was invited to speak on men's fashion at a roundtable discussion at a high-end coffee house called "The Essence of Europe." Mr. Zhu hoped that I could offer a Western critique of the fashion choices of Chinese men. An article that later appeared in *First Class* summarizing the event quoted a Beijing city official from the office of "spiritual civilization" (*jingshen wenming*) on the importance of clothing:

> Dress actually doesn't completely belong to the self or one's personal behavior. It not only displays the self, but it also constitutes a form of responsibility to others and to society. It conveys an attitude of respect to the public. (Shui Shui 2005: 86)

The implication was that, in their failure to develop more sophisticated tastes, wealthy Chengduers were not only depriving themselves of an important means of status display, but were letting society down as well. As reform-era China's most exemplary citizens, they had a responsibility to put the tastes of Chinese, as the CCP campaign urges, "on the global track" (*yuguoji jiegui*). Their failure to qualitatively better themselves constituted a shirking of their responsibility to society as a whole.

A phrase repeated in nearly every interview I conducted and in countless conversations was, "Chinese people have no beliefs" (*Zhongguoren meiyou xinyang*). This notion was often contrasted with an understanding of the West as a land anchored in Judeo-Christian values and morality. The statement was offered to explain everything from hedonistic consumption practices and dishonesty in business to the lack of philanthropy and sophisticated tastes among the wealthy in China. Many successful entrepreneurs saw themselves as actively searching for a model or a framework of belief to anchor their newfound autonomy. Drinking, gambling, consumerism, and womanizing were seen as clear symptoms of having no beliefs.

Only healthy habits, such as golf, art collecting, travel, and religious devotion were understood to fill the void and provide a positive orientation for one's consumption. Ms. Long saw her training programs and attention to health as preventing her from feeling directionless like her friends. Other entrepreneurs I interviewed highlighted their religious beliefs to differentiate themselves from their "lost" peers. However, rather than offering a genuine alternative to the competitive consumer display associated with elite social networks, emerging forms of religious devotion are generating their own modes of status display and hierarchy.

Xiao Lin was the son of a wealthy entrepreneur now working for his father. He wore Polo shirts, smoked high-grade *Yuxi* cigarettes, and drove an Audi A4, the de rigueur car of the successful businessman in Sichuan in the early 2000s. At a sidewalk barbecue stand late one night he described his typical day to me, which resembled the typical day of the majority of the entrepreneurs I worked with. He woke up late, ate lunch as his first meal of the day, and spent his afternoon in teahouses discussing business or playing cards. Occasionally he would drop in on his businesses, and sometimes he would exercise in the afternoons. He then spent his evenings out on the town with friends, business associates, or girlfriends into the early morning. He claimed to lack nothing: "I've got a nice car, a nice apartment, and no shortage of beautiful women." But he quickly qualified his boast by confessing, "My life is empty and without value" (*meiyou jiazhi, hen kongxu*). Recently he had become interested in Tibetan Buddhism and had met with a "living Buddha" (*huofo*). I mentioned that I had traveled to Kampa in western Sichuan and was familiar with some lamas there. "Lamas are nothing," he told me, "knowing a *huofo* ("living Buddha," i.e., a high-ranking, reincarnated lama) is what really counts."

For Xiao Lin and many others, the search for value and meaning itself had become a form of distinction. Very few Chinese have the free time and the access to four-wheel-drive vehicles needed to access high-ranking Tibetan lamas in their remote mountain temples. For Xiao Lin, his connection to a huofo, much like his Audi and ties to powerful officials, helped to demonstrate that he was no ordinary nouveau-riche baofahu but a man of quality and status.

Conclusion

These narratives of wealth and lifestyle among the new rich point to a fundamental contradiction. For most of the entrepreneurs I worked with, blind conformity to the consumption habits, brands, and activities of their social circle was the mark of the "low-quality" nouveau riche. Yet to refuse to participate in conventionalized forms of consumption and leisure is to endanger the very grounds of entrepreneurs' financial success and undermines the foundation of their social power: having "face"—i.e., recognition by their peers.

As the notion of conspicuous conformity suggests, state officials and the business class dictate many of the forms of elite consumption in China. To violate its conventional symbolic order is to risk exclusion from powerful elite networks. For the new rich, to transgress the recognized modes of elite status is to risk being illegible and viewed as outside the network of power. To order Macallan instead of Chivas Scotch whiskey might lead to one being viewed as an imposter, or even worse as a culturally suspect foreign-loving "banana."[18]

Yet the persistent desire to be recognized by an elite elsewhere, to "get on the global track," generates contradictions with the exigencies of their local worlds. Ms. Long's model of a successful, cultivated elite individual was defined primarily by autonomy and independence from others. She understood this autonomy as creating a space for the cultivation of the inner self rather than a flashy exterior and for the satisfaction of personal desires rather than pandering to the perceptions of others. Recognition for these "true elites" was granted not by proximate others but by imagined foreign "aristocrats" (*guizu*) and invisible market forces who will ultimately confirm who is truly worthy of their wealth. In the meantime, as they wait for the market to usher in a neoliberal rapture, this distancing from social networks creates a kind of invisibility, which undermines the very foundations of their local prestige.

Many wealthy Chinese confront multiple, often conflicting modes of naturalizing and legitimating their wealth and achieving social recognition (see Lamont 1992 for a similar argument about the United States). We can question the extent to which individuals in this social field are independently or straightforwardly maximizing their economic, social, and cultural capital, as in the Bourdieuian (1984) model of distinction. While individual Chinese entrepreneurs are clearly seeking to convert their quantitative differences in wealth into other forms of qualitative value—status, suzhi "quality," morality—they are acutely aware that their ability to do so depends on the cooperation and recognition of others and that their attempts to establish their prestige, status, or wealth in one context or with one audience can threaten their recognition in another.

More fundamentally, the anxieties of my informants are spawned by an assumption that recognition and status do not accrue automatically from the possession of money or luxury goods, but are an outcome of the subjective states—"the hearts and minds" (*xin*)—of others. According to this understanding, which resonates with scholarly interpretations of *mianzi* (face) (Hu 1944; Kipnis 1995), status is conferred by the recognition of others in specific social contexts. While particular objects might be used to communicate status to others, this process, to borrow a phrase from Webb Keane (1997), is subject to the "hazards of representation." These objects might fail to deliver what they promise—your business partner might not recognize your subtle Hermes tie. Or, your Louis Vuitton wallet's value might be degraded by its adoption by other members of the nouveau riche—what McCracken (1988) calls the "chase and flight" dynamic.

But more significantly, this anxiety is rooted in the deeper uncertainty and risk associated with seeking recognition from unseen, unknown others who are often presumed to be hostile—foreign businessmen, European aristocrats, overseas Chinese, and the more established nouveau riche. The entrepreneurs I spent time with in Chengdu feared that the terms of status were constantly shifting in ways that disadvantaged them: not only were they concerned that they were not fully proficient in the symbolic language of elite brands and tastes, but they harbored a suspicion that the game was rigged against them from the beginning.[19]

The imaginary of a boss as an autonomous executor of his own desires informs the fantasies of future success and the critiques of the present for many Chinese businessmen; but those with the means to realize this imaginary find that it only generates contradictions. Withdrawing from the outside world of business entertaining, as Wang Jianjun did, led people to question his elite status. They wondered why a successful businessman would live like a laid-off factory worker, despite Wang's assertion that his life resembled that of an upper-class American. And for Mr. Pan, bosshood drove him toward a paranoid, self-destructive retreat into the controlled environment of the baofang. Despite the toll on his body and attempts to limit his interactions with others, he vowed to sustain his business for the sake of all those who depended on him.

About a year after returning to the United States, I received a call from Mr. Pan late one night. He began telling me in a very upbeat tone, "I've done it. I've really become the biggest boss in Chengdu" (*Wo zhende chengwei laoda*). He had sold his year-old Toyota Crown and bought a brand new 700–series BMW.[20] His real estate business was booming, and his fame and reputation had spread from Chengdu to neighboring counties.

After we had updated each other on our lives, he mentioned that he was calling from the hospital. Previously, during my fieldwork, he had been hospitalized for a few weeks because of stomach problems caused by excessive drinking. He informed me that it was stomach problems again that had sent him back to the hospital. When I asked why he had endangered his health again, he

FIGURE 4.1. The "European" wing of a high-end foot massage parlor (*xijiaofang*).

FIGURE 4.2. The "Chinese" wing of the same establishment shown in Figure 4.1.

explained that he had to drink a lot because of all the yingchou associated with his business. I told him he needed to take better care of himself and that his health was more important than anything. It was the foundation of any other success. He replied to me, "I can't stop or slow down. I have many people whose livelihoods depend on me (literally "depend on me to eat," *kao wo chifan*). I've got about fifty employees and even more xiongdi. Their livelihoods depend on my success. I have to keep going."

WOMEN ENTREPRENEURS AND THE "BEAUTY ECONOMY"

Sexuality, Morality, and Wealth

"Gray" Women and the "Beauty Economy"

In a 1997 essay, the feminist economist He Qinglian (2005) suggests a new label to capture the new "types" of women that have emerged in the reform period. She dubs them "gray women" (*huise nüxing*) to account for their liminal position between proper women who belong to the morally upright and legitimate "white" world of marriage and prostitutes who belong to the illegitimate and immoral "black" underworld of sex work. Gray women include the mistresses and second wives (*ernai*) of wealthy, powerful men as well as the hostesses and massage girls who entertain the elite. She argues that this class of women is a direct product of the current period of "primitive accumulation" in China. They are often the beneficiaries of the ill-gotten wealth of shady businessmen and corrupt government officials, and they play a key role in mediating ties between elite men. She states:

> Their "career" and means of making a living are different from normal society, so they are viewed by society as "gray." However, their existence is precisely bound up with normal society, that is the "big shots" of the legitimate world [*baise shijie*]. You could even say that without the big shots who like to spend money on fleeting pleasures and keeping mistresses this type of person wouldn't exist in this world. (He 2005)

Despite the fact that many "gray women" hold positions in the "white," legitimate world as secretaries or public relations girls (*gongguan xiaojie*), He

Qinglian, and many other critics of these women, view the difference between "chickens by the road" (i.e., the lowest class of prostitute, *lubiande ji*) and the concubine of an official as one purely of status and income level.[1] For many critical observers, these women simply "eat the rice of youth" (*chi qingchun fan*).[2] Like rent-seeking, corrupt government officials, they make money off of their youthful beauty without creating anything of value for society or the economy. Their critics describe them as parasites (*jishengchong*) who leech off the wealth of others, often funneling it away from its "proper" channels of investment and family support. They not only sacrifice their feminine virtue for money and material comfort but also contribute to the breakup of families and an overall decline in human dignity in Chinese society (He 2005).

In countless movies and television shows these young women are the dreaded "third parties" (*disanzhe*) who lure men (and their wealth) away from their family responsibilities. They have been blamed for contributing to the corruption of upright officials and are often portrayed as spurring their official patrons to accept more bribes and gifts. Intellectuals and scholarly observers cite them as prime evidence of the abandonment of socialist goals such as gender equality and hold them up as examples of a more general loss of belief and values seen to be afflicting Chinese culture.

Closely associated with gray women is what has come to be termed the "beauty economy" (*meinü jingji*). This term refers to a marketplace in which young, attractive women are used to promote commercial products and services (Southcn.com 2007; see also Hansor 2005, 2008; Otis, 2011). (Jobs in the broadly defined "beauty economy" are also referred to as "pink-collar" jobs; see Zhen 2000: 98.)

In China the importance of young, attractive women in sales promotions extends beyond conventional television and print ads to the employment of models and female university students at car shows, in company booths at business conventions, and in public relations; (often fictitious) photos of "beautiful woman authors" are used to sell books. An increasing number of businesses, from insurance companies to real estate developers, sponsor beauty contests, fashion shows, song and dance performances, and even underwear modeling to attract customers (Hanser 2005, 2008; Otis 2011). The sales agents who work in the showrooms of real estate developments are overwhelmingly attractive young women. Many entrepreneurs in the real estate business described real estate development showrooms as a prime site in which wealthy men find mistresses and young women find wealthy male patrons. Many of the women who participate in the beauty economy as models and actresses also become involved in the "gray" world of accompanying wealthy businessmen and serving as mistresses.

These blurred and shifting boundaries between prostitution, concubinage, the beauty economy, and even some legitimate careers have generated a great deal of discursive boundary work for urban Chinese women. Moralizing critics see mistresses as sex workers with better working conditions, and they view car show models and massage girls as ultimately in the same business: trading feminine sexuality for money.

But in interviews and narratives, participants in the broader beauty economy tend to answer their critics with two discursive moves. First, they employ the trope of a competitive market to argue that all women, even women in marriages and legitimate careers, trade their sexuality for material comfort provided by men. They figure all sexual relations, from a single paid sex act to marriage, as part of a single market in which women trade their sexuality for financial security. In their accounts of themselves, mistresses, models, and hostesses frequently invoke the authoritative discourse of market competition and portray themselves as entrepreneurs rationally exploiting the market realities of sexual relations.

The second discursive tactic, articulated by many women who actually serve as "gray women," is to make very minute status distinctions among the ways in which they employ their sexuality and the types of compensation they receive for it (see Zelizer 2005). Thus, mistresses distinguish themselves from hostesses, and hostesses differentiate themselves from massage girls.

This social field, in which sexuality and beauty are presumed to be the primary forms of capital employed by women looking to succeed in the market economy, poses special problems for women entrepreneurs, however. Businesswomen are often accused or suspected of using (or of having used) their sexuality to get ahead. In short, while mistresses and prostitutes frame themselves as entrepreneurs, actual female entrepreneurs are constantly suspected of being current or former "gray women."

This chapter begins by examining the discourses surrounding "gray" women as well as other categories of women whose status is defined by their position within a matrix of wealth, femininity, and sexuality. These other categories include female entrepreneurs (*nüxing qiyejia*), "career women" (*nüqiangren*), white-collar (*bailing*) women, and "rich ladies" (*fupo*)—the older wives of wealthy and powerful men. I examine the stereotypes surrounding these women, and the ways in which they both appropriate and subvert them. I analyze how these higher-status women position themselves within narratives of entrepreneurialism and material success in China and how their experiences of the contradictory ideologies surrounding gender and wealth form the basis of their critique of both wealthy Chinese men and gray women.

I also look at how female entrepreneurs navigate the masculine, sexualized spaces of business entertaining described in Chapter Two. Their marginal positions within this social field afford them a critical perspective on ways of doing business and the status concerns of elite Chinese men. During the time I was accompanying and interviewing them, female entrepreneurs and professionals were very eager to tell "their side of the story," and their voices and perspectives largely frame my discussion.

While female entrepreneurs and wealthy women were often eager to talk to me, younger, unmarried women, especially those who were the girlfriends (or potential girlfriends) of rich men, were often quite wary of me. They were aware that openly associating with a foreigner would likely lead the Chinese men in our group to call their purity into question. Foreigners were understood to be promiscuous and sexually "liberated," and Chinese women who freely socialized with them were suspected of having loose morals. Furthermore, any request on my part to meet with individual women alone for an interview, without the presence of others, could easily have been interpreted by both them and their boyfriends as a gesture of courtship.

Because many of these women were the actual or potential girlfriends of my key informants, I was very cautious and conservative in my interactions with them. Thus, in formulating my understanding of how they conceived of their relationships with wealthy men, I had to rely largely on secondhand sources: discussions with their peers, published interviews and biographical narratives, and depictions and debates in the Chinese media. Some of these representations are sympathetic, focusing on factors such as poverty, oppressive kin relations, and lack of job opportunities that lead women to become sex workers, hostesses, and mistresses; but others emphasize their calculating nature, worship of consumerism, and disregard for moral propriety, the integrity of the family, and feminist ideals.

The vast majority of the women who serve as hostesses and sex workers are from rural areas.[3] Many have tried other forms of service work before embarking on hostessing, including factory and restaurant work (see Zheng 2007, 2009). In many instances, circumstances force women to become hostesses, such as job loss, divorce, or other family emergencies, but some see the job as a way to quickly amass capital for other endeavors. The compensation they receive from hostessing and sex work is often orders of magnitude greater than that offered by any salaried work in manufacturing or service industries open to women of their educational levels.

Some use hostessing to support their kin, including parents back in their rural villages, and a large percentage of them are in fact married (Pan 2000). Some view it as a path to a comfortable city life in the future and an escape from rural agricultural labor. Many save money to start their own business in the city or back in their hometowns.

Because a hostess's career is usually over by her late twenties, her best bet for remaining in the city is to become the mistress, second wife, or wife of an urban, preferably wealthy man. In her ethnography of hostesses in Dalian, Tiantian Zheng (2007: 127) argues that "hostessing is these hostesses' only way to bid for equal status with urbanites. It is their answer to, and act of defiance against, the rural-urban dualistic society."[4] While the desire for urban status and a comfortable urban life no doubt factors heavily into their motivations, this argument overlooks the desire of many to return to their hometowns, as well as the weight of kin obligations in the decision to become a hostess. This account of the motivations of "gray women" also neglects changing family structures and their corresponding shift in gendered kinship expectations in rural China.

A wealthy factory owner in Guangdong once summarized the different motivations for male and female migrants to me in these terms: "Men come here to work so they can save up money to get married; women come so they can support their parents." Because men are expected to have the assets to establish a new household (most often an apartment or house, but increasingly also a car in big cities), they have less disposable income to use to support their parents and siblings. Women, on the other hand, are expected to "marry up" into a better economic and social environment provided by their husband. Thus, I would argue, poor rural and urban families are increasingly reliant upon financial support from daughters, who don't have to "save up for marriage," for financial support. This is an important reconfiguration of filial piety and the economic logic often used to justify the "traditional" preference for sons (see also Fong 2002).[5] And as I demonstrate below, this expectation of hypergamy (marrying up) creates several contradictions and dilemmas for wealthy female entrepreneurs.

In this chapter I analyze several ethnographic examples that involve the intersection of sexuality with wealth. More broadly, these cases reveal anxieties and underlying folk theories about the different effects money has on men's and women's motivations, relationships, desires, and morals. After outlining the characterizations that have arisen to capture the different types of professional and wealthy women in contemporary China, I look at female entrepreneurs' strategies for business entertaining, the role of sexuality in corruption accounts and anti-corruption legislation, the associations between sex work and entrepreneurialism, and the dilemmas surrounding marriage for both female entrepreneurs and young women who have served as mistresses.

The cases I examine—marriage, prostitution, the "beauty economy," and sexual bribery—all constitute important cultural battlegrounds for disputes over the proper relationship between intimacy, morality, and money (Zelizer 2005). Gail Hershatter (1994: 149) has argued in her work on the sale of sexual services in early twentieth-century Shanghai that "prostitution was not only a changing site of work for women, but also a metaphor, a medium of circulation in which the city's competing elites and emerging middle classes discussed their problems, fears, and agendas." In the reform period, prostitution, and the "beauty economy" more generally, have become important sites for discussions of the differing effects of money on men and women and the proper place and value of money within social relations. This transformation is often summarized with the phrase, "As soon as a man gets rich he goes bad, as soon as a women goes bad she gets rich" (*Nanren yiyou qian jiu huaile, nüren yihuaile jiu you qian*).

Since the May 4th Movement of 1919, Chinese reformers, including the Communist Party, have sought to purge marriage, and relationships between men and women in general, of material transactions.[6] While the notion of pure love and romance untainted by interest and familial interference continues to serve as an important reference point for many young and middle-aged urban Chinese in imagining and negotiating their romantic relationships, the examples below demonstrate the ways in which not just money but other forms of value—political status, family background, perceived sexual purity, educational level—continue to operate in the domains of marital and sexual relationships.

The narrative of economic success in a competitive environment and its concomitant pressures hovered over nearly all the discussions I had and articles I read that dealt with the sexuality of women. Many Internet discussions, scholarly analyses, and narrative accounts that focus on women who serve as paid mistresses and hostesses in fact frame the sale of sex as a "developed" form of entrepreneurialism: as the rational exploitation of marginalized women's only resource in a competitive economic environment. These discussions illustrate how market ideology has increasingly become the authoritative discourse through which many Chinese make sense of their own lives and the world around them.

In the examples below I look at instances in which women who serve as the lovers of rich men appropriate this discourse of entrepreneurialism to justify their choice of work and material success. Female entrepreneurs, perhaps the harshest critics of these women, however, argue that the women of the gray world are simply lazy, lacking in ability (*benshi*), and of low quality (*suzhi*). In my interviews with successful businesswomen, they were at pains to explain that—unlike young beauties (and unlike many men who relied on guanxi)—they had earned their wealth through their ability and hard work. Not only did they earn their success, they said, but ultimately they paid a bigger price: because they operate in the interstices of the sphere of masculine network building and the beauty economy, their femininity and sexual morality are under constant suspicion, often rendering them less-than-ideal marriage partners.

Character Types:
The Matrix of Wealth, Status, and Sexuality

During my first year in Chengdu I rented an apartment directly across the street from a large chain supermarket. On weekends, at a disturbingly early hour, it held "commercial performances" (*shangye biaoyan*) to promote a particular product, usually one marketed to young people. Soft drinks and instant noodles seemed to be the most common products being touted.

A stage and a shockingly loud sound system were set up in front of the supermarket, where dancers and singers, often scantily clad young women, performed to attract the attention of shoppers and passersby. These performances were interspersed with games in which audience members were brought on stage to participate. Prizes consisted of free samples of the product being promoted, and the games often integrated the products themselves, such as juice-drinking contests and quizzes about the product.

Meinü and *Shuaige*: Beautiful Women and Handsome Men

These performances drew large crowds, and audience members seemed eager to participate in the emcee-led games. Younger audience members, from preteen to mid-thirties, were usually the most common participants. The occasional child participant was addressed as "little friend" (*xiao pengyou*), and older adults were addressed by proper kinship terms such as "auntie" (*ayi*) or "uncle" (*daye*), but the vast majority of young participants were addressed by the increasingly hegemonic terms of address of both pop culture and the leisure industry: "handsome guy" (*shuaige*) and "beautiful woman" (*meinü*).

Many scholars have noted the shift from the gender-neutral address of comrade (*tongzhi*) from the Maoist period to the gender differentiated "mister" (*xiansheng*) and "miss" (*xiaojie*) during the reform period, a shift that signaled the relegitimization of naturalized femininity and masculinity in China (Rofel 1999, 2007, Yang 1999). In the new commercial spaces of department stores and high-end restaurants, *xiansheng* and *xiaojie* continue to be the preferred forms of address. But alongside mister and miss, shuaige and meinü are increasingly being used to hail a new type of subject. Both terms embody a gender ideal: Meinü are properly feminine, attractive, decorous, and fashion-conscious. Shuaige are masculine, cosmopolitan, and romantic. Among the entrepreneurs I worked with, meinü and shuaige were the preferred terms of address during banqueting and business entertaining. Not just paid hostesses, but female employees and entrepreneurs often called their male bosses or clients shuaige when toasting them. Businessmen also called female business associates meinü. While sometimes used playfully, these terms were employed as strategic forms of flattery that figured their addressee as a desirable, properly gendered subject.

In other contexts, meinü is often used to modify an occupation. When introducing me to the writers for *First Class* magazine, Mr. Zhu, the editor, described one of the magazine's columnists, matter of factly, as a "*meinü zuojia*," "a beautiful woman writer," implying that this was a special type of writer. Similarly, when his magazine did a profile of local female real estate entrepreneurs, they were labeled "*fangdichan meinü*," "the beautiful women of real estate," rather than simply women entrepreneurs (Liang 2005). The combination of *meinü* with their occupation served to indicate that these women were not *nüqiangren* (strong, career-oriented women) but women who, despite their achievements in the rough-and-tumble business world, have managed to retain proper femininity. While profiles of businessmen might describe them as handsome (*shuaiqi*), among other qualities, I never once encountered a male entrepreneur reduced to being labeled a "handsome businessman."

The key point here is that the notions of meinü and shuaige convey a particular status. This status is promoted and celebrated in popular culture, utilized by business, and aspired to by many young people. From the perspective of an aspiring female pop star, model, secretary, or flight attendant, the problem then becomes, how does a person know she is a meinü?[7] In the examples I describe below, I show how meinü status must be reflected and confirmed by other forms of value, among which the wealth and status of one's male partner are most important.

Nüqiangren: Strong Women, Female Entrepreneurs, and White-Collar Women

In all of my interviews with male entrepreneurs, I asked about their perceptions of female entrepreneurs and their experiences doing business with them. They almost universally expressed a disdain for female entrepreneurs. Their first criticism centered on their notion of nüqiangren (literally, "strong women"), a derogatory term for independent, career-oriented women. Nüqiangren were understood to lack feminine charms and virtues. Although most male entrepreneurs expressed a willingness to do business with them, they complained about any business entertaining that involved nüqiangren. When I asked Mr. Wu how he felt about participating in yingchou (entertaining) when women were present, he explained, "I don't like it when women [businesswomen] are there. It's hard to let loose." Ms. Li, the mining entrepreneur, who often had to pay for her male clients' and partners' entertainment, explained that she was usually expected to leave the men to themselves after inviting them to a KTV. She felt that it was "easier for men to build relationships" when she wasn't around.

To most wealthy men, nüqiangren were not considered desirable sex or marriage partners, despite the widespread belief that they possessed a voracious sexual appetite. Nüqiangren's lack of desirability was attributed to their deficient femininity and perceived sexual promiscuity. My interviewees attributed their lack of feminine virtue to two primary factors. First, their purity was under constant suspicion: most men and many women I interviewed assumed that any wealthy woman's path to success involved a man in some way. It was most often assumed that these women had at some point used their sexuality, either by serving as a mistress or by strategically sleeping with the right man, to acquire capital, move up in an organization, or secure a business deal. (In other words, they were suspected of being or having been "gray" women.) Because women were presumed to be less capable of bearing the pressures associated with business, they were more likely to be accused of "taking the shortcut" (zou jiejing)—using their sexuality to get ahead. This strategic use of older, wealthier men by young women to acquire apartments, cars, and startup capital for a business was also often referred to (without irony) as a form of "primitive accumulation" (*yuanshi jilei*).

Second, while most businessmen I worked with were quick to acknowledge that there were many capable (*hen nenggande*) businesswomen worthy of their admiration (*peifu*), these talented female entrepreneurs, who by virtue of age or appearance were assumed to have achieved their own success without relying on sexuality in some way, were frequently accused of being "masculine" (*you nanren wei*) in personality and demeanor. In particular, their refusal to perform the types of flattery, flirtation, and deference that businessmen were accustomed to from mistresses and hostesses led several entrepreneurs to describe them as "no fun" (*buhaowan*) or as making them feel "awkward" (*ganga*).

The means by which female entrepreneurs achieved success were under constant suspicion and subject to much speculation by both their male and female peers. Mr. Liao, the drinks distributor, asserted that "behind every nüqiangren there's a man supporting her." By this he meant not only that they had used their sexuality to achieve success, but that in their business dealings, many successful women stood on the shoulders of husbands or other male kin who had done the real work of guanxi and business for them. Even the female entrepreneurs I worked with differentiated between those who had received assistance from men or received their initial capital from divorces and those whose success was solely a product of their own efforts.

The lack of desirability of nüqiangren contrasted strongly with the sexual idealization of "white-collar women" (*bailing nüxing*) among the businessmen I interviewed and in many popular film and literary representations. White-collar women's careers were understood to be products of their own hard work and education and to reflect their overall quality (*suzhi*). Unlike female entrepreneurs, they were seen as less exposed to the polluting effects of the outside world of business because they had a fixed, stable income and worked in organizations where they were constantly monitored by their peers. In many magazine articles, white-collar women were depicted as having liberated views on sexuality that derived from their high levels of education and cultural sophistication rather than desperation (like the *fupo*, or rich women, below), poverty (like sex workers), or predatory nature (like nüqiangren). Bars and nightclubs sought to bring in white-collar female customers with discounts, prize giveaways, and shopping vouchers as a way of attracting more male customers hoping to meet them. Next to female university students, white-collar women were the most idealized group from which to find a lover.

Fupo: Rich Women and Parallel Forms of Sexual Patronage

Closely associated with *nüqiangren* was the category *fupo* (rich woman). Fupo were often portrayed as bored, hedonistic women of leisure playing with their husband's (or ex-husband's) money. Many fupo in Chengdu and many of the wives of the businessmen I knew did in fact spend most of their time shopping, playing mahjong or cards, and traveling. Most of their households' domestic work and child care was carried out by paid nannies and domestic servants (*baomu*). Some characterized themselves as *shuajia*—a term in the Sichuan dialect referring to those who live a life of full-time leisure free from work. Because they are assumed to have been sexually abandoned by their husbands, who presumably keep younger mistresses, fupo are understood to possess a voracious sexual appetite.[8] Others explained the appetites and hedonistic lifestyle of fupo as a product of their secure financial and social position. Because most husbands feared the loss of wealth that would result from a divorce, and fupo didn't have to worry about preserving their virtue in order to attract a husband, they could safely pursue their own desires.[9]

Despite the stereotype that they are hedonistic women of leisure, many fupo are involved in their husbands' businesses or have started businesses themselves. Ms. Sun's marriage was typical of the financial and domestic arrangements of many of the fupo I interviewed. Ms. Sun's husband made his fortune in the early 1990s as a car parts distributor and the owner of a taxi company. She explained that after their two children left for boarding school in Europe she was bored and lonely. Her husband gave her control of a few of his businesses and access to capital that she used to open a foot massage parlor (*xijiaofang*). She spent most of her time with her own circle of friends and business associates and managing her many enterprises. This is how she characterized her relationship with her husband:

> He doesn't supervise me, and I don't supervise him (*Wo buhui guan ta. Ta ye buhui guan wo*). We both come home whenever we want, and neither can ask the other any questions. We've come close to divorcing a few times but decided that there are still feelings between us. So we've decided it's best to stay together.

Since getting started in business, Ms. Sun had done very well. She was fond of singing karaoke, and would often invite a group of wealthy women to sing and drink in a KTV baofang. Occasionally they would bring along their husbands or boyfriends as well. Her social and professional activities were almost entirely separate from her husband's. It was nearly two years after I met her, at a formal banquet for her birthday, that I finally met her husband.

Increasingly there are clubs and bars in China's urban centers that aim to attract fupo and nüqiangren. The services offered in these clubs mirror almost exactly those found in clubs catering to men. In fact the imagined desires of wealthy women and the types of sexual relationships they are presumed to favor closely parallel those of rich men. In an online investigative exposé of a "rich woman's club" (*fupo julebu*) in Haikou, a tropical tourist destination in the south known for its sex industry, the author describes its workings in great, somewhat voyeuristic detail (*Da He Bao* 2007). The male author encounters a sign on the door that states, "Exclusive recreational zone for successful women, no men allowed." He's permitted to enter only after his female companion introduces him as her lover. The manager of the club describes the club's customers as follows:

> Basically, they're not just your average women. The majority are women who have started their own companies or who operate large businesses. Some are the wives of government officials whose husbands have mistresses. And of course some are the second wives of rich men, and some are single women "aristocrats" (*guizu*, i.e., the rich and powerful). . . . From our perspective it doesn't matter what kind of women they are as long as they have money. There's even a very famous female pop singer who comes occasionally. (*Da He Bao* 2007)

Significantly, the club manager lists the wives and mistresses of wealthy entrepreneurs and officials as among the club's most regular clients. Although their appetites and the types of services available to women of means closely replicate those of men, the underlying sources of their desires are accounted for in different ways.

According to popular explanations, wealthy men engage in extramarital and paid sex largely because they are constantly encountering the temptations of the outside world, which include aggressive younger women seeking male patrons. Men by their nature are believed to be unable to resist these temptations, especially in a context in which having a mistress is equated with elite status. Fupo, however, are seen to seek extramarital sex because they have been sexually and emotionally abandoned by their husbands. And because they lack youthful beauty, they are seen as having no choice but to pay. In contrast, mistresses are frequently portrayed as having a very cynical, calculating conception of sexual and romantic relationships. Their own experiences have led them to believe that sexual relationships are always mediated by money and laden with ulterior motives. Thus, in pursuing their own desires later in life they use money to recreate the same hierarchical relationships of patronage and control that they have experienced with wealthy men.

The article goes on to describe young, attractive men who work at the club and perform services nearly identical to those provided by hostesses in clubs catering to men. They drink, sing, and flirt with female customers at the club and are available for sexual services off site. These forms of female sexual patronage that closely mirror those of their male counterparts have attracted a great deal of discussion on the Internet (it is still a subject too sensitive for the print press), and they also provide fodder for jokes.

Specific labels describe the young men who make themselves available to wealthy older women for money. Male prostitutes who hang out in nightclubs, often dressed all in white, are known as "ducks" (*yazi*).[10] Certain clubs in Chengdu had a reputation for yazi, and I saw many young men who were aspirational, if not actual, yazi. Wealthy women are also purported to "support" (*baoyang*) young men, who are known as "little white faces" (*xiaobailian*). The men I encountered who served as yazi and xiaobailian were all young (in their late teens and early twenties). They sported fashionable hairstyles and clothing, often emulating the look of Hong Kong and Taiwanese pop stars. Most were from a rural background. While most had slim, youthful bodies, some made an effort to develop muscular physiques that they displayed whenever possible.

Many of the men who serve as "kept men" are aspiring actors, singers, or dancers. Just as wealthy men often speculated on the price of spending the night with an up-and-coming female pop star, wealthy women could reportedly book the services of male stars for a price. A professor at a prominent performing arts school in Beijing claimed that an increasing number of his male students hoped to be "kept" (*baoyang*) as "a way to show off their talent" (*Da Yang Wang* 2007). In addition to sexual services, they are expected to accompany their female patrons to dinner and other social engagements.

Although serving as a kept man is perhaps gaining acceptance in the world of arts and entertainment, most of my interviewees, both male and female, viewed it as unmasculine and shameful.[11] I met a few men who were rumored to be or have been yazi or xiaobailian, but they were very reluctant to talk with me about their experiences. Research informants who knew yazi would often comment on the toll it took on men's bodies. Given the belief in the voraciousness of older women, they claimed that yazi had no choice but to take harmful medicines that would allow them to perform sexually multiple times an evening.

A few months into my fieldwork in Chengdu I was contacted by a friend whose former female classmate was the entertainment manager at a popular nightclub located in the basement of a five-star international hotel. The club was popular with entrepreneurs and state enterprise managers visiting Chengdu on business, and it had a reputation for having some of the most beautiful hostesses in town. The manager told me they were looking for foreign (i.e., white) male models to do a nightly "fashion show" at their club, and she was hoping I could help recruit some foreign men to participate. When I met with her she explained that the club was hoping to expand its customer base by attracting wealthy female entrepreneurs in Chengdu on business as well as fupo who lived in the city.

Her idea for the fashion show was that the men would prance around on stage to techno music and perform sexually suggestive gyrations. The men wouldn't be asked to remove any clothing, but she hoped that they would wear partially unbuttoned dress shirts and shorts "to show off their legs." The dancers would be paid a salary to show up nightly for a seven-minute performance. And if they wished to earn extra money, they would be encouraged to make themselves available to keep female customers company (*pei*). The men would be paid a standard fee of 300 RMB for sitting and drinking with a female customer. Male dancers were told that they could expect tips on top of that, and if they were willing, they could accompany women to their rooms for whatever fee they could negotiate, from which the club expected to receive a 200 RMB kickback.

Several foreign men, mostly students and English teachers, expressed a willingness to participate and were quite enthusiastic about the prospect of potentially being paid for sexual services. However, the show ran for only a week and was then abandoned. The foreigners complained about having to show up every night to perform, but more important, the club failed to attract more than a few female customers. The club's failure suggests that perhaps fupo are not as numerous or as lascivious as they are imagined to be.

Women Entrepreneurs and the Beauty Economy

Female entrepreneurs I interviewed made a considerable effort to differentiate themselves from young women who used their youth, beauty, or sexuality to gain a comfortable life, and they frequently discussed the increasing willingness of young women to use their sexuality to get ahead. Businesswomen emphasized their own ability (*benshi*) and hard work (*nuli*) as the basis of their success. They viewed young women who "ate the rice of youth" as having a strong desire for material comfort but lacking the ability, education, or suzhi to achieve it. These women were described simply as "taking the shortcut" (*zou jiejing*).

In some interviews, businesswomen cited these young women's willingness to use sexual relationships with powerful men to get ahead as evidence of their poor upbringing, lack of cultivation (*xiuyang*), and poor overall quality (*suzhi*), regardless of what their actual educational and family backgrounds might be. In other interviews, female entrepreneurs assumed that because these women lacked a good education and family background to begin with, their only means of getting ahead was to use their sexuality strategically.

Ms. Wen, the wife of a wealthy real estate investor, explained: "these women blindly pursue fashionable, high-class things but they lack the ability to obtain them themselves. Thus they must rely on men to lead a comfortable life." Mr. Liao saw a similar discrepancy between their aspirations and their ability. He saw them as duped by media images of material comfort, luxury, and fashion: "They mistakenly think that everyone can obtain these things without much effort. When they realize how hard it is to succeed, they decide that it's easier just to rely on a man than to work hard themselves." In describing what she saw as the sad state of marriage among wealthy, urban Chinese couples, Ms. Long condemned rich men's obsession with young women, but then added, "You can't blame the men entirely because lots of women want to 'take the shortcut.' They're constantly looking for rich men to support them." To female entrepreneurs, the beauty economy was populated by women with questionable morals and unchecked ambitions looking to take the easy road to success.

Sometimes different regional characteristics were invoked to account for the behavior of these women. Ms. Hu, the owner of a national restaurant chain, was from China's northeast. As a northerner, she often attributed the moral weakness of the women around her to Sichuanese local culture. She once told me about an attempt by a famous male newspaper editor to seduce her. She was shocked by his behavior and attributed it to his having been in Sichuan too long and accustomed to the local women. She exclaimed, "Those women in Sichuan are really . . . *you know* . . . and they don't even want money!" To Ms. Hu, to sell oneself for money was shameful, but to offer oneself for free was simply irrational.

Ms. Gao's public relations company's primary business was organizing and staging events for other businesses—opening ceremonies, anniversaries, and various promotional events, activities that constitute the very core of the beauty economy. These ceremonies consisted of speeches from VIPs, songs, dances, and musical performances. Virtually all of these events employed the techniques of the beauty economy: scantily clad female dancers, beauty contests, and "fashion shows." Although she occasionally hired special performers on a per-event basis, most of the performances were by a troupe of male and female dancers, singers, and models regularly employed by her company. These young performers all aspired to be stars in the entertainment world, beyond public relations.

I first met Ms. Gao at the opening ceremony for a luxury real estate development outside of Chongqing, an event that her company had successfully bid to stage. Her company had organized all the decorations, performances, and entertainment for the multi-day event. I was invited to attend the ceremony by a friend who worked for a health clinic catering to the elite and expatriate community. The clinic was planning to open a branch in the gated community to serve its well-heeled residents. Because none of the clinic's foreign doctors was available to make the trip, I was asked to sit at their booth to give the clinic a "foreign face." (Little did I know that I would be introduced during a banquet as a Canadian doctor and asked to give a brief lecture on healthy living to a group of wealthy entrepreneurs about to begin a traditional banquet involving the exchange of cigarettes, countless shots of 112 proof liquor, and dishes of fried pork belly (*huigourou*).

The weekend featured several banquets to entertain the developers, members of the media, local government officials, and potential VIP buyers. The banquets were held in a private dining hall featuring a small stage for performances. The backdrop of the stage featured larger-than-life-sized photographs of five young women, each of which was labeled "Miss Internationals" (*Guoji Xiaojie*), giving the audience the impression that they were contestants in (or winners of) a prestigious beauty competition, when in fact no such competition existed.

At the first lunch banquet, Ms. Gao introduced the Miss Internationals to the audience, promised that we would get to know more about the Miss Internationals and see them perform later in the evening, and sent one off to each table of VIPs. The evening banquet then featured a pageant-like talent contest with the Miss Internationals singing and dancing. Afterwards they were again distributed among the VIP tables to keep important guests company while they drank and ate.

FIGURE 5.1. "Miss Internationals" being introduced to the audience at the opening ceremony of a luxury housing development.

FIGURE 5.2. Dancers performing for the same event shown in Figure 5.1.

This event was typical of the way young women are employed in these ceremonies. The subtext is that audience members might get to meet real beauties, and in the case of Ms. Gao's Miss Internationals, interaction with important VIPs was part of their work assignment (*renwu*).

Before their performance Ms. Gao went over in great detail with her performers and models their instructions for the evening. These included whether they were expected to accompany guests after their performance and what kinds of invitations they were allowed to accept. She stipulated the precise time at which they needed to be back in their hotel rooms, and if they were allowed (or expected) to consume alcohol during or after dinner. It was crucial to the effectiveness of her performances (and ultimately to the success of her business) that she manage the reputations and desirability of her female performers such that they struck a balance between appearing above board and pure (and thus immune from accusations of prostitution) and maintaining the hope in their male clients that they were available for a romantic relationship.

Months after our initial meeting at this ceremony, I asked Ms. Gao if there were any advantages or disadvantages she faced as a female entrepreneur. She said that on the whole, women have a more difficult time doing business and that women in business must "sacrifice themselves" (*xisheng ziji*) in a way that men do not. She explained that even if one doesn't literally sacrifice one's body to achieve success, women will sacrifice their reputation, femininity, and ultimately their marriageability. Because of her status as both an entrepreneur and a member of the entertainment world, men often assumed that Ms. Gao used her sexuality freely in her business dealings. This was apparent in the way some of my other informants perceived Ms. Gao. One evening, after introducing her to Mr. Wang, he whispered to me with disgust, "Just think how many men a woman like that has slept with."

However, Ms. Gao explained that there were some advantages to being a woman in business, especially in the realm of yingchou. She explained that she had become quite skilled at the techniques associated with yingchou and that as a trained actress and performer she was skilled at faking enjoyment and flattering her clients. She thought that, as a woman, she was inherently more skilled at the arts of goudui and manipulating the hearts of men, but that this skill had its inherent risks. Men sometimes took her flattery too literally and intimated that they were interested in a sexual relationship or even offered her money to drink and socialize with them. Sometimes these gestures took an indirect form—"Let's talk more about your proposal for our company over dinner," but sometimes they were very overt and presented an obstacle to business negotiations.

She explained that she employed a few techniques for dealing with overzealous men. One involved refusing to follow the script of a coquettish, innocent woman when flirting with these men. Instead, when men hinted at a sexual relationship, she would aggressively suggest that they go to a hotel room right away. This usually had the effect of embarrassing the man, or at least easing the tension. At other times she would feign interest but invent excuses to ward off any possibility of a sexual relationship.

Her preferred means of dealing with yingchou, especially when it involved "lusty, older men" (*lao selang*), however, was to have her female employees accompany her clients during evenings of entertaining. She explained, "Most of the girls in my company are like Yang Mei [one of the Miss Internationals]. They don't have much *suzhi* (quality). They want to be rich or famous, so they're willing to accompany our clients. They want to take the shortcut of 'leaning on big money' (*bang dakuan*) or 'leeching off a government official' (*zheng guanyuan*)." Referring to the aspiring singers and actresses in her company she explained, "They want to become famous. Who doesn't want to become famous? [By keeping accompany with wealthy men] they can meet people and exhibit themselves (*zhanshi ziji*)." She felt that most "mainland Chinese girls are cheap" (*jian*, which can also be understood as "low or base").

Ms. Gao explained that in the entertainment industry and businesses that employ young women, using sex to advance one's career is all but required: "They [aspiring stars] see that everyone is sleeping around, and they think I might as well sleep my way to the top as well. . . . Except that now it's even more frightening. With today's directors you don't just need to sleep with them you also have to give them money." In fact, movie stars in China are commonly divided into two categories that reflect whether their fame is based primarily on their looks (and presumably their sexual strategies) or on their artistic abilities. The former are labeled the "idol group" (*ouxiang pai*), and the latter are called the "ability group" (*shili pai*).

Despite justifying the instrumental use of her female employees by citing their low quality and high ambitions, Ms. Gao still felt that she had some responsibility to protect them. She thought it best to offer money whenever possible to a lustful client looking for a financial or libidinal kickback rather than "sacrifice" one of her female employees. However, on several occasions out with Ms. Gao and her friends, I witnessed her calling one of her female employees and demanding that she join the group for the purpose of accompanying a man, usually a business associate or a client. When the woman hesitated or said that she had other plans, Ms. Gao firmly declared, "This a work assignment (*gongzuo renwu*). Attendance is mandatory."

Despite her attempts to differentiate herself from her employees and operate above the base level of the beauty economy, Ms. Gao was not immune from the expectations of wealthy men looking to be flattered and entertained by younger women. Near the end of my fieldwork I went to meet Mr. Wei, the demolition boss, at a KTV club. When I entered the room I was surprised to find Ms. Gao there alone with him, singing a song on the karaoke machine. (Before this evening, I had never seen Ms. Gao, a formerly nationally known pop star, sing outside of formal performances.) She was embarrassed and surprised to learn that I knew Mr. Wei. She then used it as a pretext to compliment Mr. Wei, saying that he was a famous entrepreneur in Chengdu with international connections. She then quickly excused herself and left.

Female entrepreneurs were well aware that many Chinese men perceived them as either unfeminine or sexually suspect. Some took this as evidence of the backwardness or "feudal" nature of Chinese men's thinking, especially in relation to an idealized West where married women work, have successful careers, and enjoy other types of independence. But others internalized this critique and became very anxious about not projecting sufficient femininity. Another female entrepreneur, Ms. Lai, while proud of her business success and independence, feared being viewed as a nüqiangren, which she claimed was the equivalent to a "woman that no man would love" and "a woman that men dare not touch." She herself hoped that she could become a "woman with a double face—a self-confident, self-sufficient woman outside [in the world of career and society] and a little, humble woman at home. At home I can't boss men around [like I do my employees] . . . I hope I can be a feminine woman."

A self-proclaimed meinü, Ms. Lai felt that her attractiveness gave her an advantage in business. She boasted that she could arrange meetings with hard-to-meet bosses and officials, and that they were often reluctant to turn her down. She thought that women were more vulnerable in business to being cheated or taken advantage of because of their more "emotional" natures. This vulnerability, however, was counterbalanced by women's ability to pull at the heartstrings of men and take advantage of men's lascivious (semimi) nature. She felt that she could use her attractiveness to negotiate more favorable terms in a contract. And in a context in which several entrepreneurs with similar capabilities are competing to land a deal, she believed that her beauty distinguished her from the crowd. (She was careful to describe this as an extension of goudui techniques and to distinguish it from what "other women" are willing to do.)

Many female entrepreneurs have developed strategies for navigating the sphere of masculine business entertaining, but marriage, which is still largely socially compulsory in China, is a sphere of contradictory expectations and desires. For many wealthy women searching for a marriage partner, and in marital relationships, the contradictions of wealth, autonomy, and ideologies of gender often prove unresolvable.

For Status, Money, and Security: Marriage and Materiality

One of the stated goals of the Chinese Communist Party's social revolution was the elimination of the "feudal" aspects of the Chinese family. In the domain of marriage this meant the abolition of marriages arranged by parents, concubinage, polygyny, child betrothal, the buying and selling of brides, and the general conception of marriage as a material transaction involving money or gifts. The CCP promoted marriage as a contract between two individuals, entered into freely and bound by mutual love, support, and assistance; on paper (but not always in practice), the Party supported the equal rights of husband and wife within a marital relationship.

In his study of love and marriage during the Maoist years, Neil Diamant (2000: 7) argues that "alongside this May 4th–inspired notion of 'free choice' individualist marriage was a second, contradictory impulse oriented toward molding people's choices according to the state's ideology." Part of this "impulse" was to promote marriages between individuals of similar class background:

> "Real love," according to one newspaper article, "cannot exist between a feudalistic [person] and a progressive person." In practice, this meant that people who were given politically "progressive" class status, such as poor and middle peasants, workers, cadres, soldiers, and wives of revolutionary martyrs, should try to avoid fraternization with, and marriage to, people assigned to "bad" class categories, such as former landlords, capitalists, counterrevolutionaries, "bad elements," and "rightists." (Diamant 2000: 7)

Especially during the height of political campaigns directed against the counterrevolutionary elements in society, individuals were reluctant to marry or even associate with those possessing a bad class status. During the Cultural Revolution (1966–76), husbands and wives were even pressured to divorce spouses who had become the targets of political campaigns or political criticism. In contrast, men with a good class background, with official rank, or from a revolutionary family became the most desirable marriage partners, partly because of the political security and material perquisites their status brought.[12]

In addition to political status, other values, including notions of material comfort, urban residency, and social status, also factored heavily into marriage choices in the first decade and a half of the PRC (Diamant 2000: 7). Male cadres, who were mostly from rural areas, often divorced their peasant wives for women from the city who, despite their imperfect class backgrounds, were still viewed by cadres as more appropriate to their high status than peasant women (264). According to one of my interviewees, a great deal of folklore and many jokes from this era also involve the scheming of cadres hoping to marry or have sexual relationships with daughters of landlords. Despite their counterrevolutionary class status, these young women were thought to be more beautiful and refined than revolutionary peasant women.

Although the importance of political status and class background in marriages after 1978 diminished when the class status system was abandoned, the May 4th dream of removing material transactions from marriage and sexual relationships suffered a setback during the reform period. To the dismay of many intellectuals, in many rural areas brideprice and dowry exchange reemerged almost immediately after 1978 and were subject to rapid inflation as rural economies improved (Honig and Hershatter 1988; Croll 1994).

By the early 1990s, forms of prostitution, concubinage, and even the buying and selling of wives in rural areas reappeared (Gates 1989; Hershatter 1997; Evans 1997; Jeffreys 2004). And after an initial period in which male entrepreneurs were viewed with suspicion because of their uncertain political status, their growing wealth made them the most sought-after marriage partners. Once again, intellectuals were decrying the return of a "feudal" mentality in marriage. He Qinglian summarizes this constant deferment of true-love marriage as follows:

> Even in the context of the revolution and the elimination of the power of money, there were just different versions of the same story [the power of young beautiful women and successful men]. In China during the fifties, men's capital, or their resource for climbing the social ladder, was not money but their "revolutionary background." During that time, old revolutionaries became the "knights

in shining armor," while in the early seventies the "prince charmings" were military cadres and employees of state enterprises. Today countless pretty young women are dreaming of becoming modern "Cinderellas"; it's just that their "Prince Charmings" are now the entrepreneurs of the modern business world. Every Chinese woman has her own unhappy story from those times. The only thing that hasn't changed is the "same old story" of the combined development of the effective resources of men (wealth and status) and of women (youthful beauty). (He 2005)

He Qinglian, influenced by the economist Gary Becker's theory of marriage (Becker 1973; 1974), sees this exchange as transhistorical and culturally universal: men trading their assets of money and status for women's assets of youthful beauty. This view represents what Viviana Zelizer (2005) in her work on intimacy and money has called a "nothing but" argument: that intimate relations are and have always been governed by market principles despite our attempts to characterize them otherwise. While He Qinglian argues for the need to temper this market with ideals of morality and gender equality, many young women in the reform period, especially those associated with the beauty economy, have appropriated this "nothing but" argument to justify their choice of partners. In their view, if marriage is "nothing but" a transaction, and ultimately part of the same economic-sexual system as the lowest levels of prostitution, then why not pursue the best price? Against those who would condemn them as "immoral," these young women assert that they are merely following the laws of the market, if not the laws of human nature. They claim that women who think otherwise are simply naïve or deluded (Xu 1996: 394). In discussions of the marriages of the new rich, one regularly finds a great deal of these "nothing but" arguments.

Marriage ads and matchmaking services during the reform period, which operate at the intersection of ideologies of wealth, gender, and sexuality, have provoked a great deal of public discussion and debate over the proper role of money in marital relationships and the respective moralities of young women and wealthy men.

Since the late 1990s, hundreds of ultra-wealthy, middle-aged men in China have taken out marriage ads, held exclusive parties, or even organized talent competitions to find a bride. One often-noted characteristic of these competitions is that the requirements for potential brides are virtually identical in each. He Xin, a lawyer who organized ad campaigns and spousal selection competitions for three different men, each "having a net worth" over 100 million RMB, stated that they all wanted the same type of woman: "pretty, young, fair-skinned (*bai*), cute (*guai*), and a virgin (*chunü*)" (Li Haipeng 2006). He Xin surmises that they desire virgins for their increasing rarity in China.[13]

While some accounts have focused on the bride-seekers' desire for "traditional" women, the motivations of the thousands of female applicants to these competitions have received more media attention. In newspaper interviews with female contestants in these competitions, many were forthright about being motivated by money. A university student from Dalian explained that at first she was disgusted by her classmates' relationships with men old enough to be their fathers. She said that after a year in college, however, she "grew up" and came to feel that "only money could give her a feeling of security (*anquangan*)" (Li Haipeng 2006).

Many of the applicants expressed a cynicism toward marriage, asserting that in a context of little trust in marital and romantic relationships "everyone is the same." One woman from Shanghai stated, "If I marry a normal person it's possible that I'll end up with nothing. If I marry a rich man at least I'll end up with some money." While many applicants viewed the man's desire for a virgin as feudalistic and out of date, one applicant asked, "Isn't the point of keeping it [virginity] to be able to sell it for a good price?" (Li Haipeng 2006).

Many of the participants viewed success in these competitions as confirmation of their beauty and traditional feminine virtues. They framed their desire for wealthy men as a rational utilization of these "resources." He Qinglian (2005) recounts the story of a well-educated recent college graduate with a degree in business administration. She hoped to use her knowledge and ability to pursue a rewarding career. After getting fired a few times, presumably by bosses who wanted her to become their mistress, she became skeptical that relying on her knowledge and skills alone would allow her to get ahead and chose to become an *ernai* (second wife) to a wealthy businessman. She draws a parallel between men's use of their connections and women's use of youth and beauty to get ahead:

> In essence, men using their power and connections and women using their youth and beauty are the same. Both are a rational utilization of one's personal resources. When a woman marries her husband she's selling her body one time to another person. Once your husband becomes rich and famous and you are old, it's likely that you'll be dumped. However, if you are kept [*baoyang*] as a mistress you can sell your body many times to multiple men. From the perspective of efficiency, it's better than selling it to one person. Moreover, if you let the

resource of youth sit idly, after a few years it will naturally disappear, you won't have utilized its value. (He 2005)

Like many of the other applicants, this young woman depicts marriage, serving as a mistress, and prostitution as part of a single market. She justifies her decision to serve as a mistress to multiple men as the most efficient use of her resources.

Women who participate in the beauty economy often view "landing" a wealthy husband or a rich patron as confirmation of their feminine virtues. Just as the beauty of their girlfriends was understood by the entrepreneurs I worked with to be iconic of the state of a man's business ventures, the status and wealth of the man to whom a woman became sexually allied was often interpreted as reflecting her desirability and as confirming her status as a meinü.

Young women often spoke of a hierarchy of beauties based on where they could successfully compete. The most "talented" left for wealthy eastern cities such as Beijing and Shanghai, and the truly exceptional might make it to Hong Kong, Taiwan, or even Europe. An unsuccessful contestant in one of the marriage competitions for a wealthy entrepreneur consoled herself by stating, "Maybe I'm not suited for someone with a fortune of 100 million, but maybe I'm suitable for someone with 10 million" (Li Haipeng 2006).

Although female entrepreneurs condemn these women for their lack of ability and their low quality (suzhi), in many narratives, the young women in the beauty economy frame their desirability to wealthy men (especially when they shirk their familial duties or divorce their wives for them) as a form of ability (benshi). For these young women, it is the older wives who lack the ability to hang on to their husbands. Similarly, they portray female entrepreneurs and career women as inherently unattractive and unfeminine and therefore resentful of the power of young beauties to steal away their husbands and boyfriends. As one female university student put it to me, "If they weren't so ugly they [career women] wouldn't have to work so hard."

The degree of philandering tolerated by wives was often correlated with the wife's ability to support herself independently of her husband. I asked my informants how wives felt about the activities of their husbands, in particular their often not-too-concealed affairs. Ms. Long, who knew a great many married women from their early twenties to mid-forties, felt that their reaction to their husbands' affairs depended on their own ability and suzhi: "Most quietly tolerate it and focus on their children. Others get lost in shopping or playing mahjong." Ms. Zhang explained that women from rural backgrounds were more likely to tolerate affairs and even open "second wives": "Women from the city probably won't tolerate it, but women from the countryside, especially those with no education, will likely tolerate it so they can continue to live an urban life."

Despite feelings of abandonment, jealousy, and betrayal, some first wives view themselves as possessing more staying power than mistresses, who are likely to be discarded for another young woman. He Qinglian (2005) recounts an exchange between a first wife (*dapo*) and a mistress (*xiaopo*) that captures this notion: "The young, delicate and charming mistress mocks the wife by saying, 'You don't have the ability to hang on to your husband.' But the wife replies, 'Do you have the ability to stay with him until you're old?'"

In a very popular series of interviews on love in contemporary China, the Beijing journalist An Dun interviews a Beijing women, Han Yuanyuan, who has moved to Shenzhen and has been the mistress to several wealthy Hong Kong businessmen. Ms. Han views the instrumental use of her attractiveness as a rational deployment of her skills and abilities. She argues that it is an innate (*tiansheng*) characteristic of women to rely on men for support (An 2002: 275). This leads to a Darwinian struggle among women over the patronage of men:

> Why do other women detest me? Because my existence is a threat to them. All men like me, and these men include their husbands. What woman doesn't fear her husband being stolen by another woman? When a man takes off with another woman [literally, "a woman from outside," *waimiande nüren*], the woman at home doesn't dare blame her husband as being worthless, and she doesn't dare admit to herself that she doesn't have the ability to hang on to her man's heart. She can only curse the other woman for being a "chicken" [slang for prostitute] and "not wanting face" [*buyao lian*—i.e., not caring about public opinion]. (An 2002: 275)

She gives examples of all the things women do to maintain their beauty, such as putting on makeup, buying lingerie, and having plastic surgery, and asks why they go to such lengths:

> Is it to make women appreciate themselves? Is it a reflection of equality between men and women? What a load of crap! I don't believe it. They're nothing but techniques for women to better control men. Women need to operate from a strategically advantageous position [*gaowujianling*]. Look behind all those successful woman, which one doesn't have a few successful men who've served as their stepping stone [*renti*]? (An 2002: 281)

Here, she echoes many male entrepreneurs' claim against female entrepreneurs: they rely on men for their success. Ms. Han goes on to employ an ends-justify-the-means argument, asserting that material success trumps all other forms of value in contemporary Chinese society:

> My mother told me that this is an age in which "history is written by the victors" [*chengwangbaikou*], especially for women. No one cares how you succeeded, what methods you used, what you sacrificed, what price you paid, who you hurt, or whether or not you lack morals. What people pay attention to is whether or not you've succeeded. The common people [*laobaixing*] envy successful people. If you're not successful and elite [*gaoshang*], who will pay any attention to you? (An 2002: 279)

For Ms. Han, those who condemn "gray women" as immoral are both behind the times and in denial of the "reality" of contemporary Chinese society. The only form of value that matters is money, and the successful will be looked up to no matter how they've made it.[14]

Because female university students were the most sought-after group for lovers and mistresses, university students I interviewed were particularly observant and critical of the workings of the beauty economy. A group of male and female art students I met with on occasion felt that at their school the concern with maintaining the appearances of wealth had gotten "out of hand" among their female classmates: "Most female students here are embarrassed to take the bus or ride a bike to class. They think that if you're not dropped off by an imported car or at least by a taxi people look down on you." They claimed that some female students without a wealthy male patron would strategically sit alone in teahouses and coffeehouses frequented by wealthy entrepreneurs in the hopes of meeting a rich male patron.

I asked both female friends and male patrons of female university students if they hid their relationships from their classmates. Mr. Wu stated, "It used to be that they would hide it. Now they want me to introduce my friends to their friends." A roommate of a student who had a rich boyfriend paying her tuition explained, "They are not embarrassed at all. They view themselves as talented. (*Tamen juede ziji hen nenggande*), and they see this as confirmation of their abilities." When I asked entrepreneurs I knew whether their mistresses were embarrassed or felt shame about being involved with a married man, most of the men replied that their girlfriends were only concerned with how they were treated by their boyfriends. As one informant put it, "Being happy is all that matters to her" (*Ta juede ziji kaixin jiu keyile*). Others said, "she's quite proud of being with me. With me she's much better off than many of her classmates back in her hometown, and when she sees them she can show them how well she's doing."

While intellectuals and elite reformers have attempted to impose a notion of romantic purity on marriages and sexual relationships, as I argued in Chapter Two, the notion that material support is the basis of marital and other sexual relationships is quite acceptable to many working-class and rural Chinese. In my limited conversations with the mistresses of wealthy men, they often pointed out "he's good to me," which was most evidenced by his providing for their (and often their relatives') material needs. Among women from poor rural backgrounds in particular, the notion of having an easier life, often captured by the phrase "*guode hao*" (living and getting along well), was invoked to justify their relationships. In fact, providing them with material support was cited as evidence of a "responsible" man (*you zerengan*), who was willing to demonstrate his affection with his money. They often contrasted this with "playboys" (*huahuagongzi*) who promise many things but, once they get what they want, move on to other women, leaving their lovers behind with nothing.

A reporter for a local Chengdu newspaper who often wrote about family issues, including second wives and extramarital affairs, felt that mistresses' reliance on wealthy men was a reflection of the gendered upbringing of most rural Chinese:

> A lot of these women are migrants from the countryside. They just want to have a better life, and having a wealthy man provide for them is seen as an easy way. In fact, they're raised to think that way. In China, sons are taught that they have to work hard and be successful so they can support others. But girls are taught that they can just marry a good husband, and they will have an easy life.

He went on to explain that parents are often supportive of these relationships, viewing them as a way for their daughters to live a comfortable life in the city without having to work long hours for low pay in the service or manufacturing industries. Some parents have financial motives as well: a responsible male patron for their daughter would likely take care of them too, perhaps later in life.[15] The sentiment that being a capable, successful woman was a much tougher and ultimately less rewarding path than simply marrying well was often captured by the rhyming phrase, "Doing a good job can't beat marrying well" (*Gande hao buru jiade hao*). Mr. Wu, who at one point provided for three different mistresses simultaneously, could understand the appeal of relying on a man for financial security. When I asked him, "What do you think about women who just look for rich men?" he replied:

> Part of it is laziness, part of it is vanity, but if you're just an ordinary worker, think about how many years it takes just to buy an apartment. If they can find a rich man, then all their problems are solved. There's no need to put forth much more effort.

Mr. Wu points to the economic reality that buying an urban apartment is simply out of reach for many rural migrants and working-class (and increasingly middle-class) Chinese. More sympathetic media accounts of mistresses and hostesses often point to these economic pressures to explain these women's desire to rely on men for financial support.

Ms. Xu, a middle-class employee of an advertising agency, felt that all women, not just rural migrants, face the same economic uncertainty:

> Most women, even many white-collar women, have an "ulterior motive" [you mudi] in their [romantic] relationships. Why is that? Very few people's economic problems [in China] are thoroughly solved. Even white-collar workers like me face really intense competition. I might be better off than a lot of people, but I still don't really have any kind of safety net [baozhang].

Despite her self-definition as a "white-collar worker," much of Ms. Xu's income came from commissions she received on advertising she sold for a television show, and there was a great deal of fluctuation in her monthly income. Her husband was a truck driver who made a decent salary but had few prospects for advancement. She saw it as understandable and inevitable that concern about money would factor heavily into all sexual relationships, and into marriage in particular. In an interesting twist on Engels's (1972) theories of marriage, love, and class in which private property is an impediment to pure relationships rooted in "sex-love," she posited that pure love and sexual relationships untainted by other motives and economic considerations could only occur among "high-level white-collar workers" (gaoji bailing) or among the "rich and powerful" (guizu), who she presumed were the types of people most likely to have "one-night stands" (yiyeqing) that didn't involve money.

Because of their fleeting, transitory nature, "one-night stands" were often depicted by other informants as domains of pure passion untainted by considerations of money, status, reputation, or responsibility.[16] They assumed that any lasting relationship between men and women, even of a similar financial background, was bound to have an economic component.

Many mistresses and girlfriends of wealthy men portray themselves as winners in a market that trades in attractiveness for material comfort; others, in a similar reworking of Engels, frame their relationships as pure romantic love, unsullied by all the other considerations that usually factor into marriage (see also Farrer 2002; Farrer and Sun 2003). In his overview of journalistic literature on women in the reform period, Xu Xiaoqun (1996) notes that many women who came of age in the 1980s and 1990s were influenced by the writings of Engels on marriage and property. They "took to heart Engels' assertion that loveless bourgeois marriages were immoral and that in the future the sole basis for marriage would be love between the sexes, without economic or other considerations" (Xu 1996: 401).

In journalistic depictions of young women who had affairs with married men (often entrepreneurs) in the late twentieth century, writers often framed their relationship as one of love or of pure sexual passion, and the man's marriage as loveless and likely "tainted" by considerations of family background and money. This framing coincided with the ways in which many wealthy men understood their extramarital relationships as well. Because marriage was viewed as a domain of responsibility and respectability, many men viewed extramarital relationships with lovers and mistresses as the true domain of romance and passion.[17]

Women Entrepreneurs and Marriage

Despite their different characterizations of sexual and marital relationships, a stable, happy marriage was a major goal for both female entrepreneurs and participants in the beauty economy. Some characterized marriage as the only means to financial security in a job market in which women were disadvantaged, and others harbored less cynical views of marriage, characterizing it as a relationship of mutual financial and emotional support. Most of the unmarried or divorced female entrepreneurs I worked with expressed a desire to marry or remarry, but their justifications for doing so varied considerably. The majority of them, though somewhat skeptical of the possibility of a happy marriage in the moral environment of Chengdu, mentioned the pressure of compulsory marriage that came from their parents and peers. They worried about the disappointment and anxiety they caused their parents by remaining single. Others imagined marriage as a retreat from the demands of their business, as a context in which they could finally enjoy their wealth. Some had little interest in a husband but hoped to have a child someday. In a context in which being a single mother is still stigmatized, they saw marriage as their only realistic path to motherhood.

Ms. Zhang and Ms. Lai were both entrepreneurs in their early thirties and unmarried. Both hoped to get married but expressed a lot of conflicting feelings about marriage. Ms. Zhang viewed domestic life as a potential retreat from the stresses of her business, while Ms. Lai seemed to be more concerned with appeasing her parents, who worried about her "advanced age" (30 in 2006) as a single woman. At the time I met her, Ms. Zhang was in a relationship with a married man. Certain that her boyfriend would never divorce his wife, she believed that the relationship had no future but felt that, unlike many of the men she did business with, matters were relatively simple with this boyfriend and that he was someone she could trust and confide in. He also didn't make any demands on her wealth or interfere with her business in any way. However, after more than a year with this man she broke up with him and began dating a much younger man who was a recent arrival to the city from the countryside. Ms. Zhang characterized herself as his "big sister" (*jiejie*), explaining that he was new to the city and needed lots of help and guidance. Despite the fact that she assisted him financially, she was quick to clarify that he was not her "little white face" (*xiaobailian*—kept man).

All of the female entrepreneurs I talked with saw wealth as the biggest obstacle in their relationships with men. According to them, the vast majority of Chinese men would be unwilling to marry a woman with an income higher than their own, as most men would view this as a loss of face. (Marrying a wealthier woman would imply that they lacked the ability to support a family on their own.)

Ms. Li estimated that 60 to 70 percent of female bosses in China were single, asserting that women "pay a bigger price for success" by damaging their marital prospects.[19] Although most female entrepreneurs expressed a willingness to marry a man with a lower income, they feared being taken advantage of by such men, who were often seen as morally suspect given their willingness to "lose face" by marrying a wealthier woman.

Ms. Lai, still single in her early thirties, had been financially swindled by some of her previous boyfriends: "First they conned me emotionally, and then they conned me out of my money" (*xian pianle wode ganqing, ranhou pianle wode qian*). Ms. Wang was also wary of men who would marry a woman with much more money, interpreting their willingness to do so as confirmation of their lack of ambition. "There are a lot of guys out there willing to 'eat soft rice' [i.e., live off a woman, *chiruanfan*]. They might be really good-looking, but that's all they've got going for them."

In addition to the obstacles posed by their wealth, many female entrepreneurs complained about the chauvinistic thinking of Chinese men, which Ms. Lai summed up as, "[even if] they don't have much ability themselves, they still want to be the emperor at home." Although she viewed them as desirable and capable, men with higher incomes than hers were also the ones most likely to forbid her to work and force her to give up her financial independence. Because of their high status, they were the most concerned with marrying a woman of unquestioned feminine virtue. According to Ms. Wang:

> Chinese men who've spent some time overseas [*haigui*] might want an equal in their marriage, but most of the mainland guys just want a "flower vase" [*huaping*—a term for a woman desirable for her beauty rather than other personal qualities or abilities] they can show off to their friends.

Ms. Li felt that most wealthy men just wanted a young, "virtuous and dutiful" (*xianhui*) wife rather than a successful, professional woman whose income might one day surpass theirs.[18] Wealthy men were also the ones who spent the most amount of time in the outside world of business and were seen as having little time for family life. They were considered to be the most likely to be tempted by younger women looking for a wealthy male patron.

Ms. Gao's ideal husband was thus one who was not too outstanding in any one thing. "I don't want him to be too successful in his career." If he were, she explained, it would mean that he would have many obligations outside of the home and be constantly tempted by other women: "He should be nice and healthy, he should be able to help me, and he shouldn't be completely without money." Ms. Lai and Ms. Wang also expressed a similar suspicion of successful men, whom they portrayed as morally suspect. Anyone successful in today's society was likely to have employed less than wholesome means at some point in their rise. Although Ms. Lai hoped to marry a man with a "real job" [meaning a steady income], she didn't want to marry a government official because "they could end up in jail the next day." And, although she liked the idea of marrying an intellectual, such as a college professor, she felt that they were "not romantic enough."

Thus, many female entrepreneurs are faced with the choice of either continuing with their business and remaining single or giving up at least a portion of their career to get married. Some view marrying a foreigner as one way out of this dilemma, as they understand foreigners to be more likely to allow them independence. Others choose to simply continue to suffer the pressure of their parents and gossip of their peers while they wait for some cultural shift that will refigure their status.

Mistresses and Corruption

One aspect of corruption cases frequently commented upon by the Chinese media has been the keeping of mistresses and second wives by government officials. A survey of corruption cases in 2000 found that 93 out of 100 cases involved mistresses, and another study of 102 corruption cases in Guangdong province found that every one involved extramarital affairs and at least one "second wife" (*ernai*).[20] Media reports on corruption often list the number of mistresses or women "seduced" by an official as an index of the degree of his corruption. Many journalistic accounts of corruption portray mistresses as exacerbating the moral decline and enhancing the greed of corrupt officials. One commentator argues that "mistresses are corrupt official's fertilizer (*zhuzhangji*). After many officials take a mistress they increase the speed and power of their corrupt activities" (Li Chuzhi 2006).

Other commentators cast the phenomenon in more sympathetic terms, portraying philandering cadres as part of a generation who made sacrifices to the state only to find the principles they fought for abandoned, so they are now seeking personal gratification. In this sense, they argue, the dilemmas and desires that officials face in their sexual and romantic lives are no different from those of other men of their generation (Jeffreys 2006: 172). Some observers have even argued that mistresses and second wives have the potential to be invaluable allies in the war on corruption. One journalist refers to them as, "great servants in anti-corruption" (*fan fubaide da gongchen*) (Li Chuzhi 2006). He offers several examples of corrupt officials who were turned in by jealous or unsatisfied mistresses, including a former vice mayor of Beijing, Liu Zhihua. The author points out that a mistress's knowledge of her patron's dealings is often broader and more accurate than that of other members of his network.[21]

Examining the relationship between officials and their mistresses reveals another dimension of the "corruption complex" described in Chapter Three, and it also allows us to examine how differently positioned actors conceptualize and account for corruption. Most important, the discourses surrounding mistresses and government officials reveal the problematic place of sexuality in the domain of corruption.

I examine two sources that make explicit the power and value believed to inhere in female sexuality: testimonies of convicted corrupt officials and the debate over legislating "sexual bribery" (*xing huilu*). I argue that in the context of what are understood by many observers to be rational exchanges of power and money, female sexuality serves as a wild card capable of generating more than its "market value" (i.e., the cost of hiring a sex worker for the recipient of a bribe). Given its capacity for excess, female sexuality is depicted as undoing the logic of reciprocity that characterizes human relationships (*renqing*) and generating its own mechanisms of control. Because of its imagined power to cause more damage and generate more corruption than money and gifts, several legal scholars have proposed making "sexual bribery" its own criminal category.

Mistresses and second wives are not simply passive beneficiaries of ill-gotten wealth but are often active agents in the informal networks of officials. Li Zhen explains that, in addition to simply receiving gifts, apartments, and cars, some corrupt officials' mistresses help them do business and engage in the work of corruption. Mistresses can act as representatives for officials in secret business dealings and accept bribes on their behalf. Just as they do with their male associates, officials help their mistresses start up their own businesses and use their backing to ensure their success. Some even help women with whom they are involved to achieve official positions.

Li Zhen states that he primarily used his power to help his mistress do business and earn money. He reports using his influence to help her win contracts for the construction of government buildings, for example. However, he contrasts himself with the truly corrupt, who "have the gall" to get their lovers appointed to official positions (Qiao 2004: 296). Li Zhen states that he merely hoped to establish a "one in the government, one in the business world" (*yizheng yishang*) relationship with his lover, a common domestic arrangement in which a couple is able to use the complementary advantages of each arena to generate wealth.

Drawing on notions of the "naturally" predatory nature of female sexuality and the natural inability of men to resist sexual temptation, many officials in their courtroom confessionals have blamed mistresses for driving them to generate more illicit income. One head of the Chongqing Transportation Bureau was reported as defending his actions by saying, "I knelt down before her [his mistress] in my office, but she still wouldn't let me go. I was just too weak. She wanted to bleed me dry" (Yu 2007). In the chapter of *At the Gates of Hell* called "Li Zhen's View of Sex" (*Li Zhen Yanzhongde Se*), Li characterizes women as deliberately manipulating men to achieve some gain. He portrays women as having a controlling influence over his actions, blinding him to the risks of his activities:

> Actually it doesn't matter if they cry tears of sadness, fake tears, or tears of joy, they'll all pull on men's heartstrings. She [his mistress] possesses a kind of a magic that makes me unconsciously fall apart. . . . I always think of ways to please her and not let her slip away from me. Whenever she would mention something I would always think of a way to get it done. When I was doing things for her [engaging in corrupt and illegal activities] I would "whistle in the dark" and tell myself "nothing bad will happen." . . . Women—as soon as they become your plaything you become their slave. (Qiao 2004: 300)

Li Zhen sees a "natural" relationship between corrupt officials and beauties:

> There are two reasons why the exchange of power for sex is simple. The first is the temptation of women's beauty for corrupt officials. The second is that beautiful women are naturally "attracted" to corrupt officials. The only difference is that some are corrupt first, then become lustful, and others are first lustful and then become corrupt. (Qiao 2004: 295)

Here Li Zhen echoes the characterization of female sexuality by Han Yuanyuan and many of the young women quoted above. He argues that women are the real agents in these relationships, wielding power over officials to achieve their own ends. Women are "by nature" attracted to powerful men, whom they depend on to achieve status and material success, and men are merely the victims of a natural lust for women.

Businessmen I interviewed often invoked the notion that the official or client who "has it all" can still be tempted by sex, in particular by the introduction of an unfamiliar young "beauty." Li Zhen states, "It is even easier for beauty than money to incite a man's greedy desires" (*geng yi yinqi nanrende dao xin*) (Qiao 2004: 292). In her review of the sexual bribery controversy, Elaine Jeffreys found the assumption that men have uncontrollable sexual desires to underlie much of the debate:

> This reliance on "enforced-compliance" and/or "after-the-fact" punishment is premised not only on the popular understanding that corrupt government officials deserve "extra punishment," but also on a fatalistic and biologically deter-

mined view of the inability of male government officials to exercise responsible self-policing with regard to women and sex. A common argument here is that when it comes to sex-related bribery and corruption, male government officials who are otherwise "incorruptible" are soon corrupted, a view which implicitly or explicitly reinstates the traditional, derogatory conceptions of female sexuality as predatory. (Jeffreys 2006: 174)

Not only does Li Zhen portray himself as the victim of his mistress's predation; he also characterizes his own feelings for his mistress as more noble than mere lust and laden with care and affection. Here he partakes in another popular narrative—that of the high-pressured elite man, in an unhappy marriage, who finally finds his soulmate in a younger mistress. Li Zhen portrays himself as a romantic, realizing a childhood crush on his former neighbor, who later becomes his mistress. Echoing many other wealthy men's characterization of their relationships with mistresses he states, "She was the only one I could pour my heart out to, the only one that could make me laugh or cry. . . . She was the only one who could truly understand me" (Qiao 2004: 303).

However, he proceeds from describing her as a "flower" and a "little lamb" to calling her a "poisonous snake" (Qiao 2004: 303). He then expresses outrage at his mistress's betrayal of him to the anti-corruption investigators. (During his imprisonment he found out that she gave up his whereabouts when he was on the run from the police.) Shifting back to the discourse of the controlling younger women he claims that, "without her I wouldn't have committed crimes; I wouldn't have committed such big crimes, and I definitely wouldn't be [facing] death!" He ends his reflection on sexuality by proclaiming, "In this world only the kiss of a woman will send you to your doom. Really send you to your doom! I want to tell all the men of the world!" (305). He also cites a common Chinese expression, "the blade above the character 'sex' (se) is sharp" (sezi toushang lidao feng—referring to the top portion of the character se, which resembles the character for knife, dao) (306).

In this narrative, Li Zhen draws on a long-standing theme in Chinese culture of the dangers of female sexuality. Classical Chinese scholars referred to the temptations of beautiful women as "fox spirits" (hulishen) who could distract them from studying for the imperial examination. Although those who abstained entirely from the pursuit of young women were laughed at as being "henpecked" (paitaitai) by their wives, the entrepreneurs I worked with would often caution against the dangers of excessive indulgence in sex. This sentiment was most commonly expressed by phrases such as, "Too many girlfriends will wear you out (*henlei*)" or "Having too many one-night stands is troublesome (*mafan*)." Wealthy men often stressed the importance of not letting their affairs with women get out of control. The importance of moderation was often summed up by a rhyming ditty:

> Don't divorce your original wife (married in poverty).
> Like the new, but don't despise the old,
> Be debonair, not sleazy,
> Be romantic but not obscene.
> (*Caokang bu xia tang, xi xin bu yan jiu, xiaosa bu luan sa, fengliu bu xialiu*).

A businessman explained to me that many wealthy men are superstitious about leaving the spouses who accompanied them on their rise to business success. Letting one's sexual affairs get out of hand, or becoming subject to the control of a mistress, was viewed as the first step toward financial difficulty. Such loss of control had the potential to influence men's reputations among their peers and in the business world, cause strains in their primary household, and siphon away their wealth.

Sexual Bribery

Given the close association between mistresses and corruption, several Chinese legal scholars have been engaged in an ongoing debate over the proposal to make sexual bribery a crime. Proponents of this proposal point to the fact that virtually all corruption cases over the past two decades have involved some form of "trading in power and sex" (*quansejiaoyi*). They point to the draining and diversion of public money to keep mistresses and second wives by high-ranking officials, and they cite the vast amounts that have been spent by businessmen hiring hostesses and sex workers to entertain officials. They also point out that sexual bribery, as a nonmaterial form of payment, slips through a legal loophole and is unpunishable under current regulations.[22] In fact, in his confessional interview, Li Zhen explains that because it is hidden and difficult to obtain any material proof, the "exchange of power for sex" has become a "safety measure" (*anquan xiangmu*) for many corrupt officials (Qiao 2004: 298).[23] When one of the mediums of exchange in a corrupt deal is sex rather than money or gifts, it is hard for investigators to trace.

Many opponents of the criminalization of sexual bribery proposal have echoed Li Zhen's argument, stating that sexual bribery laws would be impossible to enforce in practice because the only proof of such an exchange would be the testimony of the parties involved, who would be unlikely to confess their crimes or would be likely to frame their relationship as one of love rather than as an economic transaction or bribe. Despite the recognition of the ubiquity of sexual bribery, proposals to create legislation to address the problem have generated a great deal of opposition among legal scholars in China:

> Opponents have argued that the current law on bribery refers to the offer and subsequent acceptance of money or property to a member of the working personnel of the state in return for a benefit or for the assistance to obtain a benefit. However, unlike money or property, sex does not possess a transferable or quantifiable quality. In legal terms, therefore, amending the criminal code to include the crime of sex-related bribery and corruption would have the undesirable effect of reducing the human body and human attributes to the status of commodities or "things." (Jeffreys 2006: 163)

This argument adopts what Zelizer (2005: 22) describes as a "hostile worlds" approach to money and sex: that the two belong to separate social spheres and the mixing of them leads to moral contamination or degradation. What this argument fails to capture is that most forms of intimacy involve material transactions, and much of social life consists of negotiating, defining, and matching intimate relationships with the proper forms of payment or non-payment. This is in fact what the proponents of legislating sexual bribery argue—that in both law and social life intimate relations are intertwined with material transactions already (see Zelizer 2005). While this mixing provokes considerable anxiety among intellectuals worried about the power of money to corrode other systems of value, and among social scientists who posit separate spheres of exchange, many ordinary Chinese find this to be an inevitable and natural aspect of social life.

Conclusion

Differently positioned actors narrate the roles of materiality and affect in their intimate relationships in ways that attribute value and status to their actions. Gray women depict relations between the sexes as "nothing but" a competitive market in which they strive to succeed. Female entrepreneurs critique marriage as tainted by the "feudal" status concerns of men, who devalue and fear women's wealth, and imagine a different form of marriage based on mutual aid and respect. Corrupt officials portray themselves as hapless romantics who fall victim to predatory, conniving women.

Both female entrepreneurs and gray women see themselves as embodiments of the values of the reform era. In their biographical narratives, both appeal to the master narrative of success in a competitive economy to justify their claims to status and social esteem. Female entrepreneurs depict themselves as the true heroes of the market economy who, unlike young beauties and well-connected businessmen, must possess true ability, work hard, and overcome many obstacles in order to succeed.

Many female entrepreneurs I interviewed felt that they were part of a vanguard of more rational economic organization in China, one that will slowly do away with the importance of guanxi and family background. In contrast, young beauties see themselves as entrepreneurs of a different sort—women who rationally and systematically exploit their resources of youth and beauty before they lose their value. In fact, many popular representations portray prostitution in its various forms as the essence of entrepreneurialism: generating wealth out of the bare minimum of capital, one's own body. To the critics who view them as immoral and their wealth as unearned, these women need only point to their material success: Isn't monetary yield the only value that matters in China these days? Like neoliberals criticizing idealistic socialists, they characterize wives, career women, and intellectuals as wishful thinkers in denial about the truths of human nature and relations between the sexes.

In different ways, representations of ambitious gray women and wealthy, philandering men have served as allegories of the effects of the pursuit of wealth on morality in contemporary China. According to this discourse, in an environment of constant temptation from "predatory women," esteemed and successful men who possess talent and responsibility are easily led into decadence. They quickly become unmoored from morality and social responsibility and become victims of their lustful natures. Only the most cultivated, high-quality (*gao suzhi*) men can resist such temptations.

Women tempted by the power of money in a society that only cares about material success abandon concern with morality and dignity and willingly sell themselves to the highest bidder. According to this allegory, because of the easy road to success for "beauties," young women no longer view education as a means of acquiring skills to succeed, but only as a means of increasing their value in the market for wealthy men. In the world of business populated by lustful men, women's other talents and abilities pale in comparison to the power of sexual attraction. Men, however, only need money, and even the oldest, ugliest, most uncouth country bumpkin will be transformed by wealth into an object of desire.

Importantly, in these narratives, while men are characterized as the victims of their natures and their temptation-laden environments, women are often portrayed as actively choosing to disregard morality in order to get ahead. Thus women are subject to greater condemnation. When the lawyer Zheng Baichun started a website to help inform mistresses and second wives of their legal rights and protect them from being taken advantage of, a public outcry ensued, declaring that these women were not "victims" or "weak parties" (*ruoshi tuanti*) but predators (Ren 2006). Although the disloyalty and irresponsibility of elite men is seen as an unfortunate consequence of China's opening up, it is still largely young women who "take the shortcut" who receive the most blame for speeding the pace of China's moral decline.

Countless critics, from intellectuals to everyday citizens, have called for the adoption of new systems of value and belief to help prevent intimate relations from being contaminated by market forces and to protect human qualities from being reduced to their monetary value. They view the immorality of gray women, the excesses of corrupt officials, and the dishonesty of entrepreneurs as symptomatic of a more general "loss of beliefs" in Chinese society. I return to this notion of lost belief and values and the search for new standards and models in the conclusion.

6

CONCLUSION

Elite Networks and Public Morality

Power Lines and Public Morality

In the winter of 2008, many areas of southern and central China were hit with the worst winter storm in a generation. Snow, ice, and freezing temperatures made thousands of miles of roads impassable, bringing transportation to a standstill and stranding hundreds of thousands of migrant workers returning to their hometowns to celebrate the Chinese New Year. In several cities and towns, water mains froze and power lines were brought down by the ice, leaving tens of millions of people without power and water. Guizhou, a poor, mountainous province in the south, was particularly severely hit. Millions of residents were without power and water for days.

In the aftermath of the snowstorm, the residents of Kaili in central Guizhou noticed a peculiar phenomenon. Of the more than ten thousand electrical poles downed by the storm, 90 percent of them were poles that were put up during the late 1990s; the majority of the poles from the 1950s and 1960s remained standing. This discovery contradicted the national narrative of technological and economic progress. As one commentator put it, "Under normal circumstances, one would expect the old poles to break first, particularly since newer poles are built using more advanced technology." Investigators discovered that the new poles were reinforced with inexpensive iron wire instead of standard rebar (*Xin Jing Bao* 2008).

The implications of this strange phenomenon were immediately apparent to China's Internet police, who promptly deleted the story from the website of the Beijing newspaper that first reported on it. The significance was obvious to the readers of the story as well, who saw this as another instance of *guanshang goujie*—collusion between officials and entrepreneurs for the sake of illegal profit.

The brittle wire in the electric poles constituted the final materialization of a financial scheme in which public funds were diverted and distributed among members of a network. Whether the builder was awarded the contract owing to a special relationship and kickback to his official patron and then recovered his costs by using inferior materials, or whether using cheap iron allowed him simply to maximize profits and his official patron turned a blind eye, is hard to say.

These materializations of elite diversions of public funds—buildings that crumble in a few years, highway lanes that are too narrow—are common enough to have been given a name, "tofu-dregs projects" (*doufuzha gongcheng*). While examples of tofu dregs construction are numerous, perhaps none has been as tragic as the collapse of shoddily built schools during the Wenchuan earthquake of May 2008, in which thousands of school children were killed.

The story of the shoddy electric poles is significant for its symbolism. The fact that the poles from the Maoist years stood, while those from the reform era crumpled served to undermine China's narrative of development and economic progress. Beyond representing the proliferation of corruption in the reform era, this incident exemplified another contrast between the present and the Maoist years: the "loss of belief" (*shiqu xinyang*) and lack of "public-oriented morality" (*gonggong daode*) that many Chinese feel characterizes the contemporary period. To many people, tofu-dregs construction epitomizes the limits and ultimate failure of the relational ethics of guanxi networks. Just as tofu construction fails to generate a solid, enduring national infrastructure, relational ethics have yet to serve as the moral foundation for an ethical society.

The problem of belief in contemporary China is a complex one. Many of the excesses of the Maoist era are blamed on naïve beliefs in "unscientific" ideals about the economy and "human nature." Maoist institutions and ideology are widely seen as premised on denials of basic human desires and of natural differences between men and women. While China's reforms were grounded in these apparent truths about humans and markets, what has emerged in China during the reform period is not simply an evolving form of neoliberal capitalism or consumerist individualism. In many ways, the weakening of the institutional foundations of Maoist ethics created the space for guanxi practices to evolve and proliferate, and the moral economy specific to guanxi has in many ways served as an ethical counterweight to market individualism.[1] Guanxi networks are the primary institution through which forms of capital and power have been accumulated during the reform era, but they also impose their own forms of distribution and expenditure (Yang 2002: 475).

It is worth reviewing the features of the networks depicted in this book. In the reform era, guanxi networks have been increasingly oriented toward the accumulation of wealth, power, and status, but they do so as institutions that have their own internal moral economies. At the elite level, they transcend state and society as well as legitimate and illegitimate moral worlds. For businessmen, they provide protections, competitive advantages, and forms of state-controlled prestige. For government officials, they provide the bulk of their wealth, and they are means through which they achieve the face (*mianzi*) essential to their power and authority in both official and unofficial domains of practice.

Although guanxi networks tend to exclude outsiders and provide advantages and privileges to insiders, they are by no means closed to new "members." In fact they are inherently expandable and adaptable. New projects of wealth and power accumulation require the cooperation of new individuals controlling previously untapped resources. Partly because of the expandability and permeability of membership, loyalties and obligations are never automatic but must be tested and demonstrated through various, sometimes risky projects, as well as maintained and cultivated through periodic conviviality. Finally, the ethics that characterize guanxi networks are familiar, widespread cultural discourses rooted in everyday forms of kinship, gender ideologies, and broader interpersonal ethics (*renqing*). Because they are inherently particularistic and relational, guanxi ethics have yet to provide the grounding for the public morality that is sought by—some would say remembered by—many Chinese. As the above example demonstrates, the moral economies of elite networks often generate very immoral consequences for the public good.

Mayfair Yang (1994) saw the potential for an incipient civil society in the techniques of guanxi. For those who benefit from guanxi, it "humanizes" the market economy. Entrepreneurs I worked with constantly offered each other material and immaterial forms of aid and support, exchanged information, and shared opportunities. These opportunities and benefits were not distributed purely to maximize profit but out of sentimental concern for others and relations of reciprocity. In a way, guanxi serves to "humanize" the state as well, but only for those with the resources to be part of elite networks.

Laws, policies, and bureaucracies are softened (or even dissolved) when filtered through a powerful official patron. A well-connected entrepreneur might be able to gain a special tax status or have his business exempted from regulations based on his relationships. And in some extreme cases, such as Lai Changxing's appropriation of the Fujian customs house, these networks result in the complete privatization of the state.[2]

Members of the elite view themselves as beyond the law and capable of using it toward their own ends. But this version of civil society, if one can consider it such, fails to live up to the ideal of civil society in one key area: as an autonomous realm separate from state power. An official might derive his power precisely from being positioned at a node in a "civil" guanxi network, capable of mobilizing state resources for the sake of entrepreneurs who depend on him; and his unofficial status as a *yibashou* (powerful boss-patron) might far outweigh his official title (as in the case of Li Zhen). Just as elite networks appropriate state institutions for private ends, state power is also refracted and reproduced through them. Elite networks thus challenge the zero-sum game between state and society that characterizes many depictions of contemporary China (Smart 1999).

As my informants were quick to emphasize, guanxi has failed in the domains of public morality and social justice. By personalizing and privatizing bureaucratic institutions that are intended to serve abstract citizens and the public good, they exacerbate inequalities rather than keep them in check. Elite networks are the primary mechanism that allows public assets, such as land, to be diverted into private hands. They have proliferated and become the dominant force in the real estate boom of the past decade and a half. This ongoing transfer of collective and state-owned land into the hands of private or state-owned companies for commercial development and the ensuing resettlement of millions of urban and rural residents, a process Li Zhang (2010) has dubbed "accumulation by displacement," has been enabled by networks of government officials, private businessmen, and underworld gangs.

Scholars both in China and in the West have pondered by what means the moral kernel at the heart of guanxi relations might be extended to a broader public. One such possibility lies in the prestige inherent in the generosity and expenditures that characterize guanxi relations. Mayfair Yang (2002: 476) wonders "whether guanxi principles of generosity inform not only acts of corruption, but also donations in support of civil society. Have new urban entrepreneurial, managerial, and middle classes started to feel the compulsion to compete for status through community, rather than individual, consumption and expenditure?" As Chapter Four demonstrates, Chengdu's elite is beset with anxiety over the moral and symbolic limitations of their practices and is actively looking for ways to reform them. These new anxieties, along with their quest for broader social recognition, have the potential to generate a new status-driven ethics.

A Neoliberal Order?

In scholarship and even in the popular press, the myth of China's entrepreneurs as the vanguard of liberal democracy in China seems to be quickly fading. This evolution has reopened debates surrounding the nature of the political order toward which China is headed; it even raises the question whether China is in any kind of transition at all. Some scholars have begun to argue that China is merely refining and honing its current configuration of authoritarianism and capitalism, despite the cognitive dissonance this causes for many social scientists steeped in the ideological assumption that markets beget freedom. Scholars such as Minxin Pei (2006) have argued that, owing to the inefficiencies and waste caused by corrupt, elite networks, China is stuck in a "trapped transition."

Others, such as Wang Hui (2003) and David Harvey (2005), have interpreted China's move away from a planned economy in the context of a global shift toward more neoliberal forms of economic and political organization. China's mixture of authoritarianism and free markets increasingly appears to be part of a vanguard of emerging state forms rather than an anomaly (Wang 2003; Zizek 2011). I would caution, however, against presupposing an overarching neoliberal order in China, let alone a global, neoliberal totality (see Kipnis 2007).

While the Chinese state has retreated from various domains of private life and has largely left the provision of social services such as health care and education to the whims of the market, market mechanisms have been limited and even actively resisted in other domains. The central government has sought to shape certain sectors to attract foreign capital (e.g., export-oriented Special Economic Zones), while it has sought to tightly control it in others (exhibited by the continued state control of energy, telecommunications, and much of the banking sector, as well as tight currency and financial controls, despite much pressure from the United States and from global financial institutions). Huang Yasheng's (2008) recent work has demonstrated that many companies and sectors of the economy understood to be "private" by many outside observers are in fact still owned or controlled by the state. The vast fortunes of state-controlled companies like China Mobile and Sinopec have largely undone the tendency to equate "state-owned" with moribund and unprofitable.[3]

Karl Polanyi's basic assumptions about the nature of modern economies invert the tenets of neoliberalism. Although we are accustomed to thinking of socialism in its various forms as the great utopian experiment of our times, Polanyi (1944: 252) understood the attempt to organize human society by markets as a utopian experiment doomed to fail. He argued that markets generate unsustainable contradictions that necessitate their amelioration through protectionist state policies and welfare measures. Significantly, it is not simply workers who demand protection from markets, but firms and financiers as well. They might call for the privatization and liberalization of economic domains closed to them, but the behavior of capitalists and entrepreneurs in practice often exhibits very "illiberal" tendencies toward monopoly and limiting competition by fostering relationships of privilege with the state and skirting legal regulations, for example.[4] In short, elite networks, cronyism, and protection rackets are not aberrations of market economies but are organic products of capitalism. They are cultural institutions that serve to organize economies to the advantage of powerful groups. Liberal ideologies of free markets often enable their proliferation, but they are inadequate for understanding "actually existing capitalism."

Although it might strike some observers as surprising, among my informants, the groups most likely to champion a meritocratic free market ideal were not elite entrepreneurial men, but rather those who were excluded or marginalized by elite networks: recent college graduates, struggling shopkeepers, female entrepreneurs, and salaried workers.[5] They saw their success impeded by dense webs of elite men and individuals with "background" (*beijing*) structuring business and state power to their advantage.

As Chapter Five argued, the "gray women" of the beauty economy were in fact the strongest adherents of a form of market extremism, portraying all sexual relations as a market in women's beauty for men's money, while their wealthy male patrons tended to portray their relationships with these women as rooted in romance and caring. Similarly those most likely to call for the "rule of law" (*fazhi*) rather than the "rule of men" (*renzhi*) were not necessarily "bourgeois" entrepreneurs hoping to protect their property rights but ordinary citizens denied the supra-legal protections enjoyed by the elite (the "lawlike relationships" that benefit the likes of Brother Chen, Li Zhen, and Mr. Wei).

They were ordinary farmers and urban residents, for example, who had had their property appropriated by local governments in collusion with developers for a fraction of the market price.

Another irony of my research concerns the notion of *suzhi* (personal quality), the subject of much recent attention in anthropological and sociological studies of contemporary China. My research suggests that moral concerns are increasingly being linked with forms of status and that this development has transformed the dominant understanding of suzhi.

Many anthropologists have characterized suzhi as a form of "neoliberal governmentality" (H. Yan 2003; Anagnost 2004). Hairong Yan (2003: 497) dubs it a "new valuation of human subjectivity specific to China's neoliberal reforms."[6] According to Yan, "suzhi abstracts and reduces the heterogeneity of human beings by coding their value (worth) for Development." As Yan argues, the discourse of suzhi is central to understanding the ways in which the exploitation of rural migrants is both justified and rendered invisible (511).

Given this definition of suzhi, entrepreneurs should be exemplars of high-suzhi practice and subjectivity as evidenced by their characterization by the state as the engines of development and progress. However, during my fieldwork, rarely did people equate entrepreneurs with high suzhi. In fact, new-rich entrepreneurs (in a virtual tie with peasants) were by far the group most likely to be accused of possessing poor suzhi. In countless conversations with taxi drivers and shopkeepers, and even among wealthy entrepreneurs themselves, the most common phrase uttered about the new rich was, "They might have money, but they don't have suzhi."[7]

This viewpoint suggests that suzhi has in many ways been appropriated and interpreted to denote a different kind of value than merely the capacity to generate capital and contribute to economic development. Given that suzhi refers to the overall quality of an individual, the concept is inherently polysemic and has the potential to signify different forms of value. My informants most often used it to mean an individual's level of personal cultivation as reflected in his or her demeanor, manners, tastes, and most important, morality. In other words, suzhi is gradually being refigured as a way of talking not just about the economic backwardness of the peasants but about the moral failings of the new rich. When a wealthy man endangers pedestrians by running a red light in his BMW, or when the electric poles put up by his company fall down, both instances are indicative of his low suzhi and his failure to adhere to a sense of public morality and responsibility.

Entrepreneurs were among the most insistent that they as a group and Chinese society as a whole "lacked beliefs." Many have become increasingly disgruntled by what they feel to be a steady deterioration in China's moral and physical environment. If they hadn't done so already, the vast majority of my informants were planning on sending their children abroad for their high school or college educations. They frequently denounced the Chinese educational system as producing little more than meek, obedient test takers who made for good employees but lacked the skills to survive in the world of business. Upon retiring, many hoped to join their children abroad; others were planning to emigrate as soon as possible. According to a recent survey by the Bank of China and the Hurun Report, 60 percent of the 960,000 people with assets over 10 million yuan in China are either considering moving abroad or have already started the procedures to do so (Page 2012).

Part of the desire to emigrate (or at least to secure a foreign passport) is driven by the fears and insecurities discussed in Chapter Four: they might find themselves on the wrong side of a political movement; a well-connected competitor might use state institutions to bring them down; or the state itself might find a reason to go after their assets.[8] Others cited quality-of-life issues: food safety; air quality; traffic; or a general sense that Chinese society has become warped by a toxic mix of intense competition, rampant materialism, and ubiquitous corruption. Drawing from an idealized vision of Western countries, several entrepreneurs hoped that their children could build their careers in societies where those with talent and ability rather those with connections are rewarded.

Several of my entrepreneur friends and associates had emigrated, and some had already returned, disillusion with life outside of China. Mr. Wang, who was seriously considering emigrating but had yet to take any concrete steps toward doing so, often cited the experiences of a friend who had emigrated to Canada but quickly returned to China. His friend had composed a poetic ditty, describing Canada as "beautiful mountains, clean water, and boring as hell" (*hao shan, hao shui, hao wuliao*), and China as "really dirty, really chaotic, and really fun" (*hao zang, hao luan, hao kuaile*).

Leaving the country was one solution to people's dissatisfaction with China; others were more actively engaged in the search for a new form of public-oriented morality that could replace the collectivist ethics of the Maoist era. Many pointed to religion as a possible source of collective morality.

In Chengdu, many wealthy businesspeople have become devotees of Tibetan Buddhism, and a smaller number have become followers of Christianity.[9] Others have looked to practices of "life nurturance" (*yangsheng*), Chinese philosophical traditions, and the ideal of the "Confucian business-man" (*rushang*) as models for fostering more morally conscious subjectivities. More cynically, they also recognized the limitations of social distinctions based purely on money, and the necessity of other systems of qualitative value through which they could distinguish themselves from their peers. Moral behavior and philanthropic endeavors in the public realm may prove to be one such domain.

NOTES

CHAPTER 1

1. Under the socialist system work units were more than just employers. They served as the lowest tier in a bureaucratic hierarchy that linked urban individuals with the state. Work units were responsible for implementing many major policy initiatives handed down from the central government such as the one-child policy. Work units also allocated housing, provided health care and education, and supervised the daily and personal lives of their workers. In certain occupations and industries some of the benefits of work units remain, but they no longer have control over an individual's decisions to marry, divorce, travel, or change jobs. In 1997, the work unit structure was in transition. My students were free to change their jobs, but not without reimbursing their schools for the educational benefits they had received.

2. Township-village enterprises (TVEs) brought considerable prosperity to several regions of rural eastern China, but tended to be much less prevalent (or nonexistent) in the interior and in areas far from urban markets. Because most were collectively owned, some highly successful TVEs created a privileged class of wealthy local villagers who enjoyed guaranteed jobs, high dividend payments, and generous benefits. In some instances, migrants, who were excluded from these benefits, were hired to perform most of the factory and farm work, creating a class of rentier locals. (See, for example, Gilley 2001 and Chan, Madsen, and Unger 2009).

3. While officially collectively owned, in practice local governments wielded considerable control over their operations, if not de facto ownwership. Furthermore, local governments helped TVEs secure needed capital and resources, and many of the managers, if not state officials themselves, had connections to local government bureaucracies and businesses based on kin relationships, professional ties, or friendship (Naughton 2007: 277–80). Various mid-1990s financial reforms led to TVEs losing their privileged position. Many have since declined or have reorganized as more independent private enterprises, often with incumbent managers or local government officials becoming the majority shareholders (Naughton 2007: 289). See Naughton 2007: Chapter 12, for a good overview of the rise and fall of TVEs.

4. Based on her research in Harbin in the early 2000s, Carolyn Hsu (2007) describes how Harbiners make a distinction between *getihu* and entrepreneurs (*qiyejia*). No matter how much money they possessed, the former were viewed as "low class" (*di suzhi*)

while the latter were seen as possessing high "quality" (*gao suzhi*) and thus worthy of so-cial esteem and emulation. In Chengdu, however, I rarely heard the term *getihu* applied to anyone. Instead the term *baofahu* (upstart) was primarily used to describe someone with money but lacking in taste, class, or manners.

5. *Nanxun* (Southern Tour) refers to Deng Xiaoping's 1992 visit to the Special Eco-nomic Zone of Shenzhen. There he declared that economic reforms were benefiting the country and should continue, prompting increasingly liberal economic policies and greater certainty about the political correctness of profit-oriented activities.

6. See, for example, the strong public reaction to a female dating show contestant's comment that she'd rather "cry in the back of a BMW" than be happy riding around on the back of a male contestant's bicycle (Wong 2011).

7. "No Car, No House" has arguably become the slogan for the plight of the poor bachelor in urban China. A 2010 song by Sun Hui titled "No Car, No House" (*Meiyou Che, Meiyou Fang*) offered a critique of overly materialistic attitudes toward marriage among Chinese women and provoked much discussion on Chinese Internet forums. It also spawned a parody from a group of women who felt offended by the original song and who proclaimed their right to be materialistic in a society that only values money (see Chinasmack.com, March 10, 2011).

8. Several scholars have pointed out that since the end of the Maoist years, "stra-tum (*jieceng*) has largely replaced the term "class" (*jieji*) in both scholarly and popular discourse in China owing to the latter's association with Maoist ideology and political struggle (see Anagnost 2008; Zhang 2010). As Li Zhang (2010: 6) points out, this shift in language is "itself a political act because it is a conscious effort to disengage from the Maoist form of politics that is seen by many as destructive."

9. The futility of using official income statistics to categorize urban Chinese into a socioeconomic hierarchy was revealed by a 2010 Credit Suisse report which estimated that these statistics missed 11 trillion RMB in "gray income" (*huise shouru*), which amounted to 30 percent of China's GDP in 2010 (Wang 2010). The report also found that the wealthiest households had the highest percentage of gray income. Gray income refers to money de-rived from unofficial sources such as moonlighting, bonuses, loans to other entrepreneurs, income derived from opportunities created by connections (*guanxi*), and kickbacks.

10. Many multinational firms doing business in China refer to these individuals as "relationship hires" (Garnaut 2010).

11. See Goodman (2008) for a discussion of the difficulties scholars have had on agreeing on the terms and definitions surrounding the new rich and new middle class in China. For a discussion of the complexity of defining "middle class" in China see Zhang (2010: 1–16).

12. But the agency assured the reader that this number would reach 45 percent by 2020.

13. For studies that take up the political impact of China's private entrepreneurs as their central focus, see Pearson (1997), Dickson (2003), and Tsai (2007). All these studies question any simplistic narrative that capitalism or private entrepreneurs will inevitably usher in democracy in China.

14. See my discussion of goudui in Chapter Two for more elaboration of the meanings and practices associated with this term.

15. When I asked one of my informant friends, Ms. Gao, if extramarital affairs were prevalent in Chengdu, She emphatically replied, "Are you kidding? In Chengdu even the taxi drivers who don't wash their hands or feet have mistresses."

16. See, for example, Duhigg and Barboza (2012), "In China Human Costs Are Built into an iPad."

17. In fact, promotional literature on investing in Chengdu highlights the relatively low salaries of white-collar workers as one of its selling points.

18. For an extensive review of the scholarly literature and debates surrounding *guanxi* see Gold, Guthrie, and Wank (2002) and Nathan (1993).

19. Renqing can also refer to favors or to personal relationships more generally, as in "I owe him a *renqing* (favor)."

20. The same point can thus be made about morally "good" guanxi verses "bad" corruption: one person's concern for his cousin is another person's corruption. See Chapter Three for an extended discussion of the relational ethics at the heart of guanxi.

21. Some have, for example, attempted to separate and categorize guanxi relationships along spectrums of sentiment and instrumentality (see, e.g., Hwang 1987; King 1991). These disagreements may also ultimately stem from the propensity of Western social science to separate interest from affect in categorizing relationships and action (Yanagisako 2002).

22. Scholars' assessment of the contribution of guanxi to China's development has varied considerably. Guanxi networks and practices have been framed as a more or less benign adaptation to a particular set of structures, just as they have been viewed as a pathological form of corruption that distort market forces. For example, Bian (2002) depicts guanxi networks as filling "institutional holes" in China's transitioning job market by providing employers and job seekers with information about jobs, while Guthrie (1998) has characterized them as impeding the efficiencies of markets. As Hsu and Smart note (2007: 167) the boundary between guanxi and corruption is often fuzzy. Guanxi has been praised by scholars for facilitating entrepreneurship in China by "facilitating the flow of goods and services" and "breaking rigid bureaucratic monopolies" (Hao and Johnston 1995: 140), just as it has been targeted as the root of China's corruption problem (He 1998). See Smart (1999) and Rocca (1992) for a discussion of the positive and negative effects of corruption rooted in guanxi and bribery in reform-era China.

23. For example, Potter (2002) has interpreted guanxi as functioning to complement China's opaque legal system. Wank (1996) has argued that guanxi ties to state officials help firms establish trust and greater certainty in a shifting legal and policy environment, gain access to important state controlled resources such as licenses, capital, and land (Wank 1999), and help expand business and maximize profits by appropriating state institutions for private use (Wank 2002). Ong (1999) has discussed the relationship between guanxi and "flexible accumulation" in capitalism, while Smart and Smart (1998) have analyzed the role of guanxi in foreign investment in the PRC.

24. Thus I reject the notion that guanxi is simply the "Chinese idiom" for a univer-

sal human phenomenon that arises under particular structural or institutional conditions associated with planned economies or authoritarian political systems (see Gold, Guthrie, and Wank 2002: 13). Such an understanding presupposes a universal human subject rather than a culturally situated one. See Walder (1986) and Oi (1989) for institutionalist accounts that view guanxi as the Chinese gloss for neotraditional labor relations (Walder) and clientelist politics (Oi), political forms which can be found in many societies.

25. Two exceptions need to be noted. In her ethnography of guanxi practices in the 1980s, Mayfair Yang (1994: 78–85) found that women who went around cultivating relationships with important individuals were often suspected of sexual impropriety. My research on female entrepreneurs found a similar suspicion of their sexual morality (see Chapter Five). Kellee Tsai (2002: 60–119) also discusses the role gender plays in informal financial arrangements among entrepreneurs in Fujian.

26. This framing of the study follows Susan Mann's (2000) call to study the relations between men, what she calls "the male bond," that structure many Chinese institutions (e.g., civil service exams, bureaucracies, secret societies) as specifically gendered social relationships.

27. In focusing on men's business networks, I don't intend to deny or downplay the fact that there are many highly successful women entrepreneurs in China. Rather I hope to demonstrate the ways in which business networking is a gendered social field in China that generates different consequences and dilemmas for male and female businesspeople.

28. Yunxiang Yan differentiates between "primary" and "extended" forms of guanxi (1996: 226–29). The primary forms are found among an individual's "local moral world"—family members, close friends, and neighbors—and tend to be rooted in morality and sentiment, whereas extended forms are employed when dealing with outsiders for purposes of short-term gain and characterized by instrumentality and, according to Yan, often a lack of sentimentality and morality.

29. The anthropological literature that examines the relationship between interest and affect and its relation to nonmarket (embedded) versus market (disembedded) economies is vast and cannot be adequately summarized here. For Max Weber's formulation of economic action as rational, see Weber (1978). For discussions of the relationship between how affect and interest relate to gifts and commodities see Mauss (1990 [1950]), Gregory (1982), Parry (1986), and Appadurai (1986). For a historical account of the evolution of the notion of interest in Western thought see Hirshman (1997 [1977]).

30. For an articulation of a culturally distinctive "Chinese" style of capitalism see Redding (1995).

31. The apparent universality of this phenomenon notwithstanding, differences in rationales for network building and understandings of masculinity generate significant local differences. Contemporary China can perhaps be distinguished by the ubiquity and institutionalization of certain forms of male entertainment. While some have viewed many of these practices as part of a hyper-masculinity promoted by global capitalism (e.g., Ling 1999), I would argue that they must be understood within the speci-

ficities of China's political structure, economic policies, and gender ideologies. Despite their resemblances to and historical links with forms of entertainment in Japan, Taiwan, and elsewhere in East Asia, the micropractices of entertaining and the performances of masculinity they entail have evolved along with the cultural, political, and economic milieu of post-Mao China—a context in which male networks are crucial to ensuring financial success and winning the patronage of state officials.

32. For a discussion of hegemonic masculinity and its relation to other masculinities see Connell (1995) and Donaldson (1993).

33. Kiesling's (2005) work on fraternity brothers in the United States is one exception.

34. For further discussion of the history and organization of China's sworn brotherhoods in prerevolutionary China, see Ownby (1996) and McIsaac (2000). The sworn brotherhood tradition was particularly strong in Republican-era Sichuan. During that time, a group known as the "Robed Brothers" (*Paoge*), along with a few smaller organizations, controlled the vast majority of Chongqing's male workers (McIsaac 2000: 1644).

35. I thank Prasenjit Duara for pointing out to me the strong influence of this tradition on forms of masculine sociality.

36. I thank an anonymous reviewer of the manuscript for suggesting that I emphasize that masculinity is a process not an essence. For the classic statement of the performativity at the heart of gender, see Butler (1999 [1990]).

CHAPTER 2

1. Leader (*lingdao*) most commonly refers to a high-ranking cadre in a government bureaucracy or state-owned company, but it can also refer to the bosses of private companies. Essentially it refers to anyone who has the power to make decisions that can affect (positively or negatively) one's fortunes.

2. I have used pseudonyms throughout this book to protect the identity of my informants.

3. Ten thousand RMB was equal to around $1,220 in 2002.

4. As Judd (1994) and Kipnis (2001) argue, the preponderance of male entrepreneurs is partly due to the gendered division of labor, which assigns women to the "inside" and men to the "outside." This circumstance is captured by the Chinese saying, "Men manage the outside; women manage the inside" (*Nan zhu wai, nü zhu nei*).

5. I discuss how women entrepreneurs navigate these spaces in Chapter Five.

6. On the shifting politics and meanings surrounding food, eating, and banqueting in post-Mao China, see Farquhar (2002), esp. Part I.

7. Mr. Guo, an entrepreneur in the construction industry, explained to me that his company organized pleasure trips for officials in the guise of industry conferences. To ensure that the festivities catered to each high-ranking official's pleasure, Mr. Guo said that only one boss-official (*laoda*) could be entertained per trip.

8. Throughout most of this essay I gloss *yingchou*, which in its most narrow sense refers to social engagements, as "entertaining." More specifically, I am referring to the ritualized forging and maintenance of social relationships associated with entrepre-

neurs' financial endeavors. Yingchou often bleeds into other categories of play and leisure, which I discuss below.

9. The theme of retrieving "lost masculinity" is prominent in Xueping Zhong's
(2000) study of Chinese film and literature from the 1980s and 1990s and in Everett
Zhang's (2001) essay on entrepreneurial masculinity.

10. Not surprisingly, I witnessed many American businessmen mistake these gestures as indicative of attempts at homosexual seduction.

11. One entrepreneur, who sold equipment to state-owned factories, conceived of
his dependency this way: "Without the Communist Party I couldn't make any money.
Because of them [and their desire for kickbacks] I can sell something that should cost
10 RMB for 100 RMB."

12. Entrepreneurs involved in real estate, in particular, depended on the patronage
of government officials. See Chapter Three for a discussion of real estate transactions.

13. Following Yangisako (2002: 10) I use the term *sentiment* to refer to "affective
ideas and ideas with affect" that "generate particular desires and incite particular social
actions."

14. For some of my informants' associates, especially those over the age of 40, nightlife consisted entirely of gambling, usually in the form of mahjong (*majiang)* or the
extremely popular card game "struggle against the landlord" (*doudizhu)*. Because of my
limited finances and even more limited gambling ability, I had very little access to this
form of nightlife and this group of businessmen.

15. Occasionally, younger girlfriends of entrepreneurs I knew would drag their
older male lovers to fashionable discos. On these occasions my informants would pay
for drinks and sit awkwardly in a booth or sometimes shuffle their feet next to the table.
But never once did I see them venture out on the dance floor.

16. How elite women navigate these spaces is discussed in Chapter Five.

17. Karaoke originated in Japan in the 1970s and spread to other East and Southeast
Asian countries in the 1980s. Many of the first karaoke and hostess clubs in the PRC
were opened by Hong Kong and Taiwanese businessmen who in a sense "reintroduced"
this form of masculine entertaining to China given its roots in early twentieth-century
Chinese courtesan culture. KTV refers to a specific karaoke technology. Participants
sing along to lyrics that appear in white at the bottom of a TV screen and are "colored
in" at the pace they should be sung. Unlike earlier versions of karaoke that displayed lyrics only, KTVs display videos as well. Thus singers sing along to video images that range
from the conventional, MTV-style music videos that programmatically reference the
song to somewhat random images of romance, women, and nightlife that only vaguely
relate to the song's themes.

18. In law enforcement and official government discourse these women are usually
referred to as "three accompaniment hostesses" (*sanpei xiaojie*), meaning they accompany their clients in three activities. Officially these activities are drinking, dancing, and
singing, or dining, drinking, and dancing, but in practice they are usually drinking,
singing, and sex.

19. Some KTV-goers used powered ketamine ("K" *fen* or "king," known more com-

monly as "Special K" in the United States) in addition to alcohol in private rooms, a practice referred to as *haiyao*. *Hai* is clearly a transliteration of "high" from English. "*Yao*" references medicine or beneficial drugs, distinguishing this practice from the more common term for illicit drug use, *xidu*, which literally means "inhaling poison." Much of the protocol and etiquette surrounding drinking applied to ketamine as well. Losers in dice games would have to do a line of ketamine rather than take a drink.

20. Several informal surveys of friends and colleagues from all over China suggest that *goudui* does not appear to be a commonly used term outside of Sichuan and Chongqing and has not entered the lexicon of Mandarin.

21. This argument resonates with observations by Smart (1993) and Smart and Hsu (2007), who emphasize the importance of framing and tact in determining whether actors perceive a gift as a bribe or vice versa. Many payments and gifts offered by my informants would no doubt be considered "bribes" by outsiders. When talking with me, they usually used the term "kickback" (*huikou*) to refer to payments made to clients or officials. But when these were presented to their recipients, they were almost always framed as a kind of gift. One can understand Mr. Gao's failure to bribe an official at the beginning of this chapter as largely due to his inability to convincingly frame his bribe as a gift.

22. Farquhar (2003: 147–53) gives a vivid account of how, through the right combination of convivial conversation, strong drink, and good food, sentiment is produced in these encounters. Following Kipnis (1997), she argues against the idea that such encounters can be reduced to an underlying instrumentality or utility. Furthermore, As Farquhar (2003: 151) and Kipnis (1997) both argue, reducing these encounters to the ultimate truth of the various "capital conversions" underlying them discounts the embodied nature of these experiences and the role of shared pleasure in generating sentiment.

23. See also the discussion of the "boss-patron" ideal in Chapters One and Four.

24. Many businessmen explained that one of the main challenges of entertaining was ascertaining the desires and preferred forms of enjoyment of an official or client.

25. To prevent any potential loss of face at the end of the evening, KTV patrons are usually informed in advance whether their hostesses are available for sex. In fact, the challenge of the evening for hosts is figuring out the true desires of their guests, not in securing the means to satisfy them.

26. My argument here differs from Sedgwick's model of homosociality in *Between Men* (1985). Sedgwick examines the "erotic triangles" that help orient the "homosocial continuum" of relationships between men. In the examples she analyzes, men are bound together through their rivalry for the same woman. In KTV clubs it seems rather that men are bonded through a parallel structure—participants are all figured as men who enjoy, deserve, and can afford the same luxuries.

27. I thank an anonymous reviewer of the manuscript for suggesting the applicability of Rubin's theory to my material.

28. Zheng (2006: 179) finds a similar distancing from the commodified nature of relationships with hostesses among the male clients who patronized the club in which she conducted research. The male sex clients she studied insisted that only those who can

manipulate hostesses without paying have successfully demonstrated their masculine potency.

29. See Chapter Five for a discussion of the perceived morality of female entrepreneurs and wealthy wives (*fupo*).

30. See Chapter Five for further discussion of this emphasis on male sexual moderation in the context of what is perceived to be "predatory" female sexuality.

31. Toward the end of my fieldwork the extraordinarily popular television show "Supergirl" (*Chaojinüsheng*), a talent competition for aspiring female pop singers, was airing its final episodes. My informants enjoyed speculating about how many of the finalists and semifinalists had already been "kept" (*bao*) by wealthy businessmen and the price they might have fetched.

32. There is also a verb that combines these two terms: *baoyang*. *Baoyang* is a more a general term for supporting a mistress or second wife often found in formal spoken and written contexts; it was seldom used by my informants. Thus, despite the equation of *bao* with *yang* in formal contexts, I maintain that there is an evolving distinction between *bao* and *yang* among my informants.

33. Similarly, young women often interpreted the status of their male patrons as confirmation of their beauty and charm. See Chapter Five for an extended discussion of this issue.

34. See Kipnis (1997) and Y. Yan (2003) for discussions of the relationship between feelings, speech, and actions in Chinese familial and romantic relationships.

35. This is not to suggest that mistresses of wealthy men never develop "real" affection for their lovers, but rather that the convincing performance of authentic emotion and desire through linguistic and sexual practices is what authenticates the relationship. As Cameron and Kulick argue, intimacy is an "interactional achievement" (2003: 115)

CHAPTER 3

1. More precisely, Chen's comment could be translated as "the ethics of relationships are the law."

2. Clearly, however, these modes of exchange were enabled by the loosening of state control of the economy during the reform era.

3. Anti-corruption cases are often viewed as a by-product of internal political struggles. As a new leader ascends to power, he seeks to replace his subordinates with members of his own network. This has led scholars of Chinese politics to argue that formal legal institutions are used instrumentally in the service of informal networks. For a similar argument about the prevalence of informal practices in Russia, see Ledeneva (2006, especially Chapter 1).

For example, the 2006 arrest of Shanghai's party secretary, Chen Liangyu, for the misuse of public funds—was interpreted by many domestic and foreign observers as part of President Hu Jintao's clearing out of officials and factions still loyal to former president Jiang Zemin.

4. The criminal organization described below can be understood as a formalization and institutionalization of many of the practices and ideologies associated with the ad

hoc entrepreneur/official networks described in Chapter Two. In his study of brother-hoods and secret societies during the mid- to late Qing Dynasty, Ownby (1996: 2) ar-gues that secret societies were "informal, popular institutions, created by marginalized men seeking mutual protection and mutual aid in a dangerous and competitive society." Mutual aid and brotherhood were the explicit core values of their organizations. The organizations were an attempt to overcome their marginality from elite society and were perhaps their only means to social status and wealth. In contrast, corrupt officials use al-liances with other members of the elite to appropriate public goods for private ends and as a way of meeting the constant demands associated with the "face" of being an official.

5. For useful overviews of different scholarly approaches to corruption and their application to post-1949 China, see Lü 2000: Chapter 1 and Sun 2004: Introduction.

6. For a sophisticated analysis of corruption in China from the perspective of incen-tive structures see Sun 2004. For analyses of Chinese politics in terms of essential cultural and psychological tendencies see Pye 1992, 1995.

7. See Chapter Five for a discussion of "sexual bribery" and the legal debates sur-rounding it.

8. That men are more likely to become "corrupt" or misuse public money is a tenet of development economics and enshrined in many development policies, but why this is the case is often left unexplained.

9. In my search for an electronic copy of the text on the Internet I came across several excerpts from the book reproduced on Chinese government and Party websites. The most commonly cited passages were those in which Li Zhen warned of the dangers of sexual temptation.

10. This phrase mirrors another commonly quoted phrase that suggests that public moral condemnation can be overcome with enough wealth, "*Xiao pin, buxiao chang*" (People laugh at you if you're poor but not if you're [making good money as] a prostitute).

11. Jiao Yulu was a famous Communist Party official who embodied the virtues of self-sacrifice and simple living. A popular movie was made about his life in 1990. Li describes seeing it and being moved to tears.

12. I encountered the most elaborate example of this commemoration of ties to the state at the Wuliangye Liquor factory in Yibin, Sichuan. Wuliangye is the one of the best-selling and most prestigious *baijiu* (Chinese grain liquor) brands in the nation, and the factory has hosted visits from all the major post-Mao leaders: Deng Xiaoping, Jiang Zeming, Hu Jintao, and Yibin native son Li Peng. Each of these visits was commemorated with its own memorial hall (*jinianguan*) displaying photographs, quotations, and artifacts. When I was there in 2005, even though Hu Jintao had not yet paid the company an official visit, the company had already completed the construction of his memorial hall, the big-gest of the set. (Each successive hall was bigger and more elaborate than the previous one as a way to flatter the current leader).

13. When asked to explain what he means by "tacitly consented to by the leader-ship," Li Zhen freezes up and asks to talk about a different topic. Presumably Li Zhen knew that explicitly implicating the leadership in his activities would ruin any chance he had of commuting his sentence.

14. How people determine which status-seeking behaviors add to one's face and which ones diminish it is discussed in Chapter Four.

15. For example, he got his superior to approve the purchase of imported equipment for the tobacco company and to exert pressure on the bank manager to give the company the loan, but he doesn't explain why his boss would be so willing to help with such a suspect transaction.

16. When bosses are entertaining in clubs, their subordinates usually answer their multiple mobile phones. As I became closer to Brother Fatty and Brother Chen, I was often given new numbers to call, suggesting a hierarchy of phone numbers, from those for the unfamiliar to those for more intimate associates.

17. After my fortuitous meeting with Brother Chen, I began to ask my other research informants about the power and organization of the heishehui. Some confessed their ignorance or suggested books or movies for me to see, but a vast majority replied, usually without any sense of irony, "The Communist Party is the biggest mafia group in China" (*Gongchandang shi Zhongguo zuidade heishehui*).

This comment is revealing in a number of ways. First, it reveals the widespread assumption by many Chinese that corruption and self-enrichment are the default practices of most officials and that the CCP has abandoned its commitment to "serve the people" and become a predatory organization whose primary purpose is to generate wealth for its members at the expense of the public good. Second, it suggests parallels in the ideology and organization between the CCP and illicit organizations. The Communist Party, just like the mafia, demands a cut of the profits of operations under their "protection." Its members receive benefits, perks, and protection from the law unavailable to ordinary citizens. Like the mafia, they are organized around a well-defined hierarchy, but this structure is under constant threat from secret machinations, alliances, and betrayals.

18. However, Fatty and his associates often made reference to Fatty's famed martial arts skills. Over dinners with his associates, Fatty told stories illustrating his fighting prowess and capacity for violence.

19. Known most commonly as "special K" in the United States, this drug produces a dissociative, sometimes hallucinatory state in users. It is most commonly snorted in powdered form.

20. Because of the amount of drinking entailed in toasting dozens of xiongdi, managers, and associates, Brother Fatty and Brother Chen often ordered drinks with low levels of alcohol. I was surprised to see them drink cocktail combinations that would be considered "feminine" in the West, such as Bailey's Irish Cream mixed with Evian spring water.

21. My sense of etiquette was conditioned by an egalitarian notion that everyone should be treated with equal respect, or by my assumption that whomever I toasted was of higher status. This seemed at the time to be the safest mode in which to operate and the least likely to offend.

Later I learned that not accepting deferential protocol could also be offensive. Months later, when having dinner in a seafood restaurant with some friends, one of

Brother Fatty's associates whom I recognized from Fatty's nightclub approached my table and deferentially toasted me. He then informed me that he would pay for my dinner because "you are a friend of my big brother (*gege*), and my big brother's friend is my big brother." I was embarrassed but grateful and later in the evening went over to his table and deferentially toasted him and his associates as a way of showing thanks. I later learned however that this was viewed as a violation of protocol: I failed to properly accept the status accorded to me by this associate. Later Brother Chen informed me that my trip to their table had "embarrassed" the group.

22. Fatty's investigation by the police, which occurred a few years before the start of my fieldwork, resembled a negotiation much more than a struggle. I am still gathering the exact details of his mediated "fall" and hope to make them the subject of a future paper.

23. It is thus rather appropriate that the heishehui refer to their protection rackets and control of the underground economy as "management" (*guanli*).

24. In many rural areas and small towns, this merging of "black" and "white" forms of governance is even more apparent. According to He Qinglian, heads of "criminal and semi-criminal syndicates have become the effective rulers at the local level" in a countless number of small towns and villages in rural China (He 2002: 43).

25. At this time, around 2000, Chengdu entered into its most ambitious stage of urban "renewal," launched by the mayor, Li Chuncheng, nicknamed "Li Chaicheng" (literally, "Tear down the city Li"). In 1999 one-story, traditional wooden houses were still a common sight in the city, but by 2003 they had all but vanished. Thus there was no shortage of demolition projects for Mr. Wei's company.

26. His propensity to lecture others about business techniques led some other research informants to whom I introduced him to dub him "the entrepreneur" (*qiyejia*). Some of his friends saw Mr. Wei's underworld aspirations as somewhat juvenile, if not irrational and dangerous. Mr. Zhou, in particular, often dismissed Mr. Wei as copying what he saw in Hong Kong movies and trying too hard to construct a "powerful" (*quanwei*) image for its own sake.

27. I learned from a few of his xiongdi that they took protection money from one of my favorite noodle shops. They told me I could ask for free noodles anytime I went there, but I reluctantly declined.

28. Increasingly there have been cases of entrepreneurs colluding with the police and/or heishehui to eliminate their competitors. See, for example, the Wang Zhenzhong "2.20 Shooting Case" (Zhongguo Wang 2007).

29. Zhou Runfa starred in many classic Hong Kong action and gangster films, including *A Better Tomorrow*, *Hard Boiled*, and *The God of Gamblers*. He came to embody what Louie (2002: 155) characterizes as "*wu* masculinity for the contemporary world."

CHAPTER 4

1. *Xiongdi* means brothers, but in this context it refers to the younger men employed by Mr. Pan. As their "older brother," Mr. Pan was responsible for their well-being and livelihoods. See Chapter Three.

2. At the time I met him, Mr. Pan's relationship with his mistress had just ended. He had come very close to divorcing his wife to marry her, but in the end decided against it. Ultimately it was her past as a dancer that prevented him from marrying her. Both Mr. Pan and his friends explained to me that a woman with that kind of background would never be able to be a virtuous (*xianhui*) wife and live a normal domestic existence. Mr. Pan's friends often cited his near-divorce as an illustration of how far he had strayed from a "normal" life.

3. Between 2 and 3 million RMB was between US$308,000 and $463,000 in 2011.

4. In his critique of Bourdieu's notion of social capital, Alan Smart (1993: 405) argues that "effective conversion strategies depend on socially defining transactions in particular—desired manners, for example—as gifts rather than bribes. Gifts, bribes, and commodities are not real entities than can be scrutinized, fitted to a formal definition, and labeled. Their constitution is a practical accomplishment; success in presenting an exchange as the appropriate kind of transaction in not always achieved." Thus, the "transactions" which convert capital from one form to another are not as mechanistic and seamless as Bourdieu's model implies. Each capital form contains its own "constraints" (405).

5. For a sophisticated discussion of the complexities and contradictions underlying the concept of recognition and the limitations of recognition-based politics see Markell (2003). While my use of recognition is partly inspired by Markell's discussion, my use of the term is meant to be more specific to the Chinese context and therefore does not fully reproduce the nuances of Markell's and others' formulations (cf., e.g., Hegel 1977; Taylor 1994).

6. The ways in which status is rooted in the perceptions of and relations with others is captured by the notion of face (*mianzi*) discussed in Chapter 3. See also Kipnis's (1995) article on face.

7. Chinese cigarettes are marketed according to a hierarchy. Several different grades of cigarettes, clearly identifiable by differently colored packaging, are sold under a single brand name. The highest grade might be several times as expensive as the lowest. Even famous luxury brands engage in this practice. *Zhonghua*, the cigarette of choice for high-ranking officials, for example, differentiates between its hard pack and soft pack, with the latter being the more expensive.

8. *Suzhi* is a rather ambiguous term that refers to the overal "quality" of an individual, ranging from high (*gao*) to low (*di*). Suzhi is assessed according to a combination of one's education, manners, morality, taste, and appearance. See H. Yan 2003 and Anagnost 2004 for important discussions of the political effects of evaluating Chinese citizens according to their suzhi.

9. The 2007 arrest and investigation of Yang Shukuan, a powerful gangster from a small city in Hebei, uncovered that, in addition to a Ferrari and stretch limousine, he frequently drove around town in an armored tank that he had procured through his friendship with director of the local security force (*wujing*).

10. Because of the inflationary pressures associated with elite entertaining, elites frequently shifted to venues that offered newer, rarer, and more expensive pleasures.

This "chase and flight" dynamic in choice of venue can be contrasted with their conservatism in choices of liquor, clothing, and tobacco.

11. Most of these places lacked parking lots, and patrons frequently parked on the sidewalk directly in front of the establishment. When the sidewalk was full, valets would park cars further away on the street. Customers driving expensive imported cars were always given the most prominent places on the sidewalk next to the entrance. The drivers of these cars were often important businessmen and officials, sometimes meeting with each other to make deals. Instead of parking their cars far away or in a concealed area, parking valets covered their license plates with a sign displaying the name of the establishment in order to prevent journalists, anti-corruption officials, or perhaps suspicious wives from verifying their presence at these places. This way the club could still advertise its exclusive, upscale status without the identities of its patrons being inconveniently revealed.

12. While the Forbidden City is perhaps the most obvious historical example of the relationship between status, invisibility, and secrecy, the current residential compound for high-ranking party members, Zhongnanhai, is equally as "forbidden" to commoners as its imperial predecessor.

13. In her discussion of the two types of new rich, Ms. Long emphasized the low levels of education and rural origins of the appearance-obsessed nouveau riche; she contrasted their circumstances with the sheer amount of wealth of the more cultivated and philanthropic super-rich rather than their family backgrounds and education, implying that at a certain level of wealth one overcomes the stigma of a "low-quality" upbringing.

14. Since her friend conducted his philanthropic work anonymously and the beneficiaries were strangers outside of his social circle, these activities were not interpreted as an example of the "living for others" mentality Ms. Long consistently denigrated in our conversations.

15. See Chapter Five and the Conclusion for further discussion of this issue.

16. Mr. Zheng, the owner of a public relations company in Chengdu, saw this movement away from a guanxi-based economy to one more oriented around free and open competition reflected in the changing spaces of China's nightclubs: "I think China's nightclubs are moving toward more public halls (*dating*) and toward fewer private rooms (*baofang*). Baofang suggest that something secret is going on, that we're making secret plans based on our guanxi. Now things are more out in the open. People are finding out that relying on guanxi to do business is unreliable."

17. The value accorded to "international standards" is exemplified by the ubiquitous "ISO 9002" international quality certification stamped on much product packaging in China. This certification is used for American products as well, but it is virtually unknown to American consumers and is rarely displayed on product labels in the United States.

18. "Banana" (*xiangjiao*) is a derogatory term for Chinese who are perceived as being overly fond of Western culture and tastes to the extent that they betray their "racial" identity. Hence they are described as being "yellow on the outside but white on the inside."

19. Despite the iron grip that certain European luxury brands seem to have on the Chinese market, consumption of these objects is tinged with nationalist fears. Wealthy Chinese consumers I interviewed claimed that European luxury brand producers sold markedly different, often inferior goods in the Chinese market. One owner of a mining company in Chengdu interpreted the broken handle of her Gucci purse as evidence that European luxury companies sell lower-quality merchandise in China. When Gucci informed her that it would take six months to repair, she was further enraged, since the purse would be out of style by the time they sent it back. She enlisted me to assist her in dealing with Gucci customer service in the hope that they would be more likely to respond to the complaints of an American. In its most extreme form, this fear included a not entirely unfounded suspicion that the styles and product lines of luxury goods sold in China served to further mark them as "Asian consumers" and distinguish them from Westerners.

20. By 2009, he had already upgraded from the BMW to a chauffeur-driven S-class Mercedes.

CHAPTER 5

1. The status hierarchy of women who depend on sexuality to make a living has been officially codified by the police, who rank long-term *ernai* (concubines) at the top and sex workers who service migrant workers and lack any fixed workplace at the bottom (Jeffreys 2004: 168–69).

2. See Zhen 2000 and Hanser 2005 for analyses of this term.

3. For an excellent ethnography of hostesses and sex workers in contemporary China, see Tiantian Zheng's *Red Lights: The Lives of Sex Workers in Postsocialist China* (2009).

4. Pun (2003) makes a similar argument about young rural women who migrate to coastal areas to work in factories. She views these women as primarily attracted to the trappings of urban modernity and consumer capitalism. Although overcoming their stigmatized rural status is no doubt part of their motivation, her argument downplays the importance of care for parents and other social obligations in these women's lives. For comparison, see Leslie Chang's (2009) discussion of the support migrant women offer their families and the resulting power this gives them in family affairs.

5. Whether this support continues after a daughter's marriage or whether a son's support increases after he establishes his own household are important questions requiring further research.

6. For overviews of marriage and marriage law in the PRC, see Croll 1981 and Diamant 2000. For a history of the concept of romantic love in early twentieth century China see Lee 2007.

7. Since I am primarily interested in outlining the "beauty economy" I focus more on meinü. But there appear to be an increasing number of relationships in which wealthy women provide financial support for young men in exchange for companionship and sexual services such that one can posit the existence of a nascent "*shuaige* economy." I describe some of these below.

8. This characterization is also rooted in the popular notion that the sexual appetites of women increase in their thirties and forties.

9. This same argument was used to account for the imagined behavior of elite women from wealthy and powerful families (*guizu*). Because their financial and social statuses were secure, they could freely pursue romantic and sexual relationships (as long as they didn't cause a public scandal).

10. The term "duck" (*yazi*) parallels the slang term for a female prostitute, "chicken" (*ji*).

11. Because I often met wealthy female entrepreneurs and fupo for interviews in teahouses and coffeeshops, many of my male friends joked that I was a *xiaobailian*. I once poked fun at myself in this manner to Brother Chen, and he mistook me as serious. He looked at me uncomfortably and said, "Men in that business can't enter our group" (*Gao neige hangyede jinrubuliao womende quanzi*).

12. Women's political status was less important given the long-standing tradition of hypergamy in China.

13. In his 2009 novel, *Brothers* [*Xiongdi*], Yu Hua provides a satirical depiction of a "virgin beauty pageant" in which none of the entrants is an actual virgin, and the finalists are those who are willing to sleep with the judges.

14. One can contrast this assertion with the constant scrutiny and discussion of each other's backgrounds among the new rich I worked with, especially among female entrepreneurs.

15. Urban entrepreneurs often portrayed rural women as "money pits" with never-ending networks of relatives in need of assistance.

16. This idealization of one-night stands was premised on that fact that, especially for women, these affairs remain secret from their peers. See Farrer 2002 for a discussion of one night stands and the rhetoric surrounding forms of romantic and sexual "play" in reform era China.

17. Gail Hershatter notes a similar logic in elite men's relationships with courtesans in early twentieth-century Shanghai. Because most elite marriages at the time were arranged by parents, courtesans were idealized as romantic companions desired as much for their conversational skills and artistic cultivation as for their sexual attractiveness (Hershatter 1994: 172; 1997).

18. Ms. Li, a mining entrepreneur, recounted a story that she felt allegorically exhibited the dynamics of wealth and marriage. She knew a wealthy entrepreneur from a rural background who divorced his rural wife for a younger, educated, urban woman. After a while, at his new wife's insistence, he gave her some money to "play around with" and keep her occupied. She started investing in real estate and in a few years had done quite well. Meanwhile her husband's ventures were failing left and right, and he was quickly losing his money. Deciding that he wasn't as successful and competent as she originally thought, she divorced him.

19. Unmarried women professionals and entrepreneurs make up the bulk of the growing category dubbed "leftover women" (*shengnü*) in China. This derogatory term

refers to unmarried women over the age of 27. The stereotypical leftover woman has both a high level of education and a high income.

20. The most egregious case involved the vice secretary of the Xuan Cheng City Municipal Party Committee, Yang Feng, who had eight formal mistresses in addition to his wife. He is described as using "modern enterprise management theory" to run his households (Li Chuzhi 2006).

21. The extent to which corrupt officials are associated with younger mistresses is exemplified by a video game entitled "Honest and Upright Warrior" (*Qinglian Zhanshi*) developed by the local Communist Party branch's disciplinary committee (*jiwei*) in Ningbo, Zhejiang. In the game, players complete missions in which their primary goal is to kill high-ranking corrupt officials. Along the way, however, they also encounter corrupt officials' sons and daughters, their bodyguards, and bikini-clad mistresses (*qingren*).

23. Sexual bribery is, however, forbidden by Communist Party guidelines governing personal conduct for Party members.

23. The most famous example of "sexual bribery" comes from the Lai Changxing smuggling case in Fujian province in the late 1990s. See the discussion of Lai Changxing in Chapter Three.

CHAPTER 6

1. This is not to say that guanxi has humanized all capitalist relations; far from it. As Mayfair Yang puts it, "while there may be renqing between business managers, often very little is practiced when it comes to the extraction of surplus value from workers" (Yang 2002: 468). See also Ong's account of the exploitation and symbolic violence that guanxi tends to conceal (Ong 1999: 116–17).

2. There are many other tales of business owners using state services for their own instrumental ends, such as shutting down a competitor or locking up a labor organizer. For example, in the 2009 mafia crackdown in Chongqing, many entrepreneurs claimed they were targeted because they were business competitors of allies of Bo Xilai (see Higgins 2012).

3. This shift was made particularly clear to me in a conversation I had with a Chinese friend who first went on the job market in 2004. At that time he was choosing between working for a private computer company and a state-owned tobacco company. My advice to him at the time was to go to work for the private company, imagining less room for growth at a "backward" state-owned company. Perhaps somewhat influenced by my advice, he decided to work for the computer company. Later, at a dinner in 2011, he half-jokingly complained that I had given him terrible advice and said he was full of regret. When I asked why, he explained, "State-owned companies have so much money! If I had taken a job with [the tobacco company] I wouldn't have anything to worry about now."

4. One can look to the privatization of military services in the United States for a clear example of how the ideology of neoliberalism generates its ideological opposite in practice. The privatization of the war in Iraq in the name of efficiency, competition, and

small government often led to its polar opposite on the ground: cronyism, corruption, and government waste (See Chandrasekaran 2007).

5. Entrepreneurs I knew who were familiar with liberal theories that champion free markets sometimes dubbed their situation in China as "abnormal" (*buzhengchang*), but they still admitted to the benefits of both official and unofficial forms of state backing. Mr. Wen, who had spent several years doing business in Australia and South Africa, characterized the primary difference between foreign countries and China as follows: "Overseas (*guowai*) if you have a million dollars you can only set up a million-dollar business, but in China [with the right relationships] if you have a million dollars you can do a 10 million-dollar project."

6. Kipnis (2007: 390) demonstrates how the notion of suzhi, which many scholars have associated with neoliberalism, is in fact often employed to justify "decidedly unliberal" hierarchies. He argues that quite often neoliberal ideas are invoked and neoliberal policies implemented disingenuously in a "crass attempt to grab power and exploit others" (386).

7. In her seminal work on China's economy during the reform period, *The Pitfalls of China's Modernization*, He Qinglian (1998) in fact refers to the new rich throughout the text as "those with low suzhi" (*di suzhizhe*).

8. Several entrepreneurs pointed to the 2009 anti-mafia campaign in Chongqing as justification for their sense of insecurity.

9. Even one of the "elder brothers" (dage) in Brother Fatty's organization was a Buddhist convert who abstained from drinking alcohol and supported several orphans in rural areas.

GLOSSARY OF KEY CHINESE TERMS

anquangan   a sense of security and safety

bailing   white-collar

bang dakuan   to be supported by a wealthy male patron; to date a rich guy

bao ernai   to take on and support a de facto second wife or concubine

baofahu   a derogatory term for a nouveau riche; an "upstart"

baofang   a private room in a club, disco, or restaurant

baohusan   "protection umbrella"; an official who uses his or her high position and influence to protect corrupt officials or criminal groups from prosecution

baoyang   to financially support a mistress or young male lover

beijing   background; refers to having political connections, a wealthy family, or influential friends

benshi   talent; ability

biaozhun   standard

bieshu   a villa; a free-standing house as opposed to an apartment or townhouse

chiku   literally, to "eat bitterness"; the ability to endure hardships

chi qingchun fan   literally, to "eat the rice bowl of youth"; refers to a woman using her youth and beauty for material gain

dage   literally, "big brother"; an older male patron; a leader of a criminal gang

danwei   work unit

disanzhe   a "third party"; refers to the male or female lover of a married person

doufuzha gongcheng   "tofu dregs engineering"; poor quality construction due to corrupt diversion of funds

fubai   corruption

fupo   a rich woman

furen   rich person

furen jieceng   rich stratum

fuza   complex; complicated

ganqing   sentiment; affect; emotion

getihu   a household or individual engaged in private business

gonggong daode   public-oriented morality

goudui   a term found in several Sichuan dialects that refers to cultivating a
    relationship with someone for an instrumental purpose

guanshang goujie   illegal collusion between entrepreneurs and government officials

guanxi   social connections and relationships

guanxiwang   an individual's personal network of connections and relationships

guanyuan   government official

guizu   noble; aristocrat; refers to the highest-level stratum in a society

heishehui   literally, "black society"; the criminal underground; organized crime

jiali   home; the domestic sphere

jianghu   the knight-errant culture depicted in classical Chinese novels that is an
    important reference for contemporary Chinese masculinity

jiaoyi hunyin   a "transaction" marriage; a marriage rooted primarily in financial
    concerns

kaifang   socially or culturally "open" and tolerant; the opposite of conservative

laoda   a boss or patron; an informal leader; a gang leader

liegenxing   deeply rooted bad traits

lingdao   leader

liyi   economic interest; profit

luohou   economically or culturally "backward"

meinü   beautiful woman

meinü jingji   the "beauty economy"; the use of young, attractive women in
    advertisements, sales, corporate ceremonies, and conventions

mianzi   "face"; social prestige and reputation

mingpai   famous brand

mingyu   reputation

nüqiangren   a derogatory term for a successful female professional or businesswoman

pengyou   friend

pinwei   taste

qianguize   hidden or unwritten rules in business or politics

qianquan jiaoyi   the trade in power for money

qingfu   mistress

qingren   lover

qiyejia   entrepreneur

renqing   literally, "human sentiments"; affective relationships; the norms and values
    that regulate interpersonal relationships; a favor

shangliu shehui   high society; the upper crust

shili   tangible value or benefit

shuaige   a handsome guy; a term of address for a young man

siying qiye   private firm

suzhi   an ambiguous term that refers to the overall "quality" of an individual, ranging from high (*gao*) to low (*di*). Suzhi is assessed according to a combination of one's education, manners, morality, taste, and appearance.

taizidang   the "princeling faction"; refers to the children of high-ranking Communist Party officials who often occupy high positions in government and business in large part because of their family connections

tiefanwan   iron rice bowl; refers to the system of guaranteed employment, housing, and benefits in the state-run economy

teigemen'er   literally, "iron brothers"; close male friends

tubaozi   a country bumpkin; a derogatory term for someone who is unfashionable or unsophisticated

waimian   outside, often used in contrast to the domestic sphere of home and family

wan   to play; to have fun

xiahai   literally, "to jump into the sea"; to leave one's work unit (*danwei*) in order to go into business

xiagang gongren   laid-off factory worker

xiaobailian   literally a "little white face"; a younger, financially dependent boyfriend of a wealthy woman

xiaojie   a term of address for a young woman; a euphemism for a female sex worker

xijiaofang   establishments that specialize in foot bathing and massage based on the principles of reflexology; a foot-massage parlor

xinfu   new rich

xing huilu   sexual bribery

xinyang   beliefs

xiongdi   brother; a close male friend; the junior member of an underground criminal brotherhood

xiuxian   laid back; leisurely

xiuyang   cultivation in morals and manners

yang   to provide for; to care for

yazi   a duck; slang for a male prostitute

yibashou   a powerful boss-patron; a capable person

yingchou   work-related entertaining; a dinner party

yiqi   honor or a sense of obligation in personal relationships; code of brotherhood

youhuo   temptation

you tiaojian   to possess the necessary material prerequisites for marriage, often referring to a man's possession of a house and car

yuguoji jiegui   to get on the global track; to make practices conform to global norms and standards

zerengan   sense of responsibility

zhishifenzi   an intellectual

zou jiejing   taking the shortcut, often used to refer to using unethical or immoral means to get ahead

BIBLIOGRAPHY

Allison, Anne. 1994. *Nightwork: Sexuality, Pleasure, and Corporate Masculinity in a Tokyo Hostess Club*. Chicago: University of Chicago Press.

An Dun. 2002. *Juewu Jinji, Juedui Yinsi: Dandai Zhongguoren Qinggan Koushu Shilu Zhi Si (Without Taboo, Absolute Privacy: A Record of Contemporary Chinese Oral Narratives About Romance, Number Four)*. Beijing: Beijing Chubanshe.

Anagnost, Ann. 2004. "The Corporeal Politics of 'Quality' [Suzhi]." *Public Culture* 16(3): 189–208.

———. 2008. "From 'Class' to 'Social Strata': Grasping the Social Totality in Reform-Era China." *Third World Quarterly* 29(3): 497–519.

Andreas, Joel. 2008. "Changing Colours in China." *New Left Review* 54: 123–42.

Appadurai, Arjun, ed. 1986. *The Social Life of Things*. New York: Cambridge University Press.

August, Oliver. 2007. *Inside the Red Mansion: On the Trail of China's Most Wanted Man*. New York: Houghton Mifflin.

Becker, Gary S. 1973. "A Theory of Marriage: Part I." *Journal of Political Economy* 81(4): 813–46.

———. 1974. "A Theory of Marriage: Part II: Marriage, Family, Human Capital, and Fertility." *Journal of Political Economy* 82(2): S11–S226.

Bian, Yanjie. 1994. *Work and Inequality in Urban China*. Albany: State University of New York Press.

———. 2002. "Institutional Holes and Job Mobility Processes: Guanxi Mechanisms in China's Emergent Labor Markets." In *Social Connections in China: Institutions, Culture, and the Changing Nature of Guanxi*, Thomas Gold et al., eds. New York: Cambridge University Press.

Boretz, Avron. 2011. *Gods, Ghosts, and Gangsters: Ritual Violence, Martial Arts, and Masculinity on the Margins of Chinese Society*. Honolulu: University of Hawai'i Press

Bourdieu, Pierre. 1984 [1979]. *Distinction: A Social Critique of the Judgment of Taste*. Trans. Richard Nice Cambridge, Mass.: Harvard University Press.

———. 1987 [1979]. "The Forms of Capital." In *Handbook of Theory and Research for the Sociology of Education*, John G. Richardson, ed. New York: Greenwood Press.

Brownell, Susan. 2001. "Making Dream Bodies in Beijing: Athletes, Fashion Models, and Urban Mystique in China. In *China Urban: Ethnographies of Contemporary Culture*, Nancy Chen et al., eds. Durham, N.C.: Duke University Press.

Bruun, Ole. 1993. *Business and Bureaucracy in a Chinese City: An Ethnography of Private Business Households in Contemporary China*. Berkeley, Calif.: Institute of East Asian Studies.

Buckley, Christopher. 1999. "How a Revolution Becomes a Dinner Party: Stratification, Mobility, and the New Rich in Urban China." In *Culture and Privilege in Capitalist Asia*, Michael Pinches, ed. New York: Routledge.

Butler, Judith. 1999 [1990]. *Gender Trouble: Feminism and the Subversion of Identity*. New York: Routledge.

Chan, Anita, Richard Madsen, and Jonathan Unger, 2009. *Chen Village: Revolution to Globalization*. 3rd ed. Berkeley: University of California Press.

Chandrasekaran, Rajiv. 2007. *Imperial Life in the Emerald City: Inside Iraq's Green Zone*. New York: Random House.

Chang, Leslie. 2009. *Factory Girls: From Village to City in a Changing China*. New York: Spiegel and Grau.

Chinasmack.com. 2011. "No Car No House Song, Chinese Leftover Women Version." http://www.chinasmack.com/2011/videos/no-car-no-house-song-chinese-leftover -women-version.html (accessed May 19, 2011).

Collier, Jane, Michelle Rosaldo, and Sylvia Yanagisako. 1997 [1981]. "Is There a Family?" In *The Gender/Sexuality Reader*, Roger Lancaster and Micaela di Leonardo, eds. New York: Routledge.

Connell, R. W. 1995. *Masculinities: Knowledge, Power, and Social Change*. Berkeley: University of California Press.

———. 2001. *The Men and the Boys*. Berkeley: University of California Press.

Cameron, Deborah, and Don Kulick. 2003. *Language and Sexuality*. New York: Cambridge University Press.

Croll, Elisabeth. 1981. *The Politics of Marriage in Contemporary China*. New York: Cambridge University Press.

———. 1994. *From Heaven to Earth: Images and Experiences of Development in China*. New York: Routledge.

Da He Bao. 2007. "An Fang Haikou Fupo Julebu" (An Undercover Investigation of a Rich Ladies' Club in Haikou). *Da He Bao-Da He Wang*. http://news.tom.com/2007 -07-24/0027/11186753.html (accessed September 18, 2008).

Davis, Deborah, ed. 2000. *The Consumer Revolution in Urban China*. Berkeley: University of California Press.

Da Yang Wang. 2007. "Jingjiren 'Xiangjie' Qianguize Jiemi Nüxing Peike Neiqing" (Manager Explains the "Hidden Rules" and Reveals the Inside Story of Female Stars Being

Paid to "Accompany" Clients). http://news.tom.com/2007–07– 23/0027/30753041.html (accessed September 17, 2008).

Diamant, Neil J. 2000. *Revolutionizing the Family: Politics, Love, and Divorce in Urban and Rural China, 1949–1968*. Berkeley: University of California Press.

Dickson, Bruce. 2003. *Red Capitalists in China: The Party, Private Entrepreneurs, and the Prospects for Political Change*. New York: Cambridge University Press.

Dilley, Roy, ed. 1992. *Contesting Markets: Analyses of Ideology, Discourse, and Practice*. Edinburgh: Edinburgh University Press.

Donaldson, Mike. 1993. "What Is Hegemonic Masculinity?" *Theory and Society* 22: 643–57.

Duhigg, Charles, and David Barboza. 2012. "In China Human Costs Are Built into an iPad." *New York Times*, January 25.

Engels, Frederick. 1972 [1884]. *The Origin of the Family, Private Property, and the State*. New York: International Publishers.

Evans, Harriet. 1997. *Women and Sexuality in China: Dominant Discourses of Female Sexuality and Gender since 1949*. London: Blackwell.

———. 2002. "Past, Perfect, or Imperfect: Changing Images of the Ideal Wife." In *Chinese Femininities, Chinese Masculinities: A Reader*. Susan Brownell and Jeffrey N. Wasserstrom, eds. Berkeley: University of California Press.

Fairbank, John, and Merle Goldman. 1998. *China: A New History*. Enlarged ed. Cambridge, Mass.: The Belknap Press of Harvard University.

Farquhar, Judith. 2002. *Appetites: Food and Sex in Post-Socialist China*. Durham, N.C.: Duke University Press.

Farrer, James. 1999. "Disco 'Super-Culture': Consuming Foreign Sex in the Chinese Disco." *Sexualities* 2(2): 146–66.

———. 2002. *Opening Up: Youth Sex Culture and Market Reform in Shanghai*. Chicago, Ill.: University of Chicago Press.

Farrer, James, and Sun Zhongxing. 2003. "Extramarital Love in Shanghai." *China Journal* 50: 1–36.

Fei, Xiatong. 1992 [1948]. *From the Soil: The Foundations of Chinese Society*. Trans. Gary Hamilton and Wang Zheng. Berkeley: University of California Press.

Feng Xiaogang. 2001. *Da Wan (Big Shot's Funeral)*. Sony Pictures. Beijing, China.

Fong, Vanessa. 2002. "China's One-Child Policy and the Empowerment of Urban Daughters." *American Anthropologist* 104(4): 1098–1109.

Gal, Susan, and Gail Kligman. 2000. *The Politics of Gender after Socialism*. Princeton, N.J.: Princeton University Press.

Garnaut, John. 2010. "Macquarie's Getting Well Connected in China." *Sydney Morning Herald*, October 2.

Gates, Hill. 1989. "The Commoditization of Chinese Women." *Signs: A Journal of Women in Culture and Society* 14(4): 799–832.

Gilley, Bruce. 2001. *Modern Rebels: The Rise and Fall of China's Richest Village*. Berkeley: University of California Press.

Gold, Thomas. 1991. "Urban Private Business and China's Reforms." In *Reform and Reaction in Post-Mao China: The Road to Tiananmen*, Richard Baum, ed. New York: Routledge.

Gold, Thomas, Doug Guthrie, and David Wank. 2002. *Social Connections in China: Institutions, Culture, and the Changing Nature of Guanxi*. New York: Cambridge University Press.

Goodman, David. 2007. "The New Rich in China: Why There Is No New Middle Class." *Asian Currents* (July). http://iceaps.anu.edu.au/ac/asian-currents-07-07.html (accessed September 10, 2008).

———, ed. 2008. *The New Rich in China: Future Rulers, Present Lives*. New York: Routledge.

Granovetter, Mark. 1985. "Economic Action and Social Structure: The Problem of Embeddedness." *American Journal of Sociology* 91(3): 481–510.

Granovetter, Mark, and Richard Swedberg. 2001. *The Sociology of Economic Life*. Boulder, Colo.: Westview Press.

Gregory, Chris A. 1982. *Gifts and Commodities*. New York: Academic Press.

Guthrie, Doug. 1998. "The Declining Significance of *Guanxi* in China's Economic Transition." *China Quarterly* 154 (June): 254–82.

———. 1999. *Dragon in a Three Piece Suit: The Emergence of Capitalism in China*. Princeton, N.J.: Princeton University Press.

Hanser, Amy. 2005. "The Gendered Rice Bowl: The Sexual Politics of Service Work in Urban China." *Gender & Society* 19(5): 581–600.

———. 2008. *Service Encounters: Class, Gender, and the Market for Social Distinction in Urban China*. Stanford, Calif.: Stanford University Press.

Hao, Yufan, and Michael Johnston. 1995. "Reform at the Crossroads: An Analysis of Chinese Corruption." *Asian Perspective* 1(1): 117–49.

Harvey, David. 2005. *A Brief History of Neoliberalism*. New York: Oxford University Press.

Hasty, Jennifer. 2005. "The Pleasures of Corruption: Desire and Discipline in Ghanaian Political Culture." *Cultural Anthropology* 20(2): 271–301.

He Qinglian. 1998. *Zhongguo Xiandaihuade Xianjing: Dangdai Zhongguode Jingji Shenhui Wenti. (The Pitfalls of Modernization: Contemporary China's Socio-Economic Problems)*. Beijing: Jinri Zhongguo Chubanshe.

———. 2001. "Chapter 4. The Origins of Rent-Seeking Behavior in the Chinese Economy." *The Chinese Economy* 34(2): 49–72.

———. 2002. "Chapter 9. Varieties of Social Control and the Emergence of a Social Underground." *The Chinese Economy* 35(1): 33–50.

———. 2005 [1997]. "Huse Nüxing Ji Qita: Yuanshi Jilei Shiqi de Zhongshengxiang" (Gray Women and Others: The Social Creatures Produced by the Period of Primi-

tive Accumulation). *Zhongguo Baogao Zhoukan* (*China Report Weekly*). http://www
.china-week.info/html/2358.htm (accessed September 18, 2008).

Hegel, Georg W. F. 1977. *Hegel's Phenomenology of Spirit.* Trans. A. V. Miller. Oxford:
Oxford University Press.

Hershatter, Gail. 1994. "Modernizing Sex, Sexing Modernity: Prostitution in Early
Twentieth Century Shanghai." In *Engendering China: Women, Culture, and the State*,
Christina K. Gilmartin, Gail Hershatter, Lisa Rofel, and Tyrene White, eds. Cam-
bridge, Mass.: Harvard University Press.

———. 1997. *Dangerous Pleasures: Prostitution and Modernity in Twentieth Century
Shanghai.* Berkeley: University of California Press.

Heyman, Josiah, ed. 1999. *States and Illegal Practices.* New York: Berg.

Higgins, Andrew. 2012. "Fugitive Chinese Businessman Li Jun Details Struggle over
Power and Property." *Washington Post*, March 4.

Hirschman, Albert O. 1997 [1977]. *The Passions and the Interests: Political Arguments for
Capitalism before Its Triumph.* Princeton, N.J.: Princeton University Press.

Ho, Karen. 2009. *Liquidated: An Ethnography of Wall Street.* Durham, N.C.: Duke University Press.

Honig, Emily, and Gail Hershatter. 1988. *Personal Voices: Chinese Women in the 1980s.*
Stanford, Calif.: Stanford University Press.

Hsu, Carolyn. 2001. "Political Narratives and the Production of Legitimacy: The Case of
Corruption in Post-Mao China." *Qualitative Sociology* 24(1): 25–54.

———. 2007. *Creating Market Socialism: How Ordinary People Are Shaping Class and
Status in China.* Durham, N.C.: Duke University Press.

Hu, Hsien Chin. 1944. "The Chinese Concepts of 'Face.'" *American Anthropologist*, New
Series 46(1): Part 1:45–64.

Huang, Yasheng. 2008. *Capitalism with Chinese Characteristics: Entrepreneurship and
the State.* New York: Cambridge University Press.

Hwang, Kwang-kuo. 1987. "Face and Favor: The Chinese Power Game." *American Journal of Sociology* 92(4): 944–74.

Jacobs, Andrew. 2009. "Chinese Trial Reveals a Vast Web of Corruption." *New York
Times*, November 4.

Jeffreys, Elaine. 2004. *China, Sex, and Prostitution.* New York: Routledge Curzon.

———. 2006. "Debating the Legal Regulation of Sex-Related Bribery and Corruption in
the People's Republic of China." In *Sex and Sexuality in China*, Elaine Jeffreys, ed.
New York: Routledge.

Jia Zhangke. 2006. *San Xia Hao Ren (Still Life).* Hong Kong: Xstream Pictures.

Jiu Yue. 2004. "Yi Ben Zazhi He Yige Jieceng" (A Magazine and a Stratum). *Toudengcang
(First Class)* 2: Preface. Chengdu, China.

Judd, Ellen R. 1994. *Gender and Power in Rural North China.* Stanford, Calif.: Stanford
University Press.

Keane, Webb. 1997. *Signs of Recognition: Powers and Hazards of Representation in an Indonesian Society*. Berkeley: University of California Press.

Kelly, John D. 2007. "Market, Shop, Store, and Empire: Morality, Economy, and Luxury Reconsidered." Paper presented at the conference "Economies of Empire: British Political Economy and Modernization." Nicholson Center for British Studies, University of Chicago, February 9.

Kiesling, Scott. 2005. "Homosocial Desire in Men's Talk: Balancing and Re-Creating Cultural Discourses of Masculinity." *Language in Society* 34: 695–726.

Kimmel, Michael. 1994. "Masculinity as Homophobia: Fear, Shame and Silence in the Construction of Gender Identity." In *Theorizing Masculinities*, H. Brod and M. Kaufman, eds. Newbury Park, Calif.: Sage.

King, Ambrose Yeo-chi. 1991. "Kuan-hsi and Network Building: A Sinological Interpretation." *Daedalus* 120(2): 63–84.

Kipnis, Andrew. 1995. "Face: An Adaptable Discourse of Social Surfaces." *Positions* 3:1.

———. 1997. *Producing Guanxi: Sentiment, Self, and Subculture in a North China Village*. Durham, N.C.: Duke University Press.

———. 2001. "Zouping Christianity as Gendered Critique? An Ethnography of Political Potentials." *Anthropology and Humanism* 27(1): 80–96.

———. 2007. "Neoliberalism Reified: *Suzhi* Discourse and Tropes of Neoliberalism in the People's Republic of China." *Journal of the Royal Anthropological Institute*, New Series 13: 383–400.

———. 2008. "Audit Cultures: Neoliberal Governmentality, Socialist Legacy, or Technologies of Governing?" *American Ethnologist* 35(2): 275–89.

Lamont, Michele. 1992. *Money, Morals, & Manners: The Culture of the French and American Upper-Middle Class*. Chicago: University of Chicago Press.

Ledeneva, Alena. 2006. *How Russia Really Works: The Informal Practices That Shaped Post-Soviet Politics and Business*. Ithaca, N.Y.: Cornell University Press.

Lee, Haiyan. 2007. *Revolution of the Heart: A Genealogy of Love in China, 1900–1950*. Stanford, Calif.: Stanford University Press.

Li Chuzhi. 2006. "Ernai Yu Tanguan Mi Bu Ke Fen" (Second Wives and Corrupt Officials are Inseparable). *Shijie Ribao* (*World Journal*), November 26.

Li Haipeng. 2006. "Fuhao Zhenghu Ji" (Notes on Marriage Advertisements among the Wealthy). *Nanfang Zhoumo* (*Southern Weekend*). http://www.southcn.com/weekend/commend/200601050010.htm (accessed September 18, 2008).

Li, Minsheng. 2001. "Entrepreneurs from Non-Public Sector Hail Jiang's Speech." *Beijing Review* 31 (August 8): 11–13.

Liang, Chen. 2005. "Fangdi Si Meinü, Shei Bi Shei Geng Jujiao" (Four Beauties of Real Estate, Who Attracts the Most Attention?) *Toudengcang* (*First Class*) 2: 44–47. Chengdu, China.

Ling, L. H. M. 1999. "Sex Machine: Global Hypermasculinity and Images of the Asian Woman in Modernity." *Positions* 7(2): 277–306.

Liu, Xin. 2002. *The Otherness of Self: A Genealogy of the Self in Contemporary China*. Ann Arbor: University of Michigan Press.

Louie, Kam. 2002. *Theorising Chinese Masculinity: Society and Gender in China*. New York: Cambridge University Press.

Lü, Xiaobo. 2000. *Cadres and Corruption: The Organizational Involution of the Chinese Communist Party*. Stanford, Calif.: Stanford University Press.

Mann, Susan. 2000. "The Male Bond in Chinese History and Culture." *American Historical Review* 105(5): 1600–14.

Markell, Patchen. 2003. *Bound By Recognition*. Princeton, N.J.: Princeton University Press.

Mason, Katherine. Forthcoming. "To Your Health: Toasting, Intoxication and Gendered Critique Among Banqueting Women." *The China Journal*.

Mauss, Marcel. 1990 [1950]. *The Gift: The Form and Reason for Exchange in Archaic Societies*. New York: Norton.

McCracken, Grant. 1988. *Culture and Consumption: New Approaches to the Symbolic Character of Consumer Goods and Activities*. Bloomington: University of Indiana Press.

McIsaac, Lee. 2000. "Righteous Fraternities and Honorable Men: Sworn Brotherhoods in Wartime Chongqing." *American Historical Review* 105(5): 1641–55.

Meisner, Maurice. 1999. *Mao's China and After: A History of the People's Republic*. 3rd ed. New York: Free Press.

Nathan, Andrew. 1993. "Is Chinese Culture Distinctive?—A Review Article." *Journal of Asian Studies* 52(4): 923–36.

Naughton, Barry. 2007. *The Chinese Economy: Transitions and Growth*. Cambridge, Mass.: MIT Press.

Nonini, Donald. 2008. "Is China Becoming Neoliberal?" *Critique of Anthropology* 28(2): 145–76.

Oi, Jean. 1989. *State and Peasant in Contemporary China: The Political Economy of Village Government*. Berkeley: University of California Press.

Olivier de Sardan, J.-P. 1999. "A Moral Economy of Corruption in Africa?" *Journal of Modern African Studies* 37(1): 25–52.

Ong, Aihwa. 1999. *Flexible Citizenship: The Cultural Logics of Transnationality*. Durham, N.C.: Duke University Press.

Otis, Eileen. 2011. *Markets and Bodies: Women, Service Work, and the Making of Inequality in China*. Stanford, Calif.: Stanford University Press.

Ownby, David. 1996. *Brotherhoods and Secret Societies in Early and Mid-Qing China: The Formation of a Tradition*. Stanford, Calif.: Stanford University Press.

Pan Suiming. 2000. *Shengcun yu Tiyan: Dui yige Dixia "Hong Deng Qu" de Zhuizong Kaocha* (*Subsistence and Experience: An Investigation of an Underground Red-Light District*). Beijing: Zhongguo Shehui Kexue Chubanshe.

Page, Jeremy. 2012. "Plan B for China's Wealthy: Moving to the U.S., Europe." *Wall Street Journal Online*, February 22.

Parry, Jonathan. 1986. "The Gift, the Indian Gift, and the 'Indian Gift.'" *Man* 21(3): 453–73.

Parry, Jonathan, and Maurice Bloch, eds. 1989. *Money and the Morality of Exchange.* New York: Cambridge University Press.

Pearson, Margaret. 1997. *China's New Business Elite: The Political Consequences of Economic Reform.* Berkeley: University of California Press.

Pei, Minxin. 2006. *China's Trapped Transition: The Limits of Developmental Autocracy.* Cambridge, Mass.: Harvard University Press.

Pieke, Frank. 1995. "Bureaucracy, Friends, and Money: The Growth of Capital Socialism in China." *Comparative Study of Society and History* 37(3): 494–518.

Polanyi, Karl. 1944. *The Great Transformation.* Boston, Mass.: Beacon Hill Press.

Potter, Pittman. 2002. "Guanxi and the PRC Legal System: From Contradiction to Complementarity." In *Social Connections in China: Institutions, Culture, and the Changing Nature of Guanxi*, Thomas Gold et al., eds. New York: Cambridge University Press.

Pun, Ngai. 2003. "Subsumption or Consumption: The Phantom of Consumer Revolution in Globalizing China? *Cultural Anthropology* 18(4): 469–92.

Pye, Lucian. 1992. *The Spirit of Chinese Politics.* Cambridge, Mass.: Harvard University Press.

———. 1995. "Factions and the Politics of Guanxi: Paradoxes in Chinese Administrative and Political Behavior." *China Journal* 34: 35–53.

Qiao Yunhua. 2004. *Diyu Menqian: Yu Li Zhen Xing Qian Duihua Shilu (At the Gates of Hell: A Record of Conversations with Li Zhen before His Execution).* Beijing: Xinhua Chubanshe.

Redding, S. Gordon. 1995. *The Spirit of Chinese Capitalism.* Berlin: Walter De Gruyter.

Ren Yuan. 2006. "Qiangdiao Ernai Ruoshi, Zengjia Shehui Duili" (Emphasizing Second Wives as Weak Parties Will Increase Society's Opposition [to them]). *Shijie Ribao (World Journal)*, November 26.

Renmin Wang. 2007. "China's Middle Class Defined by Income." http://english.people-daily.com.cn/200501/20/eng20050120_171332.html (accessed September 10, 2008).

Rocca, Jean-Louis. 1992. "Corruption and Its Shadow: An Anthropological View of Corruption in China." *China Quarterly* 130: 402–16.

Rofel, Lisa. 1999. *Other Modernities: Gendered Yearnings in China after Socialism.* Berkeley: University of California Press.

———. 2007. *Desiring China: Experiments in Neoliberalism, Sexuality, and Public Culture.* Durham, N.C.: Duke University Press.

Rubin, Gayle. 1975. "The Traffic in Women." In *Toward an Anthropology of Women*, Rita Rayner, ed. New York: Monthly Review Press.

Ruwitch, John. 2002. "China to Make Private Entrepreneurs Model Workers." Reuters News Service, April 20.

Sahlins, Marshall. 2000 [1988]. "Cosmologies of Capitalism: The Trans-Pacific Sector of the 'World System.'" In *Culture in Practice*. New York: Zone Books.

Schein, Louisa. 2000. *Minority Rules: The Miao and the Feminine in China's Cultural Politics*. Durham, N.C.: Duke University Press.

———. 2001. "Urbanity, Cosmopolitanism, Consumption." In *China Urban: Ethnographies of Contemporary Culture*, Nancy Chen et al., eds. Durham, N.C.: Duke University Press.

Schneider, Jane, and Peter Schneider. 2003a. "Power Projects: Comparing Corporate Scandal and Organized Crime." *Social Analysis* 47(3): 136–40.

———. 2003b. *Reversible Destiny: Mafia, Antimafia, and the Struggle for Palermo*. Berkeley: University of California Press.

Sedgwick, Eve Kosofsky. 1985. *Between Men: English Literature and Male Homosocial Desire*. New York: Columbia University Press.

Scott, James. 1976. *The Moral Economy of the Peasant: Rebellion and Subsistence in Southeast Asia*. New Haven, Conn.: Yale University Press.

Shui Shui. 2004. "Nanshi Yipin" (Men's Taste In Clothing). *Toudengcang (First Class)* 10: 82–86. Chengdu, China.

Smart, Alan. 1993. "Gifts, Bribes, and Guanxi: A Reconsideration of Bourdieu's Social Capital." *Cultural Anthropology* 8(3): 388–408.

———. 1999. "Predatory Rule and Illegal Economic Practices." In *States and Illegal Practices*, Josiah Heyman, ed. New York: Berg.

Smart, Alan, and Carolyn Hsu. 2007. "Corruption or Social Capital: Tact and the Performance of Guanxi in Market Socialist China." In *Corruption and the Secret of Law*. Monique Nuijten and Gerhard Anders, eds. Burlington, Vt.: Ashgate.

Smart, Josephine, and Alan Smart. 1998. "Transnational Social Networks and Negotiated Identities in Interactions between Hong Kong and China." In *Transnationalism from Below*, Michael P. Smith and Luis Guarnizo, eds. New Brunswick, N.J.: Transaction.

Smith, Daniel Jordan. 2007. *A Culture of Corruption: Everyday Deception and Popular Discontent in Nigeria*. Princeton, N.J.: Princeton University Press.

Southcn.com. 2007. "Meinü Jingji Da Saomiao" (An Overview of the Beauty Economy). *Nanfang Wang (Southern Web)*. http://www.southcn.com/finance/cjzt/caijingzhuanti /200208290756.htm (accessed September 18, 2008).

Sun, Yan. 2004. *Corruption and Market in Contemporary China*. Ithaca, N.Y.: Cornell University Press.

Tang, Zhihao, 2009. "Never Too Old: More Seniors Filing for Divorce in Shanghai." *China Daily*. http://www.chinadaily.com.cn/china/2009-10/26/content_8845700.htm (accessed September 22, 2012).

Tatlow, Didi Kristin. 2011. "Gang Busting Cop Is One for the History Books in China." *New York Times*, November 2.

Thompson, E. P. 1993 [1971]. "The Moral Economy of the English Crowd in the Eigh-teenth Century." *Customs in Common: Studies in Traditional Popular Culture.* New York: New Press.

Taylor, Charles. 1994. "The Politics of Recognition." In *Multiculturalism: Examining the Politics of Recognition.* Amy Gutmann, ed. Princeton, N.J.: Princeton University Press.

Tsai, Kellee. 2002. *Back Alley Banking: Private Entrepreneurs in China.* Ithaca, N.Y.: Cornell University Press.

————. 2007. *Capitalism without Democracy: The Private Sector in Contemporary China.* Ithaca, N.Y.: Cornell University Press.

Uretsky, Elanah. 2007. "Mixing Business with Pleasure: Masculinity and Male Sexual Culture in Urban China in the Era of HIV/AIDS." PhD dissertation, Department of Sociomedical Sciences, Mailman School of Public Health, Columbia University.

Walder, Andrew. 1986. *Communist Neo-Traditionalism: Work and Authority in Chinese Industry.* Berkeley: University of California Press.

Walter, Carl E., and Fraser J. T. Howie. 2011. *Red Capitalism: The Fragile Financial Foun-dation of China's Extraordinary Rise.* Singapore: John Wiley & Sons.

Wang, Gan. 2000. "Cultivating Friendship through Bowling in Shenzhen." In *The Con-sumer Revolution in Urban China,* Deborah Davis, ed. Berkeley: University of Cali-fornia Press.

Wang, Hui. 2003. *China's New Order: Society, Politics, and Economy in Transition.* Trans. Ted Huters and Rebecca E. Karl. Cambridge, Mass.: Harvard University Press.

Wang, Xiaolu. 2010. "Analyzing Chinese Grey Income." *Credit Suisse Asia Pacific/China Equity Research,* August 6.

Wank, David. 1996. "The Institutional Process of Market Clientism: *Guanxi* and Private Business in a South China City." *China Quarterly* 144: 820–38.

————. 1999. *Commodifying Communism: Business, Trust, and Politics in a Chinese City.* New York: Cambridge University Press.

————. 2002. "Evolving State-Business Clientelism in China: The Institutional Organiza-tion of a Smuggling Operation." Paper Presented at the American Political Science Association's Annual Meeting.

Weber, Max. 1978. *Economy and Society: An Outline of Interpretive Sociology.* Vol. 1. Berkeley: University of California Press.

Wilson, Scott. 2002. "Face, Norms, and Instrumentality." In *Social Connections in China: Institutions, Culture, and the Changing Nature of Guanxi.* Thomas Gold et al., eds. New York: Cambridge University Press

Wolf, Margery. 1972. *Women and the Family in Rural Taiwan.* Stanford, Calif.: Stanford University Press.

Wong, Edward. 2011. "China TV Grows Racy, and Gets a Chaperone." *New York Times,* December 31.

Xian, Yan. 2007. "Gong'anjude Yifu Kezhang Nenggou 'Baohudeliao' Yongyou Jiazhuangchede Yang Shukuan Ma?" (Can a Section Chief from the Public Security Bureau "Protect" an Armored Car Possessing Yang Shukuan?) *Boxun.com*. http://news.boxun.com/cgi -bin/news/gb_display/ print_version.cgi?art=/gb/pubvp/2007/06&link=200706222322 .shtml (accessed September 17, 2008).

Xin Jing Bao. 2008. "Xuezai zhi Hou, Gaoceng Zhennu: Yi Duo Wan Gen Zheduan Di-anganli Jing Mei Ganjin" (After the Snowstorm, High-Level Outrage: More than Ten Thousand Broken Electrical Poles Didn't Contain Any Rebar). *Boxun.com*. http:// www.peacehall.com/news/gb/china/2008/02/200802292312.shtml (accessed September 18, 2008).

Xu, Xiaoqun. 1996. "The Discourse on Love, Marriage, and Sexuality in Post-Mao China: A Reading of the Journalistic Literature on Women." *Positions* 4(2): 381–414.

Yan, Hairong. 2003. "Neoliberal Governmentality and Neohumanism: Organizing Suzhi/ Value Flow through Labor Recruitment Networks." *Cultural Anthropology* 18(4): 493–523.

Yan, Yunxiang. 1996. *The Flow of Gifts: Reciprocity and Social Networks in a Chinese Village*. Stanford, Calif.: Stanford University Press.

———. 2003. *Private Life under Socialism: Love, Intimacy, and Family Change in a Chinese Village 1949–1999*. Stanford, Calif.: Stanford University Press.

———. 2009. *The Individualization of Chinese Society*. New York: Berg.

Yanagisako, Sylvia Junko. 2002. *Producing Culture and Capital: Family Firms in Italy*. Princeton, N.J.: Princeton University Press.

Yang, Mayfair Mei-hui. 1989. "The Gift Economy and State Power in China." *Comparative Studies in Society and History* 31(1): 25–54.

———. 1994. *Gifts, Favors, and Banquets: The Art of Social Relationships in China*. Ithaca, N.Y.: Cornell University Press.

———. 1999. "From Gender Erasure to Gender Difference: State Feminism, Consumer Sexuality, and Women's Public Sphere in China." In *Spaces of Their Own: Women's Public Sphere in Transnational China*, Mayfair Mei-hui Yang, ed. Minneapolis: University of Minnesota Press.

———. 2002. "The Resilience of Guanxi and Its New Deployments: A Critique of Some New Guanxi Scholarship." *China Quarterly* 170: 459–76.

Yi Hui. 2004. "Toudengcang, Huozhe Shouxi Fengdu" (First Class, Or Elite Style). *Toudengcang (First Class)* 1: Preface. Chengdu, China.

Yu Hua. 2009. *Brothers: A Novel*. New York: Pantheon.

Yu Huazhang. 2007. "Lingren Jingtande Tanguan Heise Youmo (The Impressive Black Humor of Corrupt Officials)." http://www.chinaelections.org/NewsInfo.asp?News ID=120144 (accessed September 17, 2008).

Zelizer, Viviana. 2005. *The Purchase of Intimacy*. Princeton, N.J.: Princeton University Press.

Zhang, Everett Yuehong. 2001. "*Goudui* and the State: Constructing Entrepreneurial Masculinity in Two Cosmopolitan Areas of Post-Socialist China." In *Gen-*

dered Modernities: Ethnographic Perspectives, Dorothy L. Hodgson, ed. New York: Palgrave.

Zhang, Li. 2010. *In Search of Paradise: Middle-Class Living in a Chinese Metropolis*. Ithaca, N.Y.: Cornell University Press.

——, and Aihwa Ong, eds. 2008. *Privatizing China: Socialism from Afar*. Ithaca, N.Y.: Cornell University Press.

Zhen, Zhang. 2000. "Mediating Time: The 'Rice Bowl of Youth' in Fin de Siècle Urban China." *Public Culture*: 12(1): 93–113.

Zheng, Tiantian. 2006. "Cool Masculinity: Male Clients' Sex Consumption and Business Alliance in Urban China's Sex Industry." *Journal of Contemporary China* 15 (46): 161–82.

——. 2007. "From Peasant Women to Bar Hostesses: An Ethnography of China's Karaoke Sex Industry." In *Working in China: Ethnographies of Labor and Workplace Transformation*. Ching Kwan Lee, ed. New York: Routledge.

——. 2009. *Red Lights: The Lives of Sex Workers in Postsocialist China*. Minneapolis: University of Minnesota Press.

Zhong, Xueping. 2000. *Masculinity Besieged? Issues of Modernity and Male Subjectivity in Chinese Literature of the Late Twentieth Century*. Durham, N.C.: Duke University Press.

Zhongguo Wang. 2007. "Zhongguo Waitao Zui Gao Jibie Jingguan Wang Zhenzhong Yin Zhongliu Si Meiguo" (The Highest Level Police Officer to Flee Abroad Dies in America of Cancer). http://news.tom.com/2007-09-14/OI27/85674618.html (accessed September 17, 2008).

Zhou, Yuming, and Shao Yong. 1993. *Zhongguo Banhui Shi* (*A History of China's Secret Societies*). Shanghai, China: Shanghai Renmin Chubanshe.

Zizek, S. "Capitalism with Asian Values." Interview on Al Jazeera. http://www.aljazeera.com/programmes/talktojazeera/2011/10/2011102813360731764.html.

INDEX

Note: Page numbers in italic type indicate photographs.

Entertainment industry, 161

Entrepreneurs: anxiety of, 127; attitudes of, 22; Communist affiliations of, 8; in competitive markets, 133; interdependence of, 21–22; male predominance among, 38, 197*n*4; as marriage/romance prospects, 6, 164–66, 174; officially connected, 7–9, 13–14, 20, 31–33, 42–43, 58–59, 106–9, 124–25, 186, 188; rise of, 5–9; self-assessment of, 130–31; social status of, 6; successful, factors contributing to, 132; typical activities of, 16, 19, 137. *See also* Elites (new rich); Female entrepreneurs

Ethics. *See* Morality

Etiquette: in business relationships, 53; in drinking, 50; in entertainment, 60–61, 203*n*21; in social relationships, 56; for women, 133–34. *See also* Toasting

Extramarital sex and affairs, 40, 65–72, 154, 167–68, 172, 179, 195*n*15. *See also* Lovers; Mistresses

Face (*mianzi*), 23, 34, 55, 73, 88, 89, 93–95, 103–4, 124, 139, 173

Family: CCP reform of, 163; daughters' support of, 147, 206*n*4; men's responsibility for, 67, 72

Farrer, James, 44

Fei Xiaotong, 84

Female entrepreneurs, *See* Women entrepreneurs

Femininity, traditional, 2

Film industry, 161

Foot massage parlors (*xijiaofang*), 141

Foreign investment, 7

Forms of address, 150

Foxconn, 20

Fox spirits, 178

Free market ideal, 132–33, 188

Fruit plates, *49*, 49, 122–23

Fujian province, 109–10

Fupo (rich women), 153–56

Gambling, 198*n*14

Ganqing (feelings), 43–44, 56

Gao guanxi (relationship cultivation), 19. See also *Goudui*; *Guanxi*

Gender: business and, 26, 31; Chinese reform and, 148; forms of address and, 150–51; *guanxi* and, 25-26; roles, 65–66. *See also* Masculinity; Women

Getihu (independent households), 5–6, 193*n*3

Girlfriends, 65, 67–71. *See also* Mistresses

Godfather (*jiaofu*; criminal boss), 77

Goodman, David, 12

Goudui (relationship cultivation), 15, 19, 38, 51–53, 56, 59, 62, 99–100, 131, 160, 163, 199*n*20. See also *Gao guanxi*

Government: business relations with, 5, 7–9, 13–14, 20, 31–33, 42–43, 58–59, 77–80, 86, 89–92, 106–9, 111, 124–26, 184, 186–89; corruption in, 87–97; marginal activities of, 86; market reform's impact on, 5; organized crime's relations with, 34, 86, 104–5, 108–11, 203*n*24; privileges of, 124–25

Government officials. *See* Officials

Gray income, 194*n*8

Gray women, 143–47, 169, 180–82, 188

Great Leap Forward, 5

Guangdong, 68

Guangzhou, 1, 68

Guanxi (social networks): by business sector, 19; contemporary manifestations of, 24–27, 111, 122–25, 185–86; elite use of, 78, 91, 132; and gender, 25; humanizing aspect of, 185; individualism vs., 25–26, 128–31; limitations of, 36, 185–86, 205*n*16; masculine character of, 25–26; moral and sentimental aspect of, 23, 24, 27; nature of, 22–24; prestige associated with, 23–24; reciprocity inherent in, 23; *renqing* compared to, 23; scholarly opinions on, 24–25, 195*nn*21–23

Guan Yu, 30

Gucci, 206*n*19

Guizhou province, 183

Guizu. See Elites; Nobility

Han Yuanyuan, 168–69, 177

Harvey, David, 187

Hasty, Jennifer, 81–82

Health, 128–30, 137, 140, 142, 155

Made in the USA
Lexington, KY
13 January 2015